I0165820

More Praise for
Desiring to Desire God

"In *Desiring to Desire God,* David Fagerberg's voice merges
pensively with those of the great ascetical writers and spiritual
directors whose now neglected writings once fruitfully guided
Catholics over four centuries (1500–1900). Fagerberg's chosen
theme of the soul's desire—of such fundamental, perennial
importance—is all the more crucial in our own day, when so
many suffer from either a numbing loss of desire and sense of
purpose or from an addictive enslavement to worldly desires.
Fagerberg urges us to recognize, value, trust, and cultivate the
heart's true desire—that which pleases God and finds its fulfillment in God's own desire for us. 'With desire I have
desired…' (Luke 22:15)."—ANN W. ASTELL, University of
Notre Dame

"To read this work is to drink at the wells of the classic Catholic mysticism of abnegation that blossomed between the sixteenth and nineteenth centuries. Its chapters are best savored
over and over again! We learn how desire attracting us to God
already attaches us to God, and how abnegation spurns desire
for anything not God's will, thereby correcting any misalignment of our desires. To desire to love God is truly to love God.
Desiring to love *is* love; desiring to pray *is* prayer; devoutness *is*
piety. The desire is both ours and implanted by God. Professor
Fagerberg beautifully illustrates how desiring relates to the
theological virtues. Faith, for example, is the human side of
desire meeting desire, whereas from God's side it is grace. A
new angle thus appears on grace and free will: God's desire for
us is the foundation of our affectionate desire for him. Two
wills become one. God's part is grace; the human part is desire.
God energizes, the human synergizes. God does not react to a
contribution we make of our share of the labor; God replies to
the desire that has responded to his. Now, death is the gate to
what desire hoped for; it tests the sincerity of desire; it forces

desire's choice, and is thus a servant of God. In beguiling, simple language accessible to the ordinary reader, the author has woven a spiritual and mystical classic in its own right out of the warp and weft of the Catholic classics."—JAMES OKOYE, former Director of the Center for Spiritan Studies, Duquesne University; General editor of the *African American Catholic Youth Bible*

"David Fagerberg offers a fresh look at the essential role desire plays in deepening a life of faith or re-igniting a faith grown cold. With apt quotations drawn from his vast knowledge of classical spiritual writers, he convincingly demonstrates that, even when suffering the greatest spiritual darkness, we can grow closer to God simply by *choosing to desire to desire God.* There, where desire begins, we can find the love of God we are seeking—'for love is the root of all desires.'"—REV. MOTHER LUCIA KUPPENS, OSB, Abbey of Regina Laudis

Desiring to Desire God

DAVID W. FAGERBERG

Desiring
to Desire God

❧

✠ Angelico Press

First published in the USA
by Angelico Press 2024
© David W. Fagerberg 2024

All rights reserved

No part of this book may be reproduced or transmitted,
in any form or by any means, without permission.

For information, address:
Angelico Press
169 Monitor St.
Brooklyn, NY 11222
info@angelicopress.com

978-1-62138-969-9 (pbk)
978-1-62138-970-5 (cloth)

Cover design: Michael Schrauzer

CONTENTS

Preface

THIS IS A BOOK ABOUT DESIRE. To be more accurate, it's about the *desire to desire.* To pray is best; to want to pray is good; to want to want to pray is the first touch by God. A person who is in that last condition is the subject of this book, and it turns out that even desiring to desire is an expression of love. "To desire to love God is to love to desire God, and consequently to love Him: for love is the root of all desires."[1]

Desire is a big subject, so how will we proceed? I will approach it theologically (not psychologically, historically, philosophically), I will approach it as a component of spirituality (not dogmatics, systematics, Scripture study), I will approach it as a spirituality that is Catholic (although Orthodox spirituality has much to offer), and I will confine myself to a period between 1500–1900. I am going to pick quotes from a group of authors, like picking flowers in a field to make a bouquet. This book is filled with quotations because my objective is to get out of the way, and let the reader encounter these words first-hand. It is my hope that some author's style grabs the reader's attention and he seeks that theologian out for more reading.

I call these authors *theologians of abnegation* because of the emphasis they have on denying self-will and self-love in order to make progress in the spiritual life. They emphasize abnegation, of course, because Jesus himself made it a condition for being his follower. Mark 8:34, Matthew 16:24, and Luke 9:23 are identical (except for Luke's addition of one word): "If any man would come after me, let him *deny* himself and take up his cross [daily] and follow me." Francis Libermann says "It is not I who preach abnegation, it is our Lord Himself who has set down the conditions under which He will receive us as His followers. . . . No doctrine has ever

1. Jean-Pierre Camus, *The Spirit of St. Francis de Sales* (London: Burns, Oates & Washbourne, Ltd., 1925), 69.

found more forceful expressions in the Gospels. . . . The words of our Savior allow of no quibbling."[2] John Croiset numbers the command of mortification as the first among Jesus's many teachings.

> Mortification is so necessary for the perfect love of Jesus Christ, that it is the first lesson that Jesus Christ Himself gives to those who wish to be His disciples. Without it, we can have no hope of ever being disciples of Jesus Christ. *If any man will come after Me*, says our loving Savior, *let him deny himself.* . . . For this reason all the Saints agree in considering that there is no stronger proof of real piety than perfect mortification.[3]

Once upon a time, these Catholic spiritual authors, theologians of abnegation, held the least interest for me out of all the periods of theology one could study. I was interested in patristic theology, both Latin and Greek, and I was interested in Western medieval theology, whether monastic or scholastic. I read Orthodox theologians (old and new), and a student must, of course, read modern academic theologians. But the Latin Catholic, post-Reformation, spiritual writers held virtually no attraction for me. They felt fussy, dramatic, and overly severe. They emphasized the cross and suffering, abjection and annihilation, mortification and nothingness, so I did not spend much time in their company.

Then they began to sneak up on me.

Fénelon smuggled himself into my office in a box of books a friend gave me. Libermann reached out to shake my hand from a two-volume history of spirituality. These two formed the beginning and ending parentheses, and I suppose it is telling that their major output consisted of letters to their spiritual children that still make a direct hit upon a reader. Soon the boundaries were extended. I wandered backward, to the sixteenth century (John of Ávila and Blosius) and forward to some famous preachers and writers of the

---

2. Francis Libermann, *Living With God* (New York: Catholic Book Publishing, 1949), 132–33. Publication of Libermann's *Instructions for Missionaries* found in Duquesne Scholarship Collection, https://dsc.duq.edu/spiritan-rc/1/.

3. John Croiset, *Devotion to the Sacred Heart of Jesus* (London: Burns & Lambert, 1863), 77–78.

nineteenth century (Faber at the London Oratory, Lacordaire at Notre Dame, Charles Gay at Poitier). Although a few twentieth-century authors joined them, when I speak of *theologians of abnegation,* I basically mean Catholic spiritual writers between 1500 and 1900. As I read one, he brought along another friend. A name was mentioned in a book, a footnote was included, a tribute was paid, and thus one author led me to another. This is often the best way to choose books. Although I had heard of a few of them (de Sales, Olier, Eudes, Bérulle, de Liguori, Vianney), most of them I had not (Blosius, Luis de Granada, de Castañiza, Rodríguez, de Ponte, Baker, de Bernières-Louvigny, de la Colombière, Surin, Bona, Segneri, Boudon, de Lombez, Grou, de Ravignan, and Charles Gay). I accumulated them in a large e-folder that I can search. I do not call my searches a "word study," because I am not counting words, or locating words, or comparing the way different authors use the words. I instead consider myself searching for a *grammar* of how certain keywords and concepts operate. I have treated many of these concepts in other articles and book chapters (e.g., providence, nothingness, humility) but the concept of desire swelled beyond the length of an article into this book-length study. If this were one type of book, an academic type of book, we would be asking "When were these passages written? To what school of spirituality do they belong? Who is writing to whom?" But this is another kind of book because the answer to that last question is "To me. They are writing to me." And now that I have recorded their counsel, I mean to include you, and answer the question with "To us."

The key to appreciating abnegation is liturgical theology, I hypothesize, and that stands in the background here. I have already used Orthodox authors to explore liturgical asceticism;[4] now I am using Catholic authors to explore liturgical abnegation. Abnegation is filled with words that sound harsh to our modern ears when we hear them within a limited horizon (say, of morality or psychology), but they can be better understood if we place them against a more transcendent horizon. That transcendent horizon, I hypothesize, is

---

4. David W. Fagerberg, *On Liturgical Asceticism* (Washington, DC: Catholic University of America Press, 2013).

the act of liturgizing a God whose infinite Justice demands our total worship. "God will have no Sharers."[5] Liturgy is not restricted to the sacred realm; it is rehearsed in the sacred realm in order to be lived in every realm and at every moment. Man's whole *life* should be a liturgy. The ritual cult is only the part of liturgy that we can see— like the tip of an iceberg—and is connected to a great liturgy that connects sacred and profane, cult and cosmos, Church and world, all together in one living liturgy. The little liturgy turns the great liturgy. To live liturgically requires a sinful soul to be restructured sacramentally, and the planting of sacramental graces requires tilling the ground with abnegation. The ultimate reason why Christ commanded abnegation is because it is constitutive of his program of *latria*. Only the true, Uncreated God should receive *latria*. Idolatry is bad because we worship an image (*eidon-latria*), but worse than that is to worship ourselves (*auto-latria*). Liturgical abnegation consists of forsaking autolatry. Abnegation means denial, yes, and what does a person want that is being denied? To be his own god.

Theologians of abnegation, then, write in the service of the soul's perfection. "Perfection consists in this, that the soul, looking simply to God, not only gives the preference to the Creator over all creatures in her esteem, but in truth wishes and desires nothing but Him."[6] Because original sin has wounded human nature, it is not easy for men to order their desires around God. We tend to curve back upon ourselves, per Augustine's definition of sin as *incurvatus in se*. But Christ has come to adjust our posture, like a divine chiropractor, and stand us upright again before the Father in heaven. This makes the prejudiced picture that people hold of abnegation half true: it does analyze the sickness unto death caused by inordinate desires, and prescribes denial as the cure. But this is only half the truth. Abnegation also communicates a message that is uplifting and hopeful, because it rejoices in the charity of God. This book is about that latter dimension of abnegation, so often overlooked.

5. Giovanni Bona, *Manductio ad Coelum: or, a Guide to Eternity* (London: printed for Henry Brome, 1672), 4.

6. Jean-Joseph Surin, *Foundations of Spiritual Life* (London: James Burns, 1844), 126.

I will pause in this paragraph, only to note what the theologians say about bad desires in order not to forget the problems such desires can cause. The theologians are candid about the consequences of the Fall, and I can sort their remarks into six categories, giving only a single example in each case. First, they call bad desires inordinate, unruly, irregular, or capricious. "This is a disorder into which those very often fall that are wholly addicted to impurity and vice, who seeing themselves deprived of the means to satisfy their brutish desires, do what they can to enjoy, at least in thought, their detestable pleasures."[7] Second, they call bad desires selfish, covetous, and insatiable. "It is there that are put to death all of our selfish desires, all of our self-interested turning inward upon ourselves, and all of our movements of self-love."[8] Third, they call bad desires unholy, idolatrous, and acts of self-esteem. "We have in us this miserable and idolatrous desire, to fill every one's mind with ourselves, to wish to instill the esteem of ourselves in all hearts, and to be idolized by all."[9] Fourth, they call bad desires fleshly, sensual, and brutish. "His soul is become flesh, it is sensual like the flesh, it is blind like the flesh, it seeks only the appetites of the flesh . . . in a word, it has no longer any of the feature or resemblance of God."[10] Fifth, they call bad desires natural, instinctive, human, and earthly. "All our lives long, we rush after enjoyment, after the satisfaction of the affections of the heart and our earthly desires."[11] And sixth, they call bad desires aimless, foolish, vain, lukewarm, and slothful. "As if they were strangers to eternal things, [they] allow themselves to be carried away by their unruly appetites and vain desires, and employ their thoughts and affections on objects absolutely contrary to the

7. Lewis [Luis] de Granada, *A Memorial of a Christian Life* (New York: The Catholic Publication Society, 1870), 132.

8. François Fénelon, *The Complete Fénelon* (Brewster, MA: Paraclete Press, 2008), 268.

9. Jean-Jacques Olier, *Catechism of an Interior Life* (Baltimore: Murphy & Co., 1852), 74.

10. Ibid., 89.

11. Gustave de Ravignan, *Conferences on the Spiritual Life* (London: R. Washbourne, 1873), 133.

end of their creation."[12] In summary, the world aims at having more power in our heart than God himself, which causes our desires to misfire.

The authors offer this picture regularly, it is true, but not predominantly. Much more often the theologians give a gladdening word about the desire for God that the Fall has not eradicated. Why does a soul willingly undergo mortification? In order to more perfectly love her God. The soul flees world and self in order to fly into blessedness. Abnegation does not disparage the world; it rather seeks to overcome worldliness.

> Man, in this respect, is made to the image and resemblance of God: not that he can be, as God is, sufficient to himself; but in this sense, that all his affections should have a relation to God, and assume the character of unity, by their re-union in the unity of God. In loving creatures, and loving himself, he only should love God. His love should have no other center, and whilst he takes into view diverse other objects, he should always hold fast to this only object, as to his principal and as to his term. In this manner his affections spread themselves abroad like those of God, without dissipation, and he always remains collected in God, as God is always collected in himself. But that which God is from the infinite excellency of his nature, man cannot be but from the good use of his will.[13]

Worldliness is taking the world without reference to God.

Liturgical abnegation trains the will for liturgy. It is a two-step dance. We abnegate self in order to align our desires properly; our desire for God triggers the abnegation. This is called conversion. "The first and chief effect of a true conversion, is this recollection of our dispersed affections; we were spread abroad, and God brings us home to ourselves: he gathers and re-assembles all our scattered inclinations, and reunites them in himself; and should he allow them to extend to other objects, it is not to bring on a distraction,

---

12. Jean-Baptiste Saint-Jure, *A Treatise on the Knowledge and Love of Our Lord Jesus Christ*, vol. 1 (New York: P. O'Shea, 1870), 25.

13. Jean Grou, *Morality, Extracted from the Confessions of Saint Austin*, vol. 1 (London: J.P. Coghlan, 1791), 135–36.

but to rivet them still more to himself."[14] If successful, then one can do the world the way the world was meant to be done, which is how my teacher, Aidan Kavanagh, defined liturgy.

Virtues should be animated by one single motive, directed by one single intention, and tend to one single object. "Such were the virtues of Jesus Christ. Their sole motive was the love of God; their sole intention the glory of God; their sole end the fulfilment of the will of God."[15] Our sanctification consists of being unified with the motive, intention, and end of Jesus. This is empowered by the grace of baptism, when we are grafted onto Jesus, and he takes up residence in us. Liturgical abnegation is Christ's life being lived in us. He was animated by the desire to glorify his Father, and when the Holy Spirit instills Jesus's spirit in us, then we are animated by his desire to liturgize God. A person cannot turn toward the east without turning away from the west (as ancient baptismal rites understood). Turning toward involves turning from. Most books on abnegation focus on the turning away from; this book focuses on what one turns toward, and why. What does one desire? "Oh! my daughter, those who communicate according to the spirit of the Heavenly Bridegroom, annihilate themselves and say to our Lord: feed on me, change me, annihilate me, convert me into Thyself."[16] Every word of abnegation should be understood within the environment of liturgical oblation.

We might expect these theologians to complain that our desires are too strong, too big, and too overwhelming, but much more often they complain that our desires are too weak, too small, too

---

14. Grou, *Morality, Extracted from the Confessions of Saint Austin*, vol. 1, 140.

15. Jean Grou, *The Interior of Jesus and Mary*, vol. 1 (New York: Benziger Brothers, 1893), 304.

16. De Sales's words to Camus, *The Spirit of St. Francis de Sales*, 395–96. In the classroom I would explain abnegation using an episode from the Chronicles of Narnia. When the good mare Hwin meets Aslan for the first time, she trembles all over, but says "Please, you are so beautiful. You may eat me if you like. I would sooner be eaten by you than fed by anyone else." C. S. Lewis, *The Horse and His Boy*, in *The Chronicles of Narnia*, complete set (New York: HarperCollins Publishers, 2001), 299. This is the origin of liturgical abnegation: preferring to be eaten by Christ than fed by the world.

lukewarm. They insist we should desire to desire more: this will please God. Enlarge your actions "with the desire of doing much more for God than the little that thou art doing," because here is how God will respond:

> He does the opposite of what men do: He pays the will just as He does the deed. Wherefore the last labourers, those that came into His vineyard at the eleventh hour, were made equal to the first in their wages, because if they did not work longer, at least they had the desire to do so, and had come to the market-place with their spades as early as the first, waiting to be hired. Since, then, thou hast to do with so good a Lord, do not shut thyself up like a poor snail in the shell of that simple action which thou art performing, but enlarge it with thy desire.[17]

Enlarge your actions with desire—and your spirituality, your oblation, your charity. God will give the grace that will enable you to accomplish what you intend, which is why the first stroke of desire is so important. Grace will fill the ark that desire crafts: the greater the size of the vessel, the greater the grace. "And, therefore, it will not do to walk up, [the sinner] must run—he must fly; he must 'take wings as eagles.' Divine grace is waiting to supply him with them."[18]

If we do not yet have these wings perfectly, then let us desire them; if we do not yet desire them perfectly, then let us *desire to desire* them. That is the very, very first stroke, and theologians of liturgical abnegation describe it with great hope and gladness.

Solemnity of the Immaculate Conception, 2022

17. Paul Segneri, *The Manna of the Soul: Meditations for Every Day of the Year*, vol. 1 (New York: Benziger Brothers, 1892), 186.
18. Ibid., 216.

1

Defining Desire

THERE ARE FIVE QUOTATIONS that mark the kind of desire we are going to explore here. The first comes from Ambroise de Lombez: "God looks less at what I am than what I desire to be."[1] The next two come from Jean-Pierre de Caussade, who counsels that even desiring this desire is looked on favorably by God: "If you do not feel any of these desires the mere wish to have them, the mere raising of the heart is sufficient to keep your soul recollected and united to God."[2] And "This desire to desire is the first degree from which one passes gradually to a real desire."[3] The final two come from Paul Segneri, who says we should pine for justice with hunger and thirst, as Christ intended, and "if none of the means which have been mentioned suffice to give thee such a desire, do thou at least long to experience it. Desire the desire."[4] And "this desire will be a certain sign of approaching health . . . since it is a known axiom, that to desire to be cured, is almost half the cure. *Pars sanitates est, velle sanari.*"[5]

This little book is less about *what* we desire, and more about the *state* of desiring itself, which is presented by theologians of abnegation as uplifting and hopeful. We are hopeful because the object of

---

1. Ambroise de Lombez, *Lettres Spirituelles sur La Paix Interieure* (Paris: Chez Herissant, 1774), 92. "Dieu regarde moins ce que je suis que ce que je souhaite d'être."

2. Jean-Pierre de Caussade, *Abandonment to Divine Providence* (St. Louis: B. Herder Book Company, 1921), 143.

3. Ibid., 316.

4. Paul Segneri, *The Manna of the Soul: Meditations for Every Day of the Year,* vol. 2 (New York: Benziger Brothers, 1892), 547.

5. Paul Segneri, *The Devout Client of Mary* (London: Burns & Lambert, 1857), xxvi.

our desire is God, whose love is so powerful that even desiring to desire him encourages us. "I am like a traveler who sees afar off a high mountain; but, being on foot, must labour to attain it. In like manner I have some prospect of perfection, and of the obligations of a soul longing after God, but I cannot accomplish them. However, I have the desire. . . ."[6] Even feeling the desire is fulfilling, for it is the first touch of love, and love is the fountainhead of desire. The desire is the first movement toward God, and as the first step is part of the journey, not prior to it, so the first desire is part of the ascent to God, not prior to the ascent. The lifted foot begins the journey. The spell of love stirs our desire throughout this whole ascent because "the love of Christ urges us" (2 Cor 5:14). When understood this way, there is no gap between grace and the desire. The desire for union with God is incipient union, like the drawing of breath is part of speaking a word. The first stroke of the pen has not finished writing the sentence yet, or even the word—but it has begun the writing. Desire is the acorn of love's oak. This is a remarkably hopeful perspective, and the purpose of this book is to encourage it. "It is not a question of knowing much, of having great talent, nor even of doing great things. We only need to have a heart and to desire the good."[7]

The desire that attracts us to God already attaches us to God. It is the property of the Holy Ghost to enkindle desires in the hearts of the apostles, because "desires are as precursors and fore-messengers of Almighty God in the soul, into which He is to enter."[8] The spiritual tradition spoke about "aspirations of the heart toward God." The root is *spirare*, "to breathe," and these aspirations are expressions of a soul panting for God. Aspiring means striving for, seeking eagerly to attain, or longing to reach. The desire causes something. The desire creates an effect.

We shall find, of course, that "it is true that the grace of thy Lord

6. Jean de Bernières-Louvigny, *The Interior Christian in Eight Books* (New York: The Catholic Publication Society, 1843), 78.

7. François Fénelon, *Christian Perfection* (New York: Harper & Brothers, 1947), 76.

8. Louis de Ponte, *Meditations on the Mysteries of Our Holy Faith*, vol. 5 (London: Richardson and Son, 1854), 173.

is needed for this," nevertheless, "that grace will be given to thee every time that thou askest for it, and the asking for it likewise rests always with thyself."⁹ The aspiring gaze searches the heavens because it has felt itself espied by God's loving eye: before we even look up, God has already done all he can to get the human soul to lift her eyes.

If the beloved is *present* to the lover, then rejoicing occurs; if the beloved is *hidden* to the lover, or is not felt with the fullness the lover hopes to experience, then desire occurs. "The principle of all our actions, both external and internal, and that which both begets and sets on work all other passions, is only love—that is, an internal complacence and inclination to an object from the goodness or beauty that is believed to be in it; which object, if it be absent, the first effect of love is a desire or tendence to it. But if it be present, then the effect of love is joy, rest, and fruition of it."¹⁰ Our little actions, both external and internal, become significant. A mother knows her child's work is limited by his immaturity, but his work is measured by a different standard. "We turn little actions into great ones when we perform them with a supreme desire to please God, who measures our services, not by the excellence of the work we do, but by the love which accompanies it, and that love by its purity, and that purity by the singleness of its intention."¹¹ God cannot be fooled by externals, and he always penetrates more deeply than the façade.

> He judges by the spiritual life; that is what He requires above all, and with that He is satisfied when a man is unable to combine it with outward action. He sees the intention, the upright will, and the sincere desire within the heart; and this kind of righteousness, which none but He can see, and which springs from Him alone, is the only kind that is pleasing to Him, the only kind He considers real and deserving of reward. It is by the heart alone that a man

---

9. Segneri, *The Manna of the Soul*, vol. 1, 143.

10. Augustine Baker, *Holy Wisdom, Or Directions for the Prayer of Contemplation Extracted out of more than Forty Treatises*, ed. R. F. Serenus Cressy (New York: Burns & Oates, 1911), 243.

11. De Sales's words to Camus, *The Spirit of St. Francis de Sales*, 295.

can reach His presence; it is the heart alone that makes a man righteous in His eyes.[12]

Desire leans into God: it has a tendency (*tendentia*) toward God. Love, eros, desire, longing is the principle of our actions, inside and out, which is why we can speak of the beloved object "drawing us." We lean toward it because an erotic gravity is tipping the lover. Desire that leans toward God also gives desirous love its eschatological character, because we must not, in impatience, restrict the activity of God to our timeline. If we expect him, and he does not come, then we suffer ourselves to fall into the belief that he does not love us, which is "a false and an heretical idea. He bides His time to do it all the better, He bides His time to give unto you your desire, He bides His time in order to do more. Ah! if we only understood that when He delays to help us, it is for the greater good of our souls, as we are sure to profit by the delay."[13] Desire can be intensified by such delays, and since the desire delights God, it may sometimes please him to delay our gratification. This is difficult for us to accept, unless we take desire very, very seriously.

The delay increases desire if faith holds on, if hope stands firm, and if love is unshaken. "When I find that my desire runs after my thought upon this same eternity, my joy takes an unparalleled increase, for I know that we never desire, with a true desire, anything which is not possible. My desire then assures me that I can have eternity: what remains for me but to hope that I shall have it?"[14] Providence is a difficult doctrine to understand except in retrospect. At the time of its exercise we are too eager, and cannot act with the patience Providence demands. Nothing happens in the world except by the hidden dispensations of Providence, so we should not lament at the postponement of a term, since "it is God

---

12. Jean Grou, *The School of Jesus Christ* (London: Burns Oates & Washbourne, Ltd., 1932), 125.

13. Gustave de Ravignan, *Ravignan's Last Retreat* (London: Burns & Oates, 1859), 141.

14. Francis de Sales, *Letters to Persons in the World* (London: Burns & Oates, Ltd., 1894), 461–62.

who puts obstacles to it, and thus shows you that He only requires of you the desire to make it until such time as He, Himself, gives you the means and power to do so."[15] God would not point out an end without indicating the pathway to it; he would not invite us to his home without giving us the address, or give the address without providing a map, or provide a map without empowering our legs to walk. "God only desires what we are able to give."[16] "Desire this, seek for it, think of it, pray for it, and God, Who gives you the will to serve Him, will also give you strength to do it."[17] When we think we have disappointed God because we discern the weakness of our charity and service, when we think we have disappointed God because we discern the impotence of our prayer and piety, then we are rescued by a desire that perseveres. "At times, He even prevents our prayers, and is satisfied with our desires.... God often seems not to hear us, and defers granting our petition. In this case, we must be careful not to lose courage, but persevere faithfully till our request be complied with."[18] Often, our loving Lord is accustomed to put off the fulfilling of our petition for "the better increase and enkindling of our holy desires, as may be exemplified in the Canean woman, and the Widow in the Gospel."[19]

Our eyes must be fixed on eternity even while living in the temporal. This does not mean peering through a telescope at history's conclusion, it means awakening to the sight of the eternal all around us, at every moment, which means we may begin living an eternal life now, already. The perfection lies ahead, but the beginning stands before us. "Nothing is lacking to them which they cannot acquire; they have but to will a thing, and it is accomplished. But in order to conform this will to that of God, men in such a position should seek after a perfect will, which desires nothing save His

15. De Caussade, *Abandonment to Divine Providence*, 165.

16. Ibid. The title he gives the letter.

17. Francis de Sales, *A Selection from the Spiritual Letters of S. Francis De Sales*, translated by H. L. Lear (New York: E. P. Dutton and Company, 1876), 20.

18. Jean-Baptiste Saint-Jure, *The Spiritual Man; or, The Spiritual Life Reduced to its First Principles* (London: Burns & Oates, 1878), 294.

19. Juan de Castañiza, *The Spiritual Conflict and Conquest* (London: Burns & Oates, 1874), 200.

Good Pleasure."[20] Touch a river at its source and one simultaneously touches the river at its outlet; touching eternity with desire touches heaven even now. Hence the counsel we receive from all mystics and spiritual masters: Begin! Do not expect the conclusion prematurely; in this life, it is enough for a soul to be on the way, and desire is a sign of being en route.

A teleological marker is placed on the soul by its desire, and God looks at what the soul desires to be. "[Since thou] dost desire and strive from thy heart to please Him, thou art verily dear to thy Lord, and to all the court of heaven. God, who has given thee true contrition, will doubtless also give thee pardon; nor doth He regard what thou wast formerly, but what thou now art or desirest to be."[21] What hopeful words when spoken to a sinner. What encouragement when heard by someone who is bereft of successes in the spiritual life, yet has not lost desire. "If after this their good designs do not succeed, or at least have but little success, they are perfectly content; for though they desire what is good, they desire it in the way God wills it, and desire no more than God wills. It is self-love that is ever asking for great successes."[22]

Of course, there could always be ways to counterfeit this: sinners are as cunning as the serpent whose bite they felt in Eden. One could pretend to desire to be reformed, dissembling the true state of the heart and remaining in isolation and rebellion. That is why the tradition firmly says the desire must be true, and its truth is love. A wish is different from a true desire. Why?

> It is because our heart is filled with self-love, and what we call a desire of loving Jesus Christ is nothing but a mere speculation, a barren knowledge of the obligation we are under of loving Him. It is an act of the intellect, not of the will. . . . To convince ourselves [of this] we have only to compare this pretended desire with any other desire which really influences us. How anxious we are, what

---

20. De Sales, *A Selection from the Spiritual Letters of S. Francis De Sales*, 300–1.

21. Blosius (Louis of Blois), *Spiritual Works of Louis of Blois,* ed. John Bowden (New York: Benziger Bros., 1903), 166.

22. Henri-Marie Boudon, *The Hidden Life of Jesus* (London: Burns, Oates, & Co., 1869), 52.

efforts we make, when we love anything passionately! We are wholly occupied by the desire, we think of it, we speak of it at all times, we are continually taking measures and seeking means, we even lose our sleep in order to ensure its accomplishment. And what similar effect has ever been produced in us by the desire we pretend to have of loving Jesus Christ? . . . It will never be true that we have a great desire to love Jesus Christ, as long as we love Him so little.[23]

One can will a thing, and yet not will it; Thomas calls it "the wish to will [rather] than the absolute will itself."[24] But a sign of true desire is that it produces loving effects, and then the God's-eye view of our soul looks upon its desirous affections in light of what the soul is trying to be, and where the soul is trying to go.

Desire is a sign of intention, inclination, affection. "Our desire of a thing is an evident and positive sign of our affection for it; we do not desire things that are indifferent to us, but those we hold dear."[25] Our will is aimed toward the good, and not even original sin could break the link between the two. But what sin could do, and has done, is misdirect the will toward a false good, which there-fore produces a desire that can also be called false. All false desires are fraudulent, spurious, and simulated because no finite object can fulfill a desire God planted in the soul for the infinite good that is himself. We are speaking, then, of the discovery of true desire, as opposed to false desire. "To desire is to long to unite oneself to God, to enjoy Him. If God is the only real and essential happiness, as we cannot doubt He is, naturally, necessarily, He must be what my heart always desires, aspiring only to union and joy with Him. And if I wish it, if He is the only and necessary object of my desires, will He not ever be present with me?"[26] Desire is true if it seeks a true and deserving end, as opposed to a false and unworthy end.

23. Croiset, *Devotion to the Sacred Heart of Jesus*, 46–47.

24. Gaetano Maria de Bergamo, *Humility of Heart* (Mandeville, LA: Founding Father Films Publishing, 2015), 110.

25. Jean-Baptiste Saint-Jure, *Union with Our Lord Jesus Christ in His Principal Mysteries for All Seasons of the Year* (New York: D. & J. Sadlier & Co., 1876), 429.

26. Jean Grou, *Meditations upon the Love of God* (London: T. Baker, 1905), 55.

Consider the cheerful willingness with which desire connects to an end. About our desire for Wisdom, Solomon said "She is easily discerned by those who love her, and is found by those who seek her. She hastens to make herself known to those who desire her. He who rises early to seek her will have no difficulty, for he will find her sitting at his gates" (Wis 6:12–14). Rodríguez assumes that the wisdom Solomon is speaking about is nothing else than God himself, and marvels: "But do you know with what facility it is found? . . . It is at hand the moment you wish for it."[27] A facility is not only the willingness or eagerness to do something, it includes the power and proficiency to do it. The soul has a facility for God, an aptitude and capacity, which makes it act with expedience. As Wisdom is easily discerned by those who desire to love her, so God is at hand the moment you want him. God's omnipresence means that he does not need to travel, on his part, in order to be found. The heart finds him sitting at her gates as soon as she opens the door, which is what desire does.

Sights must be raised from the image to the prototype, and desires are the wings by which we go beyond the limits of our present state, if they are holy desires. We were designed for beatitude, and though the full satisfaction will not be known until the Parousia, desire plants a first kiss of its sweetness upon our lips. Even this faint caress is enough to fortify and nerve us.

> Desires are the wings by which we rise above the earth. According to St. Lawrence Justinian, holy desire "helps our natural strength and makes difficulties appear light." Desire gives us strength for the journey toward perfection and sweetens its difficulties. Those who really want to be perfect will never stop making progress, and, unless they wander from the path, they will arrive safely at their goal. On the other hand, those who lack a genuine desire for

---

27. Alphonsus Rodríguez (Alfonso), *The Practice of Christian and Religious Perfection*, vol. 1 (London: James Duffy, 1861), 13. There are two named Alphonsus Rodríguez, who should not be confused. The *theologian* is referred to as Alfonso (he composed three volumes on Christian and religious perfection); the *saint* is referred to as Alonso (he was porter at Majorca for 46 years). See FN 136.

perfection and who allow themselves to be carried along simply by natural weakness will find themselves going backward, for, according to St. Augustine, "not to go forward is to go backwards."[28]

Supernature exceeds the natural, therefore we desire to exceed our present state. Let the desire for perfection rule, and do not cease advancing toward the consummate state God plans.

A first test to be applied to our desires is whether they are natural or spiritual. Natural desires go quiet when they are sated—hunger subsides after the meal, and thirst after the drink—but spiritual desires are further stirred when they are fed. This is what Paul meant when he said instead of resting, he continued to stretch himself to those things that are before, ever continuing to soar higher (Phil 3:13), and the tradition has used the Song of Solomon to illustrate it. There is contact with God, a real participation and deification, yet at the same time God remains constantly (apophatically) beyond, so the soul must continue to go beyond its current place. The graces we receive are immense, but they create *more* desire, they do not stifle it. Every end is but another beginning: desire sees to that. Time spent with the beloved makes one covet more time with the beloved, knowledge of the beloved makes one crave fuller insight into the beloved. These further steps are never repetitious, they always freshen the relationship. The Bride ascends to the Bridegroom, and enjoys the good, the true, and the beautiful as much as her capacity allows, and yet the Bridegroom continues to draw her on to a still greater participation, as though she had not yet so much as tasted it. Desire is not merely a first step, a rung on the ladder to be left behind once the climb begins. Desire actually creates a perpetual beginning, fresh at each advance. That is why desire remains throughout the ascent, and even the satisfactions along the way do not end it. Contentment does not end desire, rather perpetual contentment produces perpetual desire.

The fruition of a thing which always contents never lessens, but is renewed and flourishes incessantly; it is ever agreeable, ever desir-

28. Alphonsus de Liguori, *Alphonsus de Liguori: Selected Writings*, (New York: Paulist Press, 1999), 141.

able. The perpetual contentment of heavenly lovers produces a desire perpetually content, as their continual desire begets in them a contentment perpetually desired. . . .

When our will meets God it reposes in him, taking in him a sovereign complacency, yet without staying the movement of her desire, for as she desires to love so she loves to desire, she has the desire of love and the love of desire. The repose of the heart consists not in immobility but in needing nothing, not in having no movement but in having no need to move.[29]

Alas, the feeding that increases spiritual hunger is true of both vices and virtues, so a second test to be applied to our desires is knowing whether the desire is egocentric or ecstatic: does it turn one back in upon oneself or take one outside, beyond, above oneself? Only the latter knowledge will ennoble the soul and enkindle the love of the virtues. Such a desire cannot be merely intellectual: it must go straight to the heart. Then such a spiritual person

finds no difficulty in avoiding evil and doing well; he complains of no rigour in God's law, but wonders at its mildness, and loves and embraces it in all its fulness; he keeps the precepts, and the counsels too. He contemns earthly things, not judging them worthy of attention; uses them as not abusing them, and, looking not at the things seen, which are temporal, passes swiftly through them towards the things eternal. The sweetest attractions of the world do not tempt him; its dangers do not imperil him; nor do its terrors alarm him. His body is on earth; but his soul is, by thought and desire, in heaven already.[30]

Martha is on earth, fulfilling her duties, friendships, and services. Mary is in heaven already, by the desire of a good portion which will not be taken away from her. When Jesus commends Mary's choice, he is not saying Martha's *reward* is not eternal, he is saying Martha's *work* is not eternal. Mary's desire for eternal things will make tem-

---

29. Francis de Sales, *Treatise on the Love of God* (Blacksburg, VA: Wilder Publications, 2011), 178.

30. Jean Grou, *The Spiritual Maxims of Pere Grou* (London: J. T. Hayes, 1874), 3–4.

poral things pass swiftly. This kind of desire is the cause and foundation of self-abnegation.

Even natural loves give evidence of their power to turn the heart outward. We witness this in the friend, the patriot, the spouse, the parent, and both ruler and servant alike. Desire increases the greatness and capacity of a person when it is fixed on something more profound than self alone. "The capacity of our heart is measured by the greatness of its desires."[31] Remarkably (miraculously, really), a selfish person becomes a selfless person under the spell of love, and the person who has never experienced this is but a shadow of what he could be. But once this happens regularly, the art of abnegation (self-denial) is learned painlessly.

> The whole art of abandonment is simply that of loving, and the divine action is nothing else than the action of divine love. How can it be that these two loves seeking each other should do otherwise than unite when they meet? How can the divine love refuse aught to a soul whose every desire it directs? And how can a soul that lives only for Him refuse Him anything?[32]

Self-abnegation being tutored by love redirecting desire becomes an elegant, graceful art. This is true on earth, and it is also true in heaven. Like a baby in the womb, not yet born, this desire is a real beatitude, though not yet experienced in glory.

"Deep calls to deep," the Psalmist says (Ps 42:7). Desire calls to desire. Religion comes from the Creator calling to the creature.

> To love God because He desires our love, to love Him because He first loved us, to love Him because He loves us with such a surpassing love . . . this, and this alone is religion: this is what flows from the ties between the Creator and His redeemed creature; for what is redemption but the restoring, repairing, and ennobling of creation? . . . That desire of His seems the handle by which loving souls take hold of their religion, and in which they find the key to their own position of creatures, and to the rights and attractions

---

31. Croiset, *Devotion to the Sacred Heart*, 46.
32. De Caussade, *Abandonment to Divine Providence*, 86.

of the Creator; and this desire of God for our love leads straight to our desire for Him.[33]

As we shall see, God plants the desire in order that our heart may reach out to his heart reaching out to ours. When a man discovers the pearl in the field, he sells his claims on esteem, profit, and influence in order to buy the superior beauty. Then the abnegation is painless. "You may experience many heavy and wearisome days in which you cannot reckon your progress, but, only desire and you will have the disposition of heart to which God ever responds."[34]

Desire as a disposition of heart is modeled for us by the patriarchs and prophets. The entire redemptive economy was for the purpose of reviving a desire for the heavenly Father that had languished since the Fall. First, God prepared the human race by teaching about desire (through the prophets), commanding it (through the law), and then communicating it to us by the Incarnation.

> How the coming of Our Saviour was desired! Adam, Noah, Abraham, Isaac, Jacob, the prophets and patriarchs all longed for His coming. *Drop down dew, ye hevens [sic], from above: and let the clouds rain the just. Let the earth be opened and bud forth a saviour.* [Isaiah 45:8] The prophet Aggeus said: *For thus saith the Lord of hosts: Yet one little while, and I will move the heaven and the earth and the sea and the dry land. And I will move all nations: and the desired of all nations shall come. And the angel of the testament whom you desire shall come to his temple.* [Haggai 2:7–8] The coming of Jesus Christ was greatly desired and the Holy Ghost wishes to be desired. For it is fitting that the gift of the Holy Ghost should be ardently desired before we receive it.[35]

The Son of the Father became man to give us his desire for the Father. The desire being spoken about throughout these pages is a supernatural, deified desire. It is the desire of the New Adam, not the Old Adam. It is different in kind, not merely in degree. It is a

33. Frederick Faber, *The Creator and the Creature, or, The Wonders of Divine Love* (London: Thomas Richardson and Son, 1858), 424–25.

34. De Ravignan, *Conferences on the Spiritual Life*, 195–96.

35. John of Ávila, *The Holy Ghost* (London: Scepter Limited, 1959), 15.

desire the historical Jesus left as a gift in his Mystical Body, and one can only exercise it within the Church, or on one's way to her.

> Ardent desires are the sign of the coming of God into the soul, as David teaches by these words: *Fire shall go before Him and burn His enemies round about*, for the flames of holy desires precede the arrival of God in the soul, that they may consume all remains of sin and prepare His abode. The soul will comprehend that God is not far off when she feels inflamed with this sacred fire, and can say with the Prophet: *The Lord has made fire penetrate the marrow of my bones*. Our good angel takes so great a pleasure in seeing us sigh after Our Lord and burn with this beautiful fire, that he supplies fuel for it by his inspirations. . . .[36]

One possesses this desire by being born of water and the Spirit, both of which must be desired. The supernatural case can be explained by a natural example. "Listen carefully to me! If a man will not go to another man's house because he is not sure of his welcome there, will this not also be the attitude of the Holy Ghost? He wants the man who desires His presence to desire it greatly; and He wishes to be desired by many."[37] Take another natural example, that of eating.

> The dish that is good of itself is wasted on him who has no wish for food. You would imagine that a chicken or a partridge would give anyone an appetite. But the sick man to whom it is offered says "Take it away, for I have lost all interest in food! I have no taste for it." A very bad sign indeed. You have no interest in food? It is a symptom of death.
>
> The Holy Ghost will not come to you if you do not hunger for Him, if you do not desire Him. Your desires for God will bring God to you, and the proof is that if you desire God He will come to you without delay.[38]

Jesus said those who hunger and thirst after justice are blessed, for they shall have their fill. "By justice He means holiness and the whole series of virtues that compose it. For only holiness can bring

---

36. Saint-Jure, *A Treatise on the Knowledge and Love of Our Lord Jesus Christ*, vol. 1, 322.
37. John of Ávila, *The Holy Ghost*, 15.
38. Ibid., 15–16.

us near to God, who is holy in His essence and cannot be united to anything that is not so. To be happy, then, it is necessary that the Christian should desire to be holy, and make every effort to become so."[39] The ones who have no fill are the ones who have no hunger, whose hearts are not purified. But it is unheard of that the Holy Spirit will not come to those who hunger and thirst for him.

It is fitting, therefore, that the gifts and fruits of the Holy Spirit should also be ardently desired. "For these are the mystic and most secret gifts of God. These gifts no man knows, but he that receives them; no one receives but he who desires, and no one desires but he whose desire is enkindled by the Holy Ghost."[40] When the Holy Spirit floods the heart, as once he flooded the house where the disciples were, he fills it with exercises of virtues practiced with fervor, such as "the love of God, zeal for His glory, hope of His mercy, a reverential fear of His majesty, joy for His excellency, praise and thanksgiving for His benefits, sorrow for sins, and ... desires of obeying God," all of which cause changes to appetites to the point that they become "filled with Thy Divinity, to the end that my desires and my propensities might henceforth be wholly divine."[41]

And after the Holy Spirit enkindles the heart, his gifts and fruits all serve to initiate and protect a love for Jesus Christ. "This desire of having an ardent love of Jesus Christ is a disposition absolutely necessary for acquiring the devotion to the Sacred Heart, which is itself a continual exercise of this ardent love. Jesus Christ never gives this love but to those who earnestly desire it. . . . All the Saints agree that the best disposition for acquiring a tender love of Jesus Christ is to have a great desire to love Him."[42] If one worries over having not the disposition to love Jesus, the solution is simple: start by desiring to love him. The citizens of the Church Triumphant have their desire; the citizens of the Church Suffering and the Church Militant experience a suffering because they do not. "It is inevitable that this

39. Grou, *The School of Jesus Christ*, 104.

40. Giovanni Bona, *The Easy Way to God: A Manual of Ejaculatory Prayer*, trans. Henry Collins, (London: Burns Oates & Washbourne, Ltd., 1876), 82.

41. De Ponte, *Meditations on the Mysteries of Our Holy Faith*, vol. 5, 201.

42. Croiset, *Devotion to the Sacred Heart*, 45–46.

love should burn with infinite desires to see and to possess Him. But what shall we call these desires? They are a hunger, they are a thirst, they are a fever; a hunger for God, a thirst for God, a fever to possess God."[43] As the desire is purified, the love will be purified.

> A heart must necessarily be purified by this ardent desire to be in a condition to be enkindled by the pure flames of divine love. This ardent desire not only disposes our heart to be inflamed with love for Jesus Christ; it also obliges our loving Saviour to enkindle in our hearts this sacred fire. Let us desire truly to love Him. Such a desire, we may say, is always efficacious. It is unheard of that Jesus Christ ever refused it His love.[44]

Christ the Physician will destroy our feverish attention to the world, and Christ the Good Shepherd will increase our fervor for the Father. The Father could refuse nothing the Son desired, and the Son desired nothing that the Father would have refused; it should be the same with us.

Will we fall short? Of course. We are currently in the Militant, not the Triumphant, Church. But even our individual sins are a *felix culpa*. "Will she ever offend her Spouse? Perhaps; though sincere, she is so frail! though she lives, she is so tempted! But if she forgets herself, if she turns aside, if she falls, hardly is the fault perceived, but drowned in so many tears, that she appears afterwards to be still more beautiful than if she had never wept."[45] God wastes nothing, not even sin. The laws of abnegation prove that he can use our pride to produce humility, our sin to produce repentance, our offences to bring forth cries for mercy. Christian conversion is a change of the object of desire—no longer our own gains, but God's glory. Christian growth in grace is an increase of desire for that new object— may God alone be glorified. Then the spiritual Christian discovers that even sorrow, trial, and tempest can contribute to God's glory. "I am expecting a great tempest to burst over me, but I await it joy-

43. Charles Gay, *The Christian Life and Virtues Considered in the Religious State*, vol. 3 (London: Burns & Oates, 1879), 355.

44. Croiset, *Devotion to the Sacred Heart*, 46.

45. Charles Gay, *The Christian Life and Virtues*, vol. 2 (London: Burns & Oates, 1879), 277–78.

ously; and looking to the Providence of God, I hope that this will conduce to His greater glory, and the more perfect repose of my soul."[46] The beatitude to which God leads is a secret happiness, unknown to the world, because the world operates by different desires and different satisfactions. "O, my child, how often the world calls good what is evil, and still oftener evil what is good."[47] The path is inscrutable to the world, and mysterious to the pilgrim, but the telos is clear. God will hear us, not according to our thoughts, but according to his own.

> Have a little patience, and you will see that all will go well. . . . He postpones the hour of the accomplishment of your holy desires only to make you find it happier; for the loving heart of Our Redeemer arranges and adjusts the events of this world to the greater good of those who unreservedly devote themselves to His love. It will come then, the happy hour you desire, the day which Providence has named in the secrets of its mercy.[48]

The Son says he has come to do his Father's will; Mary lets it be done to her according to God's command; every martyr died with the intention of honoring God; our soul is the more purified when everything works for the same end. The desire is endless, because love is endless. "The ardours of love in prayer are good if they leave good effects and occupy you not with yourself, but with God and his holy will. In a word, all interior and exterior movements which strengthen your fidelity towards this Divine will are always good. Love, then, celestial desires, and desire as strongly celestial love. We must desire to love and love to desire what can never be enough desired or loved."[49]

46. De Sales's words to Jane de Chantal in Francis de Sales and Jane de Chantal, *The Mystical Explanation of the Canticle of Canticles by St. Francis de Sales*, and *The Depositions of St. Jane Frances de Chantal in the Cause of the Canonisation of St. Francis de Sales* (in one volume) in *Library of St. Francis de Sales* (London: Burns & Oates, 1908), 115.

47. De Sales, *Letters to Persons in the World*, 109.

48. De Sales, quoted by Jean-Joseph Huguet, *The Consoling Thoughts of St. Francis de Sales* (Dublin: M. H. Gill & Son, 1877), 129.

49. De Sales, *Letters to Persons in the World*, 4.

2

Desiring to Desire

TO PRAY IS BEST; to want to pray is good; to want to want to pray is a start—the first touch by God. The desire described in chapter one is best; to want that desire is good; to desire to have the desire is still good. That is the subject of this chapter.

Do you want God? This is the first flicker. "Oh! even in our own day, God imparts His gifts. We have only to desire them in order to receive them."[1] Do you want to want God? This is a step before the first step. Or, we could call it a medium step: a mediation. The full step is too long for our short legs, so we begin to sprint with smaller steps, better fitted to our current stride. We cannot make the leap all the way to the final desire, but the yearning for the desire can stand in the middle (*medius*), and we beg God to view even this with good favor. "If thou feelest not this desire, do thou at least desire to have the desire. Say to thy gracious Lord: 'O good Jesus, I ought and I wish to love Thee with my whole heart; deign to supply for me what is wanting to my ardent desire and love.'"[2] A person who sought spiritual direction from de Caussade wrote "I am not sure that I do love, all that I know is that I try to love," to which he replied,

> Well, that is all that God requires of you. It is a received axiom in theology that God never refuses grace to him who does all that is in his power to acquire it. Try then to love Him, and if these efforts are not the fruit of love, they will obtain for you the grace of charity. God already gives you a great favour in inspiring you with the desire to love Him. Some day, I hope, He will lead you further, and satisfy this desire.[3]

---

1. De Sales, quoted in Jane de Chantal, *Meditations for Retreats Taken from the Writings of St. Francis de Sales* (New York: Benziger Brothers, 1900), 152.

2. Blosius, *Spiritual Works of Louis of Blois*, 129.

3. De Caussade, *Abandonment to Divine Providence*, 369.

We are surely not describing here an intention to give God less than he deserves (an inferior, second best desire). Do not look upon the desire to desire as a deficient objective, like trying to get by with something less than necessary. Rather, the desire to desire already confesses a weakness so profound that we realize how far short we fall of giving adequate attention to God, or possessing satisfactory desire for God. No act merits God's grace, not even the desire-act described in the previous chapter, and so we fall on our knees before Jesus to ask "if I do not merit this grace, accept at least the true desire I have of it."[4] We admit our helplessness, confess our weakness, and beg God to receive our widow's mite. "Thou knowest, O Lord, that if I could do so, I would give Thee all the praise, glory, and honour with which Thy angels laud, magnify, and glorify Thee, with all Thy elect. But as I am helpless to do so, receive at least my desire and my goodwill."[5]

This is a realistic assessment of our soul in the state of sin. Souls made sick on the forbidden fruit from Eden must have their appetite for the Paschal banquet restored and repaired. Desires that have been misdirected must be realigned, and desires that have toppled must be turned upright again. To the man who has no hunger, the Holy Spirit must first give the hunger before giving the food. "The disgusted sick man has no appetite for eating, yet has he an appetite to have an appetite; he desires no meat, but he desires to desire it. Theotimus, to know whether we love God above all things is not in our power, unless God himself reveal it unto us: yet we may easily know whether we desire to love him; and perceiving the desire of holy love in us, we know that we begin to love."[6] A man with no appetite at all is one thing; a man with no appetite who nevertheless misses it, regrets it, and wishes to have it, is another thing. This is conversion coming to a boil, and already begins to please God, who replies to us:

Thou canst not possibly have too high an idea of My loving-kindness and mercy, as long as thou dost not abuse My mercy as a

4. Croiset, *Devotion to the Sacred Heart*, 190.
5. Bona, *The Easy Way To God*, 128.
6. De Sales, *Treatise on the Love of God*, 412.

license to sin. Thou canst not trust in Me too much. Let this then be the constant employment of thy soul, to think of My goodness and to believe that I do not desire to condemn thee; for in good truth I desire to condemn no one who desires to correct his evil ways and does not despair. It satisfies Me that thou art sorry for thy sins and art resolved not to sin again.[7]

The median is directed toward the ultimate. The mediating desire to desire feeds the final desire because they both come from the same source, namely, the will. "The desire of loving and love depend upon the same will: wherefore as soon as we have framed the true desire of loving, we begin to have some love; and ever as this desire grows, love also increases."[8] An athlete doing the long jump takes a run-up; a convert preparing to make the long leap of faith takes a run-up of desiring to desire. Begin! and it will commence a campaign from lukewarmness to zeal, from weakness to strength, from incomplete to full-hearted. In order to love, start with a desire to love.

"He who desires love ardently shall shortly love with ardour... He who has no assurance of loving God is a poor man, and if he desire to love him he is a beggar, but a beggar with the blessed beggary of which Our Saviour has said: Blessed are the beggars of spirit; for theirs is the kingdom of heaven."[9] The full desire for God lives in the hearts of the saints, but the beginning desire to have this desire is a blessed beggary. If Jesus blessed the hunger and thirst for righteousness, then the theologians of abnegation can bless the hunger for hunger, and the thirst for thirst. "Do you and I hunger and thirst after justice? And if we do not hunger, if we do not thirst, let us at least have the desire of doing so; and if we think we have not even the desire of hungering and thirsting, let us have the desire of the desire, according to the words of the prophet."[10]

The very concept of desiring to desire exposes an interior strug-

---

7. Blosius (Louis of Blois), *Comfort for the Fainthearted* (Westminster: Art and Book Company, 1908), 150.
8. De Sales, *Treatise on the Love of God*, 412.
9. Ibid.
10. De Ravignan, *The Last Retreat*, 81–82.

gle, as if one will works against another will, both inside the same person. The desire feels it falls short—the desire is not as it ought to be. If that were all, that would be the end of it. The soul would want no more, wish no more, desire God no more. It would surrender and capitulate to self, world, Satan. But another part of the soul seems to regret this loss, and wishes to renew the desire, rekindle it, perfect it. Persistence is pitted against resistance, and God approves of the contest. He favors both the ultimate desire, and the penultimate desire. At least, he has communicated such to some of his favored mystics.

> When the same virgin, St. Gertrude, once complained that she could not feel as much desire of God as she ought, she was divinely taught that it was amply sufficient in the sight of God, if a man wished to have a great desire, though he might feel little or no desire within himself; because he has before God as great a desire as he wishes to have, and God dwells in the heart containing such a desire (that is to say, the will to have the desire) more gladly than a man could dwell amid fresh and pleasant flowers.[11]

This preliminary desire is like a key that unlocks the treasury: the contents have yet to be taken in hand, but the person with the key has before God as great a desire as he wishes to have.

The soul may be dissatisfied with the desire she feels, but God consoles her that the will to have the desire pleases him. His countenance smiles at the soul's wish to have great desire. The desire may not be great, but the God to whom it attaches is great, and that is what counts. God will then dilate the heart to receive its desired desires.

> My God!
> My heart is small in substance,
> But it is infinite in its desires.
> Though your happiness be ever so great,
> My heart is capable of containing it.
> However great paradise may be,

11. Blosius, *Spiritual Works of Louis of Blois*, 221.

My heart can contain it.
I may flit, as a bee, from flower to flower,
From creature to creature,
Without finding what I seek,
Without finding rest.
But when I rest in You, O God,
I have peace, and full satisfaction.[12]

Our desire may be meagre in our eyes, in our feelings, and in the eyes of other people, but it may be sufficient for a merciful God who looks for the slightest invitation to come and dwell in the soul that has ceased trying to find its rest in the world, and looks for its rest in God alone. In another rendition of the story about Saint Gertrude's regret for not feeling as much desire as she wished, we are told she learned that even "when we feel not in ourselves any desire of heavenly things; or, at least feel but a very weak one, it suffices that we truly desire to have a very ardent one; because in the eyes of God the desire is always as great as we would have it to be."[13] When a heart creates a desire this great, then God will count the heart's desires as effects, and will come to dwell there.

God dwells [there] with greater pleasure than that wherewith any man dwells in the most delightful place or palace in the world. In effect God does not want the sublimity of your prayer; he seeks only your heart, and will effect that all the good desires and sentiments thereof shall be accounted and rewarded as effects, or good works. Offer yourself, therefore, entirely to him in prayer; give him your whole heart, and desire to have as much fervor as even the angels of the highest choir can have; he will receive that good will, and make the same account of it as of the action itself.[14]

So many things are beyond our will and control, but our desire is not one of them. We can always want to want more.

12. John Crasset, *Meditations for Every Day in the Year from the Christian Considerations of Father John Crasset, S.J.: Pentecost to Advent* (London: R. Washbourne, 1888), 87.

13. Alphonsus Rodríguez (Alfonso), *The Practice of Christian and Religious Perfection*, vol. 1, 297.

14. Ibid., 298.

Some puzzlement comes from the fact that desire belongs partially to the will, and partially to the category of affection. On the one hand, even though affections are not easily controlled, they are such a crucial part of our relationship to God that they can be described as the better way of approach.

> It is better to approach God and virtue by the affections of the heart than by the thoughts of the mind, and it is an important counsel to nourish the heart and make the mind fast; that is to say, to desire God, sigh after God, long for the holy love of God, for an intimate union with God, without amusing yourself with so many thoughts and reflexions. . . . If you do not feel any of these desires the mere wish to have them, the mere raising of the heart is sufficient to keep your soul recollected and united to God.[15]

It is more preferable and useful to have a desire that leads to interior life, humility, fervor, prayer, the love of God, and the practice of virtues, than to make a thousand reflections about them, amusing though the exercise may be. You should remain occupied with the business of belonging to God. Do you do so? Perhaps not, or perhaps not adequately. But do you want to? The wish for such affection is sufficient to recollect the soul and unite it to God.

On the other hand, even though affection plays its role, the will is necessary to move the affection toward the good, and the intellect is necessary to point out the good to the will. "The will is the faculty by which we move towards and cleave to what is presented to us as being good, that is, as satisfying a want in us."[16] Of the three faculties within a person—understanding, will, and affection—the first is presented as a torch because it is the faculty that really shows things (shows things as they are in reality). "Such is the order established by nature, that the will being a blind power, it is the function of the understanding to lead it, bearing before it the torch which directs its affections according to the nature of the knowledge it gives, and a thing is loved or hated according as the understanding

15. De Caussade, *Abandonment to Divine Providence*, 143.
16. Edward Leen, *Progress Through Mental Prayer* (New York: Sheed and Ward, 1935), 206.

represents it as being worthy of love or hatred."[17] Our will must acquiesce to God's will, which accounts for the interior civil war: the old Adam does not want to submit, but the new creation struggling for birth is willing to do so. We catch it in the act of willing. One part of the soul is resisting, the other part is willing. Thus, the conflict. "From the depths of my heart I now will and desire that what I have said may remain as my firm and unchangeable determination. And as often as through my weakness, corruption and tendency to evil, through my negligence and forgetfulness, anything may be done otherwise, I protest that this is not my will but utterly contrary to my will and determination. Help me, I beseech Thee, and strengthen this will in me to the everlasting glory of Thy Name. Amen."[18] The person commands the will to will, the desire to desire.

Accepting the providences of crosses, humiliations, and being despised by the world is difficult, yet eventually one actually comes to desire these trials. "All interior souls do not pass through trials of the same length, or involving equal suffering. God regulates the measure for each as He wills; but all do go through trials; all pledge themselves to do so, and long for them more than they dread them; fear belongs to their nature only, but desire is in their will. For the love of crosses is one of the first feelings that God implants in their hearts, and that love is always on the increase."[19] The witness of the martyrs aids us in coming to want what they wanted, even if we will not be required to do what they did. If a person longed for martyrdom, but does not die a martyr's death, the promise is fulfilled nevertheless, because God bestows

> on that soul the essential love and reward of a martyr, making it a martyr of love, granting to it a prolonged martyrdom of suffering, the continuance of which is more painful than death. Thus He bestows really on that soul what that soul desired, and what He had promised. For the substance of that desire was, not any partic-

17. Saint-Jure, *Knowledge and Love of Jesus*, vol. 1, 51–52.
18. Blosius, *Comfort for the Fainthearted*, 82–83.
19. Grou, *The Spiritual Maxims of Pere Grou*, 150.

ular kind of death, but rather the oblation to God of the obedience of a martyr, and a martyr's act of love.[20]

Martyrdom is worth nothing without the friendship of God, which is what we are really desiring. Then God gives "the love, obedience, and reward of a martyr perfectly; and the soul is satisfied as to its desires, though the death of a martyr is withheld from it. These desires, and others like them, when they spring from true love, though not fulfilled as men may understand them, are nevertheless fulfilled in another and better way, and more for the honour of God than men know how to ask."[21]

We will be going the right direction if we earnestly desire to have these desires. God knows we begin weakly.

> You say that you feel not in yourself, as yet, a desire of being despised, but that you would fain have that desire. Begin, therefore, with that desire in your prayer, to exercise yourself in the virtue of humility, and say with the prophet: "My soul has longed always to desire thy justifications." (Ps. cxviii. 20). O how far am I from having these ardent desires, which so many have had to be despised! But I would fain, O my God, come to the point at least of wishing earnestly, to have these desires. Thus will you be in the right way; for this is a good beginning and disposition to obtain them.[22]

A lower mark of humility is to bear humiliations; the highest mark of humility is to welcome humiliations. "He who is truly humble desires to be humbled."[23] In the final stage of humility, we do not merely accept whatever comes, we *want* whatever comes—it is the final stage of surrender. Desire should lead to acquisition. "We shall never succeed in acquiring humility unless we really desire to

20. John of the Cross, *Ascent of Mount Carmel*, in *The Complete Works of Saint John of the Cross*, vol. 1 (London: Longman, Green, Longman, Roberts & Green, 1864), 141.

21. Ibid.

22. Alphonsus Rodríguez (Alfonso), *The Practice of Christian and Religious Perfection*, vol. 2 (London: James Duffy, 1861), 222–23.

23. De Sales, *Maxims and Counsels of St Francis de Sales for Every Day of the Year* (Dublin: M.H. Gill & Son, 1884), 160–61.

obtain it; nor shall we ever desire it unless we have learnt to love it, nor shall we love it unless we have realized what humility really is— a great and most precious good, absolutely essential to our Eternal Welfare. Consider for a little while in what esteem you hold humility. Do you love it? Do you desire it? What do you do to acquire it?"[24] Thereupon the soul will welcome and desire contempt, not for masochistic reasons, but for theological ones. The world that does not know how to reason theologically will never understand the Christian virtue that comes out of submission to crosses. "Any one who is convinced that he is very miserable, is not offended if he is despised: he sees that it is only just. A humble man, whatever bad treatment he may receive, thinks that justice is done him. Men do not esteem me; they are right, they agree in this with God, and with the Angels. Whoever has deserved hell, thinks that contempt is his due."[25] At the end, there is happiness in humility, which is why the saints desire it; at the beginning, we can only earnestly want to have this happiness. The desire to desire is a compass, pointing the direction of the journey of the soul.

Desiring to desire the cross takes us beyond the initial mercantile deals we make with God, such as when we say that we are willing to pay the price now for eternal beatitude later. The martyr does not suffer the cross in calculation of an eternal reward. The martyr desires what Christ desired; the martyr desires the cross because Christ desired the cross; Christ desired the cross because through it he "repaired the glory of His Father, appeased His anger, and reconciled Him with the world."[26] The path to union with God is the trackway of the cross. Abnegation (denial of self-will, and self-love, and the world) is how we embrace the cross in our daily lives. The Paschal Mystery that was played out on Calvary plays out again in our lives via abnegation. "The cross is the throne of the true lovers of Jesus Christ."[27] Christ's cross was his altar; our crosses become

---

24. De Bergamo, *Humility of Heart*, 110.
25. Croiset, *Devotion to the Sacred Heart of Jesus*, 82–83.
26. Jean Grou, *Manual for Interior Souls* (London: S. Anselm's Society, 1890), 31.
27. Margaret Mary Alacoque, *The Letters of St. Margaret Mary Alacoque*, Kindle edition (Charlotte, NC: TAN Books, 2012), letter 16.

altars, too. His cross creates liturgy. "Prayer is a fire that is fed with the wood of the cross."[28]

Cruciform threads of connection run from the historical Jesus, through his Church, to each individual Christian soul, binding all together. "Cultivate the spirit, the love and desire which annihilated Christ, that you, too, may be annihilated for Him."[29] Since that path was trod by Jesus, we desire it, which requires overcoming our aversion to suffering. Desiring to desire is a petition, a request, a prayer, a supplication. It may be slow in being answered, but it will be answered over a lifetime, under the direction of God's providence, if we do not flag in desire. And then we already foretaste the end of all desire: to be united to God. So remain in God peacefully, "acquiescing heartily in His will as to what He gives or takes away without doing more than retaining in the depths of the soul a sincere desire to belong entirely to God; to love Him ardently and to be ultimately united to Him, or else, as I have explained, to wish to have these desires."[30]

We experience this, too, in the natural realm. There are sufferings we do not relish in themselves, yet are willing to undergo because we can see the good they do, for ourselves or for others. It is the constant occupation of parents, but equally regular in the lives of any persons of charity. The moments when God painfully corrects a sin, an egocentricity, a selfishness, become occasions of joy. If one feels frightened approaching another cross, one's instruction is to desire whatever will reproduce that happiness again. Deconstructing sin, and sin's consequences, is a painful business to the Old Adam, but the embrace of contrition brings pardon, and if we are not yet contrite, let us at least desire to be contrite. "If sorrow and contrition appear wanting, at least be sorry that thou art not sorry, for this indeed is sorrow."[31] The lavishness of Christ's Precious

28. Jean Crasset, in Jean Crasset and Francis de Sales, *The Secret of Sanctity According to St. Francis de Sales and Father Crasset* (New York: Benziger Brothers, 1892), 159.

29. John Eudes, *The Priest: His Dignity and Obligations* (New York: P. J. Kenedy & Sons, 1947), 193.

30. De Caussade, *Abandonment to Divine Providence*, 144.

31. Blosius, *Comfort for the Fainthearted*, 4.

Blood has, one could say, "a whole world of extra-sacramental prodigality," because "all holiness is tied to the Sacraments by innumerous, indirect, and hidden fastenings.... Even the grandeur of perfect contrition is tied to the Sacraments by desire."[32] God can therefore say that the desire for contrition is more valuable than the sentiment of contrition.

> To grieve that thou dost not grieve is true sorrow and enough for the sacrament of Penance. Grieve for thy sins because thou hast offended Me, or at least grieve because thou dost not feel that thou grievest. For very often it is more pleasing to Me and better for a man himself to will to be contrite, or devout, than to feel contrition or devotion, because to desire to have it and not to feel it produces humble sorrow of heart....
>
> This kind of contrition, although it does not affect the feelings, that is, it leaves the heart feeling hard, arid and dry, still suffices for salvation. For I am well aware of thy misery, thy weakness, thy poverty. A man of good will must never be discouraged, whatever degree of coldness or dryness of heart he may feel, as long as he wishes he had not sinned and is determined for My sake not to sin again.[33]

In the person with perseverance, desire compensates for both dry prayer and coldness of heart because God considers what we desire, not what we feel. From Scripture we learn that converted sinners are more praised "than if they had never committed such great sins, but had lived a lukewarm life, and never burnt so fervently with love for Thee. For, according to the opinion of St Bernard, Thou dost not so much attend to what a man was, as to what in his heart he desires now to be."[34]

Contrition is learned slowly, step by step. The first words in the following profession before the Sacred Heart are difficult to say, but the hook of hope appears at the end.

32. Frederick Faber, *The Precious Blood; or, The Price of Our Salvation* (London: Burns & Oates, Ltd., 1860), 243.

33. Blosius, *Comfort for the Fainthearted*, 142.

34. Ibid., 30.

Thou art in this place, oh Lord, only to do me good. Who is there then, that shall hinder it? If my imperfections are an obstacle, begin, if it please Thee, by freeing me from these imperfections. Cure these wounds, which make me displeasing in Thy sight. I have not loved Thee, it is true. I am deeply grieved that it has been so. But at least, it seems to me that I have a true desire of loving Thee, and if this desire were not sincere, I should not so often come before Thee, who seest to the bottom of the heart, to ask for Thy love.[35]

Admit wounds, admit imperfections, admit displeasing God, within the context of being deeply grieved by it, then beg God to see the true desire to love him that lies underneath these failings. "For when we no longer either desire or commit sins, but turn ourselves utterly away from them, then God also forgets them."[36]

Belonging entirely to God is the happiness for which man is created. This desire should beat in the human heart, and if the spiritual heart has gone into cardiac arrest, it must be shocked back to life by abnegation. Telling God that we desire to have the desire will mean standing before the great Judge, which is the very thing we are afraid to do. But lo! the Judge surprises us.

We have all need to be reminded of some of these painful moments in the past, which will be a joy for the rest of our life! Then what happiness! how freely we breathe, how we feel that this Paternal Judge was waiting to pardon us! woe to us if we remain cold, indifferent and insensible, without seeking to acquire true contrition! at least, let us desire that we may have it, and ask as did the prophet for the "desire of desire."[37]

The desire to desire is daring the first step. It rises from faith, it prepares for hope, and it issues in love. The desire awakens from slumber upon seeing that the Judge is a Father who wants relationship with his children. The mercy of God must pry, or extract, this from us almost by force. So, we can hear him say, in comfort for the faint-

35. Croiset, *Devotion to the Sacred Heart of Jesus*, 129–30.
36. Blosius, *Comfort for the Fainthearted*, 31.
37. De Ravignan, *Conferences on the Spiritual Life*, 244.

hearted: "Thy chief desire should be to neglect nothing that will please Me, to think of Me, long for Me and love Me always. . . . Even if thy sins were heaped up mountains high and were multiplied by thousands of thousands, I forgive all, as if they were one. For it is not less easy for Me to forgive many sins than few."[38] Here God's omnipotence works in our favor. Besides creating countless stars, and giving life to countless souls, he can forgive countless sins. Therefore, the Lord concludes:

> What I am now going to say is indeed wonderful, but must be believed with most certain and undoubted faith. If the whole world were one globe of fire, and a little shred of linen were thrown into its midst it would not be so quickly burnt up as the abyss of My mercies receives a penitent sinner who desires to be converted. For in that merely natural burning of the shred of linen, some slight fraction of time would be necessary although so minute as to be perhaps quite imperceptible, but there is absolutely no interval of time between penitence and remission, between the groan of contrition and the answer of forgiveness.[39]

Desire conditions an act—both an act of righteousness and an act of sin. We can further understand the positive result of a desire if we look at the negative result of a desire, as if in a mirror. "It is the desire alone that makes us guilty in God's eyes, whether it be executed or not, for the same reason that makes God take our good desires into account when we are not able to carry them out. . . . We perceive it to be really true, then, that sin is committed in the heart, and derives its malignity from our inward dispositions. The same reasoning applies to good actions, which God estimates and rewards in accordance with the same rules."[40] Jesus increased the reach of the law beyond external actions into the interior heart. Even someone angry with his brother is a murderer; whoever insults his brother is liable to the council; even someone looking at

38. Blosius, *Comfort for the Fainthearted*, 153.
39. Ibid.
40. Grou, *The School of Jesus Christ*, 130–31.

a woman with lustful intent has already committed adultery in his heart (Mt 5:27–28).

> For if, for example, we consent to a mortal sin, it is certain that though at the same time we feel no sensible motion in ourselves, nor any pleasure at all therein, yet we cease not to offend mortally, and to deserve eternal damnation. By consequence, therefore, if we will and desire effectually what is good, though we feel not any sweetness in conceiving this will, yet, nevertheless, we fail not to please God, and merit heaven; chiefly because God is always more ready to reward than he is to punish.[41]

Can we imagine? Not only a desire for love, not only a desire for the sacrament of love, but even a desire for the law? "Only a continual great desire to be taught by God can make us worthy of discovering the wonders of his law. Each of us receives this sacred bread to the extent that we desire it."[42]

As sin is an act of the will, so desiring God is an act of the will. The classic example in Scripture, of course, is Abraham's sacrifice of Isaac. Was it an "attempted sacrifice" (because Isaac was not immolated) or a "true sacrifice" (because Abraham was willing)? We can see that sacrifices of love are acceptable to God "from the fact of His so often inspiring His servants with pious designs, which He never intends them to accomplish, as in the case of Abraham's sacrifice of Isaac, and St. Philip's desire to go to the Indies to preach the Gospel, and to shed his blood."[43] God estimates and rewards in accordance with the same rules: a bad act derives its malignity from our inward dispositions, a good act derives its righteousness from our inward dispositions. Therefore,

> Do not even attach great importance to an actual fulfillment of this desire if it is inspired by divine grace. You are permitted to desire such a fulfillment, but let it be with great humility and only to the extent that that holy impression prompts you to do so. You

41. Alphonsus Rodríguez (Alfonso), *The Practice of Christian and Religious Perfection*, vol. 1, 289.
42. Fénelon, *The Complete Fénelon*, 179.
43. Frederick Faber, *All for Jesus*, 326.

may hope that God's goodness will grant you that great favor, but let your hope be joined with great humility, great distrust of yourself, and do not let your hope go farther than grace prompts it.[44]

Everyone has a trajectory to the Messianic banquet, a trajectory personally approved by God, leading now to the altar of the Eucharist, and then to the wedding feast of the Lamb. This eschatological hunger can be sacramentally fed already. This has been treated under the category of *spiritual communion.* "The holy Council of Trent moreover, highly commends spiritual Communion, and zealously invites all the faithful to practise it; all truly pious souls have always observed this holy exercise. And what excuse can you give for not doing so? Is it want of time? It cannot be, seeing that a single act of desire and love, as quick as thought, is sufficient."[45] Things happen in a flash in the region of a heart standing before the altar, where desires play. The soul pours out her love in sighs and desires "till they find the object of their desires in the enjoyment of the Beloved. It is but a moment—a moment so brief and yet so long!"[46] Sacramental Communion should create an excitement in a heart that has been spiritualized. This spiritual communion is not a substitute for sacramental Communion, the former accompanies the latter, both before and after. Regarding before: spiritual communion *disposes* us for sacramental Communion. "The first duty [of spiritual communion] is, duly to prepare ourselves before sacramental communion, adorning the soul with acts of virtues suitable

44. Francis Libermann, *Letters to Clergy and Religious,* Spiritan Series 7, vol. 3 (Pittsburgh: Duquesne University Press, 1963), 68.

45. Henri-Marie Boudon, *The Book of Perpetual Adoration; or The Love of Jesus in the Most Holy Sacrament* (London: R. Washbourne, 1873), 78. De Liguori's Act of Spiritual Communion was used during the pandemic. "My Jesus, I believe that Thou art truly present in the Most Blessed Sacrament. I love Thee above all things, and I desire to possess Thee within my soul. Since I am unable now to receive Thee sacramentally, come at least spiritually into my heart. I embrace Thee as being already there, and unite myself wholly to Thee; never permit me to be separated from Thee." Alphonsus de Liguori, *The Holy Eucharist,* vol. 6 of *The Complete Works of Saint Alphonsus de Liguori, The Ascetical Works* (New York: Benziger Brothers, 1887), 124.

46. Crasset, in Crasset and de Sales, *The Secret of Sanctity,* 204–5.

to this celestial banquet."[47] Then we hear Mass with profit. Regarding after:

> You should return to your own homes on leaving the Holy Altar, with more love than you carried thither with you; and so with the desire and the determination to be more firmly and closely united to God, to be more attentive and more faithful to grace; more watchful over yourselves; more courageous to fight and to do violence to yourselves; more charitable towards your neighbour, more gentle and patient in bearing with him; more careful in fulfilling the duties of your station; more generous in giving to God; stronger in suffering all those crosses which may come into your way.[48]

Had we lived while Christ was teaching in the flesh, we could have expressed our desire to meet him by going to the place where he was teaching. Today, our trip can be even shorter.

> [St Gertrude] was divinely instructed that as often as a man gazes with desire and devotion on the Host where the Body of Christ lies hid sacramentally, so often does he increase his merit in heaven; and that in the future Vision of God to all eternity there shall be to him so many special and congruous joys, as the times that on earth he gazed with desire and devotion on the Body of our Lord, or which is greatly to our present purpose, when he so much as desired to do so, and was reasonably hindered from doing it.[49]

Try to assist at Mass; if this be impossible, commune by spiritual desire. "God is pleased to attach the same promise to the desire to see Him as to the actually doing so; so that the remarkable words of St. Lawrence Justinian were no devotional exaggeration, when he said, 'Let us persist in our prayers, that better gifts may be daily given to us. For it very often happens that what merits cannot do, the intercession of desires effects.'"[50]

47. Louis de Ponte, *Meditations on the Mysteries of Our Holy Faith*, vol. 1 (London: Richardson and Son, 1852), 344. Sometimes listed as Luis de la Puente, or D'Aponte.

48. Grou, *Meditations upon the Love of God*, 120.

49. Faber, *All for Jesus*, 295.

50. Ibid.

Desire union with God and not anything short of that. God has given us many instruments by which it will come about. "Now this union is formed, practiced, and rendered perfect by sanctifying grace; by acts of the virtues, in particular of the virtues of Faith, Hope, and Charity; by the worthy reception of the sacred body of Jesus Christ in the Blessed Sacrament, which, for this reason, is called Communion; by desires, by petitions, but chiefly by imitation of our Lord, which produces his likeness in us."[51]

If, during this pilgrimage, one does not attain what one desires, do not go limp. Desire to keep the desire active. The desire of a postponed blessing creates a tension in the bow that shoots arrows of love toward God. The most substantial part of the spiritual life happens out of sight of the world: the merit is given *even if the man couldn't act.* "God is just, my dear brethren, in all that He does. When He recompenses us for the smallest good action, He does so over and above all that we could desire. A good thought, a good desire, that is to say, the desire to do some good work even when we are not able to do it, He never leaves without a reward."[52]

"This poor man cried, and the Lord heard him" (Ps 34:6); "The desire of the righteous will be granted" (Prov 10:24); "O Lord, you will hear the desire of the meek" (Ps 10:17); "Take delight in the Lord, and he will give you the desires of your heart" (Ps 37:4). Promises made; promises kept, even if not before the eyes of the world. "Many Saints have desired many things for God in this life, and their desires have not been granted; but it is certain that, as their desires were just and good, they will be perfectly fulfilled in the world to come. And as this is true, so also is it true, that God in this life performs His promise of granting their desires, though not in the way they thought."[53] Even though we sometimes cannot act, even though God will sometimes not act at the present moment, every desire is heard. Therefore, we want to keep it alive by desiring the desire.

51. Saint-Jure, *Union with Our Lord Jesus*, 14.

52. John Vianney, *The Sermons of the Curé of Ars* (Chicago: H. Regnery, 1960), 133.

53. John of the Cross, *Ascent of Mount Carmel*, in *Complete Works*, vol. 1, 141–42.

3

Desire and Act

WE NOTED IN THE LAST CHAPTER that Jesus increased the reach of the law into the interior heart, beyond external actions alone. God regards the heart because it is the place from which actions emanate. "When thou dost wish and desire to do any good work, but art not able, that holy desire is received by God as if it were the work itself."[1] God's all-searching eye is trained on the interior fountainhead most of all.

> God is a simple act. Whatsoever is done stands in a certain relation to God. . . . Words, therefore, are but accidents. Nay, overt acts add but little, comparatively, to the malice of the interior will. The thought has been assented to; the intention has been formed; the temptation has been deliberately admitted. The thing is irrevocable. It has touched God, and is stereotyped. He needs no index of the voice, nor consummation of the hands. It is an act, and ranks as such with Him, for good or evil, for reward or punishment.[2]

In God's eyes, desire is deed, even when the person does not, or cannot, bring the ambition to action. "God sees this desire, and, in His sight, desires are equal to acts, whether for good or evil."[3]

This is the subject of this chapter: if the desire is equal to an act, our authors are led to say "a voluntary thought and a deliberate desire are not less actions in the sight of God than the words of our mouths or the operations of our hands."[4] Of course, it is important and necessary to put the virtue into practice, and, of course, it is not

---

1. Blosius, *Spiritual Works of Louis of Blois*, 89.
2. Faber, *All for Jesus*, 291–92.
3. De Caussade, *Abandonment to Divine Providence*, 225.
4. Faber, *Creator and the Creature*, 220.

enough just to wish idly, abstractedly, and apathetically. But by his foreknowledge, God knows whether the present desire will grow into action, and by his knowledge of the interior God knows how much disease or health is in the heart. We may consider those desires that never issue forth in activity to be fruitless, failed, innocent, but God "raises even our ineffectual desires to the dignity of effectual acts."[5]

The tree is the consummation of the seed, but the seed is already the beginning of the tree. The act is the consummation of the desire, but the desire is already the beginning of the act. Desiring intends; desiring fixes attention upon an outcome; because the desire is original (in the sense of "that from which anything is derived") it is whence the outcome comes into existence.

> If we do not hunger and thirst, if we are still cold, let us ask of God to kindle in us the fire of His burning charity, which will give us the consummation of purest virtue, the consummation of holiness in Jesus Christ; and then abandon your heart to the zeal of holy love, to the virtues of meekness, patience, peacemaking—virtues difficult, I acknowledge, to practise, but virtues which are the strength of the soul. Ask for them, desire them; *to desire is to begin to practise already.*[6]

God's omniscient wisdom is master of cause and effect, so on the day that Saint Gertrude did not feel as devout as she wished, she offered all the preparation and devotion of Mary and the saints on her own behalf, and the Lord appeared to her and said, "Now thou dost appear before Me, and in the eyes of My Saints, clothed and adorned according to thy desire," to which Eudes concludes, "O Lord! how good art Thou to thus take our desires for effects!"[7] The divine wisdom that knows the cause also knows the results of faith and good works in his foreknowledge. "God has prepared Paradise for those He foreknows as His; let us strive to be truly His in faith

---

5. Faber, *All for Jesus*, 285.
6. De Ravignan, *The Last Retreat*, 97. Emphasis added.
7. John Eudes, *St. John Eudes: Selections from His Writings* (London: Burns Oates & Washbourne, Ltd., 1925), 97.

and in works, and He will be ours in glory. And it rests with us to be His; for though it comes of God's Gift, He never refuses that Gift to any, but offers it freely to all who will heartily consent to receive it. See, then, how earnestly God desires that we be His."[8] Love meets love, desire meets desire, God meets man. Our action is to desire God, God's action is to pull us into himself. "Let us first say:—Doth God love us? Who can doubt it! And do we love Him? If we desire to do so, we do."[9] One cannot love even other people accidentally, unintentionally, or by chance: love must be willed. One must desire to do so, and then one does. To love God is to adhere to him by the will, because charity is "an affection rather of the will, than [an affection of] the sensitive faculties."[10]

We are saved by charity. God prefers to weigh the love we have for him, rather than count up the actions we do for him, because if we did the actions, or kept the commandments, or even lived the religious life, without love, it would count for nothing. The actions must be expressions of an interior love. If the deed merits anything, it is because of the intensity of the love for God with which it is done. "We must desire our salvation; the merit lies in the will which attaches itself to the law of God, and which has eternity for this aim and object."[11] God will receive the good will for the deed because he regards the heart, and if you do not feel a fervent devotion to God, then apply yourself to the desire. "Exercise yourself in wishing to have this devotion, and these desires; and hereby you will supply what is wanting to you. For God who regards the heart, will receive your good will for the deed, according to the words of the prophet, 'the Lord has heard the desire of the poor; thy ears, O Lord, have heard the preparation of their heart.' [Psalm 10:17]."[12] There are times when we would do the deed if we could, but cannot. At such times, we can do nothing more than embrace this desire and trust that God knows all. "Accustom thyself to dispose thy will in this

8. De Sales, *Treatise on the Love of God*, 133.

9. De Castañiza, *The Spiritual Conflict and Conquest*, 450.

10. Baker, *Holy Wisdom*, 261.

11. De Ravignan, *Conferences on the Spiritual Life*, 80.

12. Alphonsus Rodríguez (Alfonso), *The Practice of Christian and Religious Perfection*, vol. 2, 437.

kind of way, and to raise and direct it to God. For then God in His loving-kindness will accept the will for the deed, where thou canst do nothing more."[13]

The gracious way by which we can come to God is by the merits of Jesus Christ, in whom our desire for justification and sanctification is satisfied. Salutary desire binds us to Christ, and Christ to us. "To put man in a state to enjoy these advantages, Jesus Christ assists him with His grace, according to these beautiful words of Peter, Abbot of Moustier: 'Jesus, with a goodness and largess truly divine, recompenses not only our good actions, but even our good desires.'"[14] In a practical world, a desire without action is useless because utilitarian consequence is the only concern. When one is only interested in a result, the motive is irrelevant. But when one is interested in a person, the motives of all the actions are immensely relevant. A parent is gratified by what his child wants, even if the child falls short, because utility is not a component of love. This is extremely important during the dark nights of the soul. Even when the inferior soul lacks sensible consolation, the superior soul can choose (will) to desire. "When God deprives you of his sensible presence, and of devotion in recollection, content yourself with having a holy desire and wish to retain it; this will suffice, as it is most pleasing to God and very meritorious."[15] Alonso Rodríguez is speaking of himself in third person when he gives "an account of conscience" about a man who fears that his Jesuit society will dismiss him. In his autobiography he admits he lived with these fears for many years, but then "he had recourse to God for consolation and heard a voice which said to him, 'It is enough that I want it,' like someone says, 'Even were all the world to contradict it, it is enough that I should want it.'"[16] And on the basis of this desire, he remained for thirty-five more years. "Oh, how much easier it is to love than to fear! Fear constrains, fetters,

13. Blosius, *Comfort for the Fainthearted*, 83.

14. Saint-Jure, *The Spiritual Man*, 228.

15. De Caussade, *Abandonment to Divine Providence*, 233–34.

16. Alonso Rodríguez (Alfonso), *St Alphonsus Rodríguez: Autobiography* (London: Geoffrey Chapman: London, 1964), 78–79. See FN 45. Though named Alphonsus, this porter is known as Alonso (see Rodríguez, page 10).

perplexes one; but love persuades, comforts, inspirits, expands the soul, and makes one desire what is good for its own sake."[17]

Jesus is the mediatorial link between his heavenly Father and us. He walks before us as guiding shepherd; he walks behind us to catch a stumble; he walks beside us to encourage.

> Jesus carries His overflowing goodness so far as to make up even this powerlessness. On our part, when it is impossible for us to follow the inclination of our piety, and to be present personally at the Celebration of His Sacrifice, He is satisfied with the desire of our hearts, and grants us therein the same share as if we were present. He bears upon the Altar, as He bore upon the Cross, all the Faithful in His Heart; they are all present to His Mind. . . . We can daily celebrate on the Altar of our hearts the Sacrifice of our salvation.[18]

It is incumbent to insist that this desire must operate on a level of sincerity to which only God can be witness. The Church accepts the witness that a desire for the sacrament was sincere if it leads to actually being baptized, or assisting at Mass, or making confession, but here we are discussing the internal desire of a heart present to Christ's mind when he is upon the altar, and upon the cross, and offering absolution through his ministers. He can recognize a desire for the Father when he sees it. Our mystical union with Christ allows him to recognize our desire for God if it looks like the desire for the Father he has, himself. To acquire this treasure of divine love

> the only thing necessary is greatly to desire it. Yes, God only asks for love, and if you seek this treasure, this kingdom in which God reigns alone, you will find it. If your heart is entirely devoted to God, it is itself, for that very reason, the treasure and the kingdom that you seek and desire. From the time that one desires God and His holy will, one enjoys God and His will, and this enjoyment corresponds to the ardour of the desire. To desire to love God is truly to love Him.[19]

17. François Fénelon, *Letters to Men* (London: Rivingtons, 1877), 3.

18. Jean Grou, *The Practical Science of the Cross* (London: Joseph Masters, 1871), 153.

19. De Caussade, *Abandonment to Divine Providence*, 87–88.

Desire enjoys. We use the latter word to indicate the pleasure or satisfaction we receive from something or someone, but the etymology indicates a second meaning. The prefix *en* means to make, to cause, or bring about—as in engender, endanger, enact—so to enjoy God could also mean "to cause joy in God." A blessed soul will have two charges in heaven: to enjoy God and to en-joy God. It is a remarkable component of the gospel that God wants our praise, even though he does not need our praise. The desire we are talking about is liturgical in nature, and a love as jealous as God's revels in our desire to love him.

We have responsibility and culpability for the deeds we do, but there are other deeds we cannot do, even if we wish to. Often, we are limited in what actions we can take by our talent, our opportunity, our circumstance, or our station. Our plans or intentions usually negotiate with the objective world, and sometimes compromise in it, so we wind up conceiving more activity than we can accomplish. But it is different with desire: we do have charge of our desire, which is why "the immense Mercy of our Eternal Creator condescends to approve not only what man can do, but what he would desire to do; for the merits of the just are counted up by the Most High, not only in the doing of the work, but in the desire of the will."[20] A parade of existential questions pass by: what can I do? what would I do? what shall I do? what do I want to do? If God takes the will for the deed, then he is even pleased by our desire for actions we cannot perform.

> After this, direct your prayer to the most Holy Trinity, and offer the praises of your heart. Have an ardent desire to praise God more than you do and more than you can. For God looks at the will, the desire; and He considers a man to have done well all that the will really desires. *He takes the will for the deed*, although the man cannot really perform and execute what he sincerely desires. Our desires are, in fact, as great before God as we truly and sincerely wish them to be.[21]

---

20. Faber, *All for Jesus*, 228.
21. Blosius (Louis of Blois), *A Book of Spiritual Instruction: Institutio Spiritualis*, (St Louis: B. Herder, 1900), 81–82. Emphasis added.

If one desires whole-heartedly, and if one does all that one can do, then one possesses virtue in the sight of God. The virtues will display greater glory to God when they come to surface in the living of a life, but God takes the kernel, too.

This sort of desire is not hypocritical puffery: we are not fooling God. Neither is it a wish to get by at a minimal level. The ardor of the desire seeks more, not less, love of God.

> Assuredly, all good things depend upon the will; and when thou earnestly desirest with thy whole heart, and doest all that lies in thy power to possess humility, charity, or any other virtues, without doubt thou possessest them in the sight of God. In like manner, when thou desirest from thy heart to do any good work, but art not able, God receives thy good will for the deed. And God accounts thy desire to be as great as thou with thy whole heart wishest it to be.[22]

Blosius goes on to counsel that it is good, and profitable, to speak in what must surely sound like hyperbole to an outside listener. "It is, therefore, exceedingly profitable to pray thus: 'Would that I might, O my Lord, for the honour of Thy name, have as much love and affection for Thee as any creature ever had.... I seek and desire with my whole heart to please Thee perfectly in all virtue and holiness, by Thy merciful will.'"[23] We know that we cannot deceive God, and this is never being attempted when we take a sincere refuge in God accounting our desires to us. Rather, this is exactly the sort of thing a lover would say to his beloved: all limits are abandoned, all practical considerations are ignored, and one is swept away with a desire stronger than any we can conceive on this side of beatitude. What a satisfaction heaven will be when the desire will be felt, and real, and satisfied! "So great is the Power of Love, that it does in a manner, transform the Lover, into the thing belov'd. It is a kind of willing Death, a voluntary Separation of the Soul and Body. He that is in Love is out of himself."[24]

---

22. Blosius, *Spiritual Works of Louis of Blois*, 151.
23. Ibid.
24. Giovanni Bona, *Manductio ad Coelum*, 105. Capitalization in original.

No excuses! No one may say that he would be more zealous if only circumstances would permit it, more charitable if only the opportunity would arise, more faithful if only the trials came as they did to the saints about whom he reads. The Master judges with a different eye. Grou describes the multiple mastery Jesus has over us. He is the Master of our reason, who gives light to every man that comes into the world; Master of our hearts, who purifies and orders their affections; a Master who teaches in the deepest places of the heart, without noise of words and without argument; a Master who teaches in one instant of time; a Master who never leaves us, and who takes the work of our sanctification into his own hands; a Master who handles our wills with equal gentleness and force, and makes us desire what he commands; a Master who began by doing what he proposed to teach; and finally, "a Master who judges with infinite justice and rewards all our good deeds with infinite generosity, testing their value by the purity, sincerity and rectitude of our motives. For He accepts a genuine desire as though it were achievement, the effort in the place of success, the intention for accomplishment, when the actual deed is out of our power."[25] Even if one fails to do the good work, God will receive the good will for the deed, because the intention is an achievement of the will.

This is the only way to make sense of the story of a foreigner who could not make confession because he found no priest who could understand his language. Saint Bridget interceded on his behalf, as saints are wont to do, and the Lord answered her:

Tell him to be of good courage. The will is sufficient, when a man is not able to do the good work that he desires to do. For what brought salvation to the thief on the cross? Was it not his good will? And what constitutes hell, but an evil will and inordinate affections? . . . Without doubt a good will is a great and sweet treasure. He who has this, desires and endeavours to obey and to please God, and to do those things which are acceptable to Him.[26]

---

25. Grou, *The School of Jesus Christ*, 4.
26. Blosius, *Spiritual Works of Louis of Blois*, 241.

Penitents who are found in Scripture and among the saints are dear to our authors. "My patrons in Heaven and my chosen favourites are those who have stolen it—like the Holy Innocents and the Good Thief. The great Saints have earned it by their works; as for me, I will imitate the thieves, I will have it by ruse, a ruse of Love which will open its gates to me and to poor sinners."[27] Priests are advised to have their penitents "recall the conversion of St. Peter, St. Paul, St. Mary Magdalen, St. Augustine, the good thief and countless others."[28]

The good thief was foremost among them because his desire was his repentance, since he was already at the end of his life. The good thief was saved by desiring to unite his cross with Christ's. "Daily does the Blood of the Saviour work upon the Altar the same miracles that It wrought upon Calvary. Here It converts, here It sanctifies sinners. . . . [When the good thief] beheld himself, he acknowledged his Savior, he united the sacrifice of a life of sin to the sacrifice of a life all holy, he asked for pardon, he obtained it, and was the first of the predestinated baptized in the Precious Blood which flows upon the Cross."[29] Jesus told us that the kingdom of heaven suffers violence (Mt 11:12), and this thief is a model of one whose suffering won the kingdom. "How was it that the good thief won [the kingdom of heaven] by violence on the cross? Because he made it his own in a few moments."[30] It is rapid, it is thorough, it is exhaustive. Theologians teach that the least act of contrition, produced in an instant, is capable of purifying a soul. Desire that opens a crack in the human heart will open a greater passage in the divine heart.

> The Jews had a very beautiful gloss on this truth: My children, says the holy and blessed God to the people of Israel, give me in your hearts an opening for penance only as large as the eye of a needle, and I will give you in Mine, in the bosom of My mercy, an opening so great that chariots can pass through it. The value of Penance, says St. Chrysostom, is not measured by length of time, but by the

---

27. Thérèse of Lisieux, *Thoughts of the Servant of God Thérèse of the Child Jesus* (New York: P. J. Kenedy & Sons, 1915), 137.

28. Eudes, *The Priest*, 178.

29. Grou, *Practical Science of the Cross*, 154–55.

30. Segneri, *The Manna of the Soul*, vol. 2, 379.

disposition of the heart. . . . Whoever asks pardon of God with a good heart, and says to Him one word of true repentance, obtains forgiveness and is restored to grace in the same moment.[31]

Even in the natural state we can understand the superiority of someone who does a deed with a good spirit, over someone who does a deed grudgingly and resentfully, even if it is a good deed. How much more obvious is this difference to the eyes of God, who can see more than we do. "Humble patience, cheerful gratitude of heart, and holy confidence in Him, will fully compensate for what may be sinful in the dissipation of the senses. God regards and delights no less in our reasonable endeavours and pious desires to do right, than in our work itself."[32]

This can be confirmed by many examples, and one of great edification comes from Saint Augustine. He was visited by an African named Potitianus, a man in the service of the emperor. While others joined the Emperor at Trier to watch the circus games, Potitianus and his three friends took a short walk out of the city and entered a hermitage where they found a book containing the hagiography of Saint Anthony. He had scarcely begun to read when he felt his heart inflamed with divine love, and he exclaimed:

What do we aspire to, for all the services we have so many years rendered the Emperor? The most we can hope for is, to obtain his favour, and than this what can be more frail or dangerous? For how much must we still encounter before we can arrive to any great fortune, which of itself is also very dangerous, and, therefore, is so much the more to be feared? But, should I endeavour to gain the love of God, I can do it with ease—I may obtain it in a moment—it suffices that I only earnestly desire it.[33]

The esteem of the world takes much labor and many years to acquire, but the love of God can be obtained in a trice. God's work

---

31. Saint-Jure, *Knowledge and Love of God*, vol. 1, 230.

32. Blosius, *Spiritual Works of Louis of Blois*, 45.

33. Alphonsus Rodríguez (Alfonso), *The Practice of Christian and Religious Perfection*, vol. 1, 331. De Granada also uses the story in *A Memorial of a Christian Life*, 10.

was perfected in his heart while he read further, and he became disgusted with things of the world, renounced all hopes upon earth, fixed his thoughts only upon heaven, and joined the hermitage immediately.

How much desire does it take? Not much, if it is humble and sincere. How much effort does it take for what follows? A lifetime of abnegating self-love, self-will, self-esteem. The first raising of the eyes is simple and tranquil, even if the enactment that follows will require effort. "Thou deliverest me from innumerable dangers, adornest me with many gifts and graces, givest me leave at all times to have free access to Thy throne of mercy, so that with one holy thought, one humble sigh, one devout desire, I may draw near to Thee, and enjoy Thee."[34] We shall later see the connection of desire to faith, hope, and love, but it is worth noting the dimension of faith being treated here. We are speaking of one holy thought, one humble sigh, one devout desire—all of which are responses of faith to the grace that God showers upon each person individually. The twitch on the line of grace by the divine fisherman is intended to catch us, and turn us away from creatures toward the Creator. Abnegation makes the desire simpler (to desire only one thing) and purer (to desire the supreme happiness, and nothing less). Purity of heart means to will one thing, and not be split in desires.

Created for conversation with Almighty God, abnegation must cure us from distracted senses and a scattered imagination.

> It does not take much time to love God, in order to renew ourselves in his presence, to raise our heart to him or to worship him in the depths of our heart, to offer him what we do and what we suffer. This is the true kingdom of God within us, which nothing can disturb.
>
> When distraction of the senses and vivacity of imagination stop the soul from recollecting itself in a quiet and sensitive manner, we must at least calm ourselves by the rightness of our will. *Then the desire for recollection is itself recollection enough.* We must turn ourselves to God, and do with a right intention all that he wants us to

---

34. De Castañiza, *The Spiritual Conflict and Conquest,* 256.

do. We must try to awaken in ourselves from time to time the desire to be with God.[35]

Desiring to love is love; desiring to pray is prayer; devoutness is piety. And these may go on even without the consolations sensibly felt. "A profound desire for recollection is a very real recollection in itself, although unaccompanied by pleasure. If less consoling than sensible recollection, it is all the more disinterested, and consequently more meritorious. In such a state one appropriates nothing to oneself because one seems to possess nothing at all."[36]

The desire to be with God animates liturgy. What are all the false motives that could bring us before the altar of the Lord? Vanity? Sanctimoniousness? Parading our virtue to the world? The mercantile motives of a slave? Liturgy must be done from the depths of a true desire to be present to God, since God has constructed the whole liturgical apparatus as a means to continue his presence with us, even after the Incarnate One has ascended. "What shall we then say of the mystery of the most holy Eucharist, which is, as it were, an extension of the Incarnation! In the holy Eucharist the Son of God, in His overflowing mercy, not content with having made Himself the Son of Man, a sharer in our humanity and our Brother, has invented a wondrous way of communicating Himself to each one of us in particular."[37] Not content with having walked the earth for one score and thirteen, not content with the thousands who heard him preach, not content with the many he miraculously cured, Jesus devised a way of continuing to offer communion with himself. Those who desired to see the Messiah had but to walk the distance to Galilee; we have an even shorter distance to walk. Love, abnegation, sacrifice—we know it would be a hollow liturgy if celebrated without these in the soul. "The increase of the desire to consecrate yourself to God is an additional grace of His mercy," and if there is a delay in accomplishing these ardent desires, it

---

35. Fénelon, *Christian Perfection*, 27. Emphasis added.
36. De Caussade, *Abandonment to Divine Providence*, 355.
37. Camus, *The Spirit of St. Francis de Sales*, 390–91.

is intended to try your fidelity. If, in the meantime, you are getting on in years, you need not consider that, because you already possess the best part of what you wish for, which is, the strong desire to consecrate yourself to God. This desire is, in the sight of God, the best part of the sacrifice, or, to speak correctly, it is the entire sacrifice since you have already given yourself to Him, in heart and soul, and are now sacrificing your most earnest desires in awaiting patiently the time chosen by His providence.[38]

We hasten to add, in concluding, that we are talking about involuntary failures to act, not deliberate avoidance when the opportunity arises. God's scale weighs genuineness, sincerity, rectitude, and purity of intention. "Purity of intention is the measure of holiness, and is proportionate to the degree of light communicated by God, and to the faithfulness of our correspondence to the same. God indeed considers, not our actions in themselves, but our motives. Therefore the slightest action of the Blessed Virgin was of greater value in the eyes of God than the noblest works of other Saints, because her intention was incomparably pure."[39] We are so accustomed to imagining that desires invade our souls unbidden, sometimes unwelcome, sometimes deceitfully, that we have a difficult time thinking of a desire as an achievement. But desire does, indeed, include intention. If a gap exists between the desire and its effectuation by reason of voluntariness then we are to blame, but we can take heart if that gap exists involuntarily. That is what these authors are telling us: the delay might be God's decision.

> Suppose I should never be able to accomplish my holy desires? Very well! that would prove to me that God does not require it, and I should be satisfied to do His holy will; because it would then be obvious that God did not wish for the sacrifice itself, but only that I should be willing to make it.... God, not permitting nor desiring the actual sacrifice, is satisfied with the sacrifice of desire, which, in His sight, is the same thing.[40]

38. De Caussade, *Abandonment to Divine Providence*, 162.
39. Grou, *The Spiritual Maxims*, 69.
40. De Caussade, *Abandonment to Divine Providence*, 165.

And when we submit to the grace that connects cause (desire) and effect (abnegation), then the desire makes everything easy.

It is difficult to agree to this providence, and even more difficult to approve of it, but one should let God be God, and trust him to bring us home by the path he has chosen. The saints of Ávila (John of Ávila, Teresa of Ávila, and John of the Cross) teach that the dark night can be a trial from God, given for the twin purposes of our good and his glory. The desire for God during the dark night is more meritorious than a desire for God in the bright sunlight of consolation. Therefore, take joy in the desire that continues to throb even in darkness, and "do not dwell on the pain that the difficulty you experience in concentrating your thoughts causes you. Remind yourself that the habitual desire of recollection alone will serve equally well, and that all that is necessary is to desire unceasingly to think of God, to please God, to obey God, in order to please and to obey Him in reality."[41]

As we have noted, one is culpable for so much as consenting to mortal sin, even if one feels no sensible motion, and even if one hasn't the opportunity to commit the deed contrived in mind. We may therefore conclude, in a reverse application, that "if we will and desire effectually what is good, though we feel not any sweetness in conceiving this will, yet, nevertheless, we fail not to please God, and merit heaven; chiefly because God is always more ready to reward than he is to punish."[42]

---

41. Ibid., 336.
42. Alphonsus Rodríguez (Alfonso), *The Practice of Christian and Religious Perfection*, vol. 1, 289.

4

Implanting the Desire

A FIRST DISTINCTION WAS MADE in the last chapter, and now we have a second to make. We denied the notion that desires always invade us irresistibly from the outside, or arise unbidden and uncontrolled from within, and we affirmed the fact that desire can be a sort of achievement by the soul. A second characteristic must now be noted: the desire achieved is not an autonomous accomplishment, but a synergistic response to the energies of God.

> It is true, that thou art a party to the various acts of virtue, by force of thy free-will. But this very concurrence thou owest to God, Who causes thee to concur, without, however, doing violence to thy natural freedom: "It is God Who worketh in you to will" (Phil 2:13). Does not the body concur in all its own operations, of seeing, dancing, speaking, and the like? And yet it could not without folly attribute to itself instead of the soul which is its guiding power, any one of these operations. Here then is a good illustration of thy free-will stripped of the grace of God; it is a body without a soul: it can do nothing: or if it can do anything, it can only commit sin, and run headlong to ruin and perdition.[1]

A person cannot attribute all his desires to himself, without God, any more than the members of the body can attribute their movement to themselves, without the soul. All the mystics describe their experience of this, because their vocation is to give words to every Christian's less perceptible experience.

> I have felt a thousand times that I could not by myself conquer my humour, nor overcome my habits, nor moderate my pride, nor follow my sense of right, nor continue to desire the good which I

---

1. Segneri, *The Manna of the Soul*, vol. 1, 9.

did at one time desire. It is thou who givest this desire. It is thou who keepest it pure. Without thee I am only a reed blown by the least wind. Thou hast given me courage, integrity, and all my noblest sentiments. Thou hast made me a new heart which desires thy righteousness, and which thirsts for thy eternal truth.[2]

God inspires, or implants, the desire, which causes reaction in us. Mary is our model. "Consider the *fervent desire which the Blessed Virgin* had for the coming of God into the world, which so much the more increased as the time of the Incarnation approached, the Holy Spirit inspiring them into her, whose property is, when He will grant anything to the elect, to inspire into them lively desires of it; that, with their desire and prayer, they may dispose themselves to receive it."[3] We have been considering the case in which someone wants to want to love God, and when the Holy Spirit grants to the elect a lively desire for this communion, it is his property to inspire into a person a lively desire for what God offers. This is the state of prayer. "What God gives is precisely what we should have desired to ask. For we will have whatever he wills, and only that. In this way, this state contains all prayer: it is a work of the heart that includes all its desire. The Spirit prays within us for those very things that the Spirit himself wills to give us."[4]

The force of God's desire for us creates a vehemence of love on our part. His desire to be with us is the stronger, but it creates a nevertheless strong desire in us for communion with him. So we admit, in prayer, that "Thou much more desirest to be with them than they desire to be with Thee: indeed, if they desire to have Thee with them, it proceeds from this, that Thou dost first infuse this desire into them, so to accomplish Thine own. I give Thee thanks for this immense charity, which Thou bearest to Thine elect, by the which I humbly beseech Thee not to exclude me from my part in it. Amen."[5] The desire is achieved in cooperation with God: God ener-

2. Fénelon, *Christian Perfection*, 124.
3. Louis De Ponte, *Meditations on the Mysteries of Our Holy Faith*, vol. 2 (London: Richardson and Son, 1852), 60.
4. Fénelon, *The Complete Fénelon*, 86.
5. De Ponte, *Meditations on the Mysteries of Our Holy Faith*, vol. 5, 73.

gizes, man synergizes. Grace has already begun work in the seed because God is the one who plants it—from where else could it come? Not the world, which tries to attract souls to itself; not ourselves, whose appetites have been misled by the Fall. The desire must be planted by God himself. Even before one prays, one makes a resolution to pray. The resolution is a product of desire and the desire is a gift of God. "If you have not yet made this resolution but feel some desire to make it, feed and strengthen your desire with frequent aspirations, spiritual reading, and profitable reflection," and you will discover that

> no man has ever desired to pray, and asked for that grace earnestly, and done everything to secure it that God suggested to him, without obtaining it. Indeed, such a supposition contradicts itself. For who is it who gives you the desire? God, of course. Does He give it in order that it may remain ineffectual? That is impossible. He implants in you a desire for the thing with the intention of giving you the thing itself; He will infallibly give it to you if you ask for it in the right way; and He begs you, He urges you, He aids you to make the request.[6]

The question in this chapter is *why* God plants the desire. The answer in this chapter is that the desire is implanted in order to give the thing itself. The expectation does not remain ineffectual, because he who is responsible for inspiring the desire will not let up until he has led someone to his full satisfaction. There is grace ahead, and grace behind; grace before, and grace after; grace without, and grace within. Pray to be provoked by God. "O King of heaven, who, like a kingly eagle, soarest in the air, and placest Thy nest in the height of heaven, provoke me that I may follow Thee with desire."[7] We might feel as though we are *pushing* our desires upward, but, we are actually being *pulled* upward by God who gives an "invitation from the Divine Heart. God knows how to draw you to Himself, by your needs and by your desires."[8] Desire is his bait and tackle. The Father is the end toward which the pilgrim travels; the Son

6. Grou, *The School of Jesus Christ*, 285–85.
7. De Ponte, *Meditations on the Mysteries of Our Holy Faith*, vol. 5, 159.
8. De Ravignan, *Conferences on the Spiritual Life*, 150.

lays his cross over the abyss of sin that separates the pilgrim from the Father; the Holy Spirit animates the pilgrim so he would traverse it. God is the goal, God is the bridge, God is the impulse. We are carried voluntarily, cooperatively, willingly in the arms of the whole Trinity. Where could we better find ourselves? What could we do better than place all matters in God's care? His providence creates security in his children. "Could our future be more secure than in the all-powerful hands of that adorable Master, of that good and loving Father? who loves us more than we love ourselves? Where could we find a safer refuge than in the arms of divine Providence?"[9] Do we have need of our own lights and certainties, ideas and reflections? Not when we are no longer walking, but being carried in the arms of divine providence.[10] God does not plant any seed with the intention of leaving it infertile, he plants it with the intention of growing it to perfection. He will bring the desire to fruition, and remove any blemish or defect from it. "A good will is a great and sweet treasure. He who has this, desires and endeavours to obey and to please God, and to do those things which are acceptable to Him. This is the foundation and the root of all holy virtues. It springs from the Holy Spirit, and is a great grace of God and an infused love. Blessed is he who has received it from God, and who studies to keep it."[11]

The first thing the Holy Spirit does to nurture our desires is to repair them at the root. Our natural desires must become supernatural desires, and grace sets to work immediately perfecting nature. Any meritorious desires, such as we have been talking about, must proceed from this divine Spirit. "We must ardently desire that the Holy Ghost may dwell in our hearts and possess us fully, that he may sweetly move us to seek God in the higher part of our souls; for our own desires do not merit to be heard of God, but only such as proceed from his divine Spirit."[12] We needn't be troubled if God

---

9. De Caussade, *Abandonment to Divine Providence*, 166.

10. Ibid., 75.

11. Blosius, *Spiritual Works of Louis of Blois*, 242.

12. Constantine Barbanson, *The Secret Paths of Divine Love* (London: Burns Oates & Washbourne, Ltd., 1928), 124.

doesn't seem to hear us initially, since it is part of the correction of our desires. "Though our first desires seem good to us and to be real and ardent aspirations after our supreme good, in truth they are often for the most part rather certain impetuous and violent natural impulses which impel us forward to search after divine things."[13] The difference between our natural desires and the spiritual desires is noticeable, because the former "are passionate and full of impatience and perplexity and trouble," whilst the latter, "which are infused by the Holy Ghost, are gentle and peaceable and wonderfully submissive and resigned to the divine will."[14] Submission is difficult for the old Adam, but faith knows God "has arranged everything for the greater good of those who submit to Him, or, at least who desire to acquire and to practice this submission."[15] What God is ultimately doing when we seek his presence earnestly

> is to purify and reform our desires from the very roots, so that we may no longer desire anything merely naturally, but in entire submission to his will, and in entire resignation as to how and when he shall please to hear us. Hence it comes to pass that we experience so many changes of our concepts and judgements, such vicissitudes in our interior life, and so many secret labours and trials; for God does require of us, however ardent our desires may be, that they be always entirely subject to his will.[16]

Or, in other words, "Do what you can and God will do what you desire. But to do what we can we must know what we ought to do."[17] Enkindling of love and fortification of will requires guidance of the intellect by God.

Coming to desire to do what we ought to do is the first step of the three estates in the spiritual soul's progress toward God, identified variously as "purgative, illuminative, unitive,"[18] or "beginning, aug-

---

13. Barbanson, *The Secret Paths of Divine Love*, 124.

14. Ibid., 124–25.

15. De Caussade, *Abandonment to Divine Providence*, 195.

16. Barbanson, *The Secret Paths of Divine Love*, 124–25.

17. Crasset, in Crasset and de Sales, *The Secret of Sanctity*, 159.

18. Alphonsus Rodríguez (Alfonso), *The Practice of Christian and Religious Perfection*, vol. 1, 249.

mentation, and perfection,"[19] or for the "beginners, proficients, and perfect."[20] In the purgative stage, the soul learns to cooperate with the mortification—even to the point of desiring it! In this beginning stage, we can hardly imagine what we're getting into, and must learn to play on God's terms. If we think our confession of faith and dabbling in piety will control God, we must think again, because he will give us a desire for mortification we did not anticipate. "Meditation is for beginners; affection for those who are advancing; contemplation for the perfect. . . . In meditation the mind seeks; in affection the heart desires; in contemplation the soul finds what it sought and enjoys what it desired."[21]

There is a divine design behind the desire God implants. "Remember also, dear friend, that God has His own views when He inspires desires in us and that we should always refrain from examining what these views are. He knows why He gives us those desires. One who reasons and draws conclusions from his desires, is already the victim of an illusion."[22] If the desires become effectual, they will conform us to Jesus to the point of possessing his desires and his dispositions as our own. And where did that lead him?

> Q. What do you mean by having the same dispositions that our Lord had?
>
> A. It is to have in one's heart and soul the same desires that he had; for example, of being humbled and crucified.[23]

Love will cause love to enter. God will cause abnegation in the open soul. "A pure and perfect love of Jesus should inspire you with a holy generosity in giving yourself to Him,"[24] and upon the beginning of perfect love, renunciation of self can occur: "You ask me whence comes that openness of heart and mind in those who give

---

19. De Ponte, *Meditations on the Mysteries of Our Holy Faith*, vol. 2, 11.
20. Baker, *Holy Wisdom*, 396.
21. Crasset, in Crasset and de Sales, *The Secret of Sanctity*, 269.
22. Libermann, *Letters to Clergy and Religious*, Series 7, 69.
23. Olier, *Catechism of an Interior Life*, 23–24.
24. Francis Libermann, *Letters to Religious Sisters and Aspirants*, Spiritan Series 5, vol. 1 (Pittsburgh: Duquesne University Press, 1962), 8.

themselves entirely to God. It seems to me that it comes naturally, and, as it were, necessarily, from this perfect love."[25] Therefore, "Do not set limits to the crosses you are willing to bear. Accept all that come as so many precious stones and be afraid to let any escape from your grasp."[26] Why crosses? Why abnegation? Why renunciation of self-love and detachment from the world? Because this is the way to union with God, a synonym for holiness. "As long as you retain desires and wishes of your own, your union with God will be neither real nor perfect."[27] Our union with God will become perfect and real when God's desires become our own.

Desire is not a way to avoid spiritual discipline, it is rather the means and willingness to embrace it. All might desire to save their souls, but not all are willing to accept the means God has established for it.

> Theotimus, we are to will our salvation in such sort as God wills it; now He wills it by way of desire, and we also must incessantly desire it, in conformity with His desire. Nor does He will it only, but, in effect, gives us all necessary means to attain to it. We then, in fulfilment of the desire we have to be saved, must not only wish to be saved, but, in effect, must accept all the graces which He has provided for us, and offers us. With regard to salvation itself, it is enough to say: I desire to be saved. But, with regard to the means of salvation, it is not enough to say: I desire them. We must, with an absolute resolution, will and embrace the graces which God presents to us; for our will must correspond with God's will. And, inasmuch as He gives us the means of salvation, we ought to avail ourselves of such means, just as we ought to desire salvation in such sort as God desires it for us, and because He desires it.[28]

It is a mystery of conversion that a person can be brought to desire what he initially resisted; it is a mystery of sanctification that grace enables the person to fulfill the desire in action.

25. Francis Libermann, *Letters to Clergy and Religious*, Spiritan Series 8, vol. 4 (Pittsburgh: Duquesne University Press, 1964), 136.

26. Libermann, *Letters to Religious Sisters and Aspirants*, 144.

27. Libermann, *Letters to Clergy and Religious*, Series 7, 4.

28. De Sales, *Treatise on the Love of God*, 269.

In the parable of the two sons, Jesus contrasts a son who says he will not work in the vineyard, but later changes his mind and goes, with a son who says he will go to work, but does not. The two states can be described like this:

> There are two sorts of good wills. The one says: I would do well, but it gives me trouble, and I will not do it. The other: I wish to do well, but I have not as much power as will; it is this which holds me back. The first fills hell, the second, Paradise. The first only begins to will and desire, but it does not finish willing: its desires have not enough courage, they are only abortions of will: that is why it fills hell. But the second produces entire and well-formed desires; it is for this that Daniel was called man of desires. May our Lord deign to give us the perpetual assistance of his Holy Spirit, my well-beloved daughter and sister![29]

God's aid finishes the willing in the person whose faith perseveres. But, as we have been insisting, even someone just beginning his way to becoming a well-formed person will find encouragement in the desire God gives at the beginning. The desire to reach the perfection of Christian life is one "you must cherish and tenderly nourish in your heart, as a blessing of the Holy Spirit and a spark of his Divine fire. I have seen a tree which was planted by the blessed St. Dominic at Rome: every one goes to see it, and is fond of it for the sake of the planter. In the same way having seen in you the tree of the desire of sanctity, which our Lord has planted in your soul, I cherish it tenderly."[30] Everyone goes to see a desire growing strong in a saint, and is fond of it for the sake of Jesus, who planted it.

Sometimes the fulfillment of the saint's desire is delayed. But often it is not. And then, remarkably, the prayer of the sinner is heard with the same immediacy as the prayer of a just man.

> The prayer of a sinner to escape from sin arises from the desire to return to the grace of God. Now this desire is a gift, which is certainly given by no other than God himself. . . . And, indeed, in the Holy Scriptures themselves there are multitudes of instances of

---

29. De Sales, *Letters to Persons in the World*, 256–57.
30. Ibid., 134.

sinners who have been delivered from sin by prayer.... Oh, the wonderful! oh, the mighty power of prayer! Two sinners are dying on Calvary by the side of Jesus Christ: one, because he prays, "Remember me," is saved; the other, because he prays not, is damned.[31]

The state of perfection will take time, but the desire for perfect union with God is alive throughout, and God will answer the intensity of that desire even at the first moment. "How often have the desires of the saints been their own immediate fulfilment, because of their intensity!"[32]

The intensity of the Virgin Mary's desire pleases our eye especially, and we rejoice in its two results.

> The desire of her heart, like a shaft that cannot be recalled, had sped its way. It reached the Heart of the Babe, and at once she felt the touch of God, and was unutterably calm, and Jesus lay upon the ground on the skirt of her robe, and she fell down before Him to adore. Twice had her pure desire drawn Him from the home of His predilection, once from the uncreated Bosom of the Father, and once from her own created Bosom which He tenanted. It was as if the sweet will of Mary were the time-piece of the divine decrees.[33]

The devout who wish to salute Mary are befriended by her. When Saint Gertrude's illness made her unable to say the Office, or even the *Ave* in its entirety, she repeated at least the first line, "whereupon, the Virgin Mother of God appeared to her, clothed in a mantle marvelously adorned with golden flowers, which represented the salutations recited by her with difficulty; and, in them shone forth brilliantly the pious affection with which she had desired to salute the glorious Virgin."[34]

31. Alphonsus de Liguori, *The Great Means of Salvation and of Perfection* (New York: Benziger Brothers, 1886), 91.

32. Frederick Faber, *Bethlehem* (London: Thomas Richardson and Son, 1860), 73.

33. Ibid., 152.

34. Blosius, *Spiritual Works of Louis of Blois*, 228.

Salutary desire is a mix of affection and will. Heaven's beatitude tomorrow comes as the consummation of such a desire today. On earth, desire creates a vessel; in heaven, God fills it full, and then souls rejoice. The desire will be fulfilled, and this will not terminate desire, it will increase it, which is why heavenly happiness will be ceaseless. To him who desires much, will more be given. It will be the same for saints then as it is for the angels now.

> How can this be understood, that the angels who see the Redeemer and in him all the mysteries of our salvation, do yet desire to see him? Theotimus, verily they see him continually, but with a view so agreeable and delightsome that the complacency they take in it satiates them without taking away their desire, makes them desire without removing their satiety: the fruition is not lessened by desire, but perfected, as their desire is not cloyed but intensified by fruition.[35]

To be satiated—without the desire being taken away! This is a profound description of the state of love, and the Church is called the Mystical Body because it is Christ's love present. No one shall become bored with God.

God wants the soul; he wants the soul to want him; he wants us to want what he wants for us. He intends to empower us to execute the desire for union with him, which means giving the soul the required strength to do so: he infuses faith, hope, and love. United to God by an intimate and immediate union, the soul "produces in an excellent degree acts of all virtues,—of faith, by involving herself in the mysterious darkness with which God environs his throne;—of hope, by depending on no creature, and remaining, as it were, suspended between heaven and earth;—of charity, by seeking God alone, and looking for no sensible consolation."[36] No one is left on his own when Jesus becomes the soul of his soul, and no one is left with an intention that is his alone.

35. De Sales, *Treatise on the Love of God*, 177–78.
36. Jean Crasset, *The Devotion of Calvary; or Meditations on the Passion of Our Lord and Saviour Jesus Christ* (Liverpool: Booker & Co., 1844), 20.

I believe that it is our Lord who has inspired your desire, and this gives me very great joy. He will live in you, dear friend; this is my firm hope. Live also in Him. Don't be satisfied with the desire of being always occupied with our Lord Jesus, but have besides a greater and more lively desire to possess Him in your soul and to be possessed by Him. He will then be the life and, as it were, the soul of your soul, so that you have no longer any actions, sentiment, desire, affection, will, or intention of your own, but Jesus Himself will animate you in all your internal and external activities. He will then live in you in "His spirit of holiness, in the fullness of His power." He will re-enact in you all the interior states of His Holy soul, states in which He wants you to have a share.[37]

This is the liturgical life: when the interior states of Jesus's holy soul are re-enacted in a person. A saint-to-be-by-desire lives in God the Father, by the presence of the Holy Spirit, as the only begotten Son lives in him. The soul is immersed in the Trinity as the only ocean in which she wants to swim.

The Divinity, moreover, is the proper, vast element, wherein the soul should find life, and an infinite life. When out of this element, the soul is like a whale that has been stranded in a brook: the great creature has not space enough to swim or plunge in its waters. Hence it ever desires the ocean, which, for its depth and wideness, is capable of containing it and millions of others. Here these huge creatures find no bottom, but can swim in all fullness, and enjoy security from danger; for here they are in their element and, as it were, in their own kingdom.[38]

Poor souls! A whale in a brook! No wonder they rest not in creatures, nor in created images; no wonder they thirst after the spaciousness and infinity of God. Liturgy draws us out into apophatic depths. God creates the desire to swim in the divine ocean, because God shows the soul she has not space enough in the world for her magnitude.

---

37. Francis Libermann, *Letters to Clergy and Religious,* Spiritan Series 9, vol. 5 (Pittsburgh: Duquesne University Press, 1966), 167.

38. Augustine Baker, *The Inner Life of Dame Gertrude More,* vol. 1 (London: R. & T. Washbourne, Ltd., 1911), 165.

The desire planted by God commences a reassembly of both our internal and external activities because it changes the object, the intensity, and the purpose of whatever other desires were planted in the soul by the world. It energizes the soul to mortification: "God will fill your vessel with precious balm, if He sees that it no longer contains this world's perfumes."[39] Worldly desires must be demolished and on their ruin a new man constructed, a man who has been drawn out of darkness, death, and the devil's realm, into light, life, and the Lord's kingdom. "What composed the old man is demolished by Christianity, all things are made new in it: new thoughts, new sentiments, new desires, are the portion of the true Christian. For this reason Isaias calls our Lord 'Father of the world to come,' because He is the Author and Founder of a new world, and in Him and by Him men are actuated by new hopes, new affections, new desires."[40]

Here is a simpler account. Instead of going one by one through all the old hopes, old affections, and old desires implanted by the world, we can speak of their exchange *in toto*. All the old desires are replaced by a single, new, overwhelming desire: the desire for Jesus, who, in turn, gives us his desires to enjoy as our own. This is the mystical union with Christ, and it is the state of believers in his Mystical Body. The Father spades our heart by the Holy Spirit in order to plant a desire for his Son, who accepts the commission because he wants to share his desire for the Father with us. "Do not desire things, but allow Jesus to act, and let Him desire in you. True, all your desires are desires of the cross and therefore they are generally those of Jesus. But I believe that not only ought He to originate them, but it belongs to Him to keep them up, perfect and execute them. . . . It should be enough that you have that desire in your soul and, while keeping it before you, look with joy and surrender upon Jesus."[41] The process we are talking about ranks as deification. "Nature is susceptible of that enlargement and transformation

39. De Sales, *A Selection from the Spiritual Letters of S. Francis De Sales*, 204.
40. Saint-Jure, *The Spiritual Man*, 16.
41. Libermann, *Letters to Clergy and Religious* (Series 8), 317.

which theology does not fear to call deifical."[42] Desire is susceptible of deifical expansion since it comes from God, exists under the hand of God, is kept alive by God, and is guided to perfection by God. It is a desire for deification: it is a deifying desire. We dare it because our deification is Jesus's ambition:

> I demand thy heart for My habitation, that I may join and unite it unto Mine; for to this end was My heart opened to thee upon the altar of My Cross. My will is, I say, O My dearly beloved spouse, that thou desire nothing, think nothing, understand nothing, see nothing, feel nothing, but Myself only; that so I only may be in thee and thou totally turned into Me; and that thou mayest possess in Me perfect quiet, and in thee pleasant content.[43]

What nerve this gives to creatures of clay! "To desire thee seems very presumptuous, and yet without desiring thee I neither will nor can live. Children of Adam, blind men, straying sheep, if this is your sheepfold, whither do you run?"[44] The creature's desire for undeserved union with his Creator could not be imagined, much less could the creature dare to desire it, except that the offer is presented by Jesus. The Son of God became man so that we might become God, said the Fathers of the Church. The desire of the *Logos* for Incarnation motivates our desire for *theopoiethomen* (participation in God). The love of mankind that brought the Son down from heaven creates a desire that raises man up to heaven. The starting point of empowerment to love God is the reception of the mysteries of the Son, given so we can offer them as our very own. We thus unite our little intents and services to the great intentions and operations of Jesus. The embedding of divine desire in a creature is a liturgical transaction. How do we love God? With *his own* perfections! Such a miracle did the hypostatic union work.

We have seen how God enables us to love Him by giving us all His own perfections, and the mysteries of His dear Son, to offer as our

42. Jean-Baptiste Henri Lacordaire, *Life: Conferences Delivered at Toulouse* (New York: P. O'Shea, 1875), 148.

43. De Castañiza, *The Spiritual Conflict and Conquest*, 188.

44. De Granada, *A Memorial of a Christian Life*, 44.

very own to His blessed Majesty.... But we may now go a step further, and say that in His anxiety to be loved, and to give us the means of loving Him, He raises even our ineffectual desires to the dignity of effectual acts, and enables us to worship Him with a most heavenly and delightful worship, with the passing wishes of our loving hearts.... The faintest heart in creation may love Him, and love Him with an abundant love.[45]

Though our desires are weak and ineffectual, God's power raises them to the dignity of effectual acts by allying them with merits of Christ, our spouse, so that we can worship God with a more than human worship. This is the purpose of the divine implantation: God does it out of his eagerness to love, and to receive our love in return. When the desire is a spark of the Holy Spirit's divine fire, then we worship the Father with the heavenly and delightful worship of the Son.

Jacob's ladder is an Old Testament type of a liturgical staircase, with traffic down and up. The desire is a restless, tumultuous state, so "on Jacob's ladder no Angel was seen to stop, for all were either ascending or descending; so in this pursuit, not to advance is to fall back, and he who ascends not descends; because between progress and failure no middle state is found."[46] The desire is a whirlwind, akin to the one that brought Elijah up to heaven. When God draws a soul after himself, he lifts it out of this world. His genesis begins the process; to it he then adds our responsive action.

Behold, therefore, I pray you, Theotimus, how gently God moves, strengthening by little and little the grace of his inspiration in consenting hearts, drawing them after him, as it were step by step, upon this Jacob's ladder. But what are his drawings? The first, by which he prevents and awakens us, is done by him in us and without our action; all the others are also done by him and in us, but not without action.... Begin thou first: I cannot awake of myself, I cannot move unless thou move me; but when thou shalt once have given motion, then, O dear spouse of my heart, we run, we

45. Faber, *All for Jesus*, 285.
46. Giovanni Bona, *A Treatise of Spiritual Life* (Poplar Bluff, MO: the author, 1893), 475.

two, thou runnest before me drawing me ever forward, and, as for me, I will follow thee in thy course consenting to thy drawing. But let no one think that thou draggest me after thee like a forced slave, or a lifeless wagon. Ah! no, thou drawest me by the odour of thy ointments.[47]

The first, the original, the primal prayer is "begin thou first. I desire you to move me." This sense of desire must pervade prayer like a perfume.

Our desire is then extroverted: what was once introvertively aimed at attaining something for ourselves is converted, turned outward to God, to receive from God, to give to God. The mercantile exchange altogether disappears from liturgy. We do not liturgize for self-gain anymore. A total reversal takes place: "it is not our own interest in our blessedness which should make us desire his glory. It is on the contrary, the desire for his glory which should make us desire our blessedness, as one of the things which he is pleased to make part of his glory."[48] The liturgy of the Mystical Body of Christ, and the liturgy of the lives of each member in it, is designed to accomplish one purpose, and one purpose only: to praise the Father, in the Spirit, with a filiality that comes from being an adopted brother of the Only Begotten Son. A soul in communion with *Theos*, through the *Logos*, is led by the Holy Spirit to commit an act of *theology*, and is indifferent to anything and everything out of God's will. Holy indifference is not inactivity. It is the renunciation of everything *except God's will*. Now God's will becomes ours.

> Such a soul absolutely ceases either to desire or to will, except in cooperation with the Divine leading. Its desires for itself, as it has greater light, are more completely and permanently merged in the one higher and more absorbing desire of God's glory, and the fulfillment of His will. In this state of experience, ceasing to do what we shall be likely to do, and what we may very properly do in a lower state, we no longer desire our own salvation merely as an eternal deliverance, or merely as involving the greatest amount of

47. De Sales, *Treatise on the Love of God*, 103.
48. Fénelon, *Christian Perfection*, 137.

personal happiness; but we desire it chiefly as the fulfillment of God's pleasure, and as resulting in His glory, and because He Himself desires and wills that we should thus desire and will.[49]

This is liturgy rising from abnegation. We don't even desire God's glory on account of our own salvation, and instead "see that our own happiness is a thing that he has been pleased to make a part of his glory."[50]

The Holy Spirit corrects and converts our prayer to make it righteous, dampening wrong prayer and exciting every desire to pray rightly. John of the Cross gives an example.

I will explain my meaning by the following illustration. A person in the State of Union is requested to pray for a certain individual. Now he will never remember to do what is asked of him, by reason of anything whatever remaining in his memory; but if it be right so to pray—which it will be when God shall be pleased to hear that prayer—God will then move the will and excite a desire to pray. On the other hand, if it be not the Will of God to hear that prayer; let that person do what he may, he will never pray as he was requested, neither will he have any desire to do so.[51]

The desire is like a key that turns a lock. God gives us the key, but it would be foolish to imagine it turns anything other than the lock it fits. If the desire is congruent with the will of God, he will receive it; if the desire is not congruent with the will of God, then the person praying will slowly stop desiring it. Some of our desires—even apparently holy ones—are misplaced. Very well! In that case, accept God's judgment.

One of the clearest and best established maxims of holiness is, that the holy soul . . . ceases to have desires for anything out of the will of God. . . . The holy soul not only desires particular things, sanctioned by the known will of God; but also the fulfillment of His

---

49. François Fénelon, *Maxims of the Saints* (https://www.ccel.org/ccel/f/fenelon/maxims/cache/maxims.pdf), 4.
50. Fénelon, *The Complete Fénelon*, 100.
51. John of the Cross, *Ascent of Mount Carmel*, in *Complete Works*, vol. 1, 210.

will in all respects, unknown as well as known. Being in faith, it commits itself to God in darkness as well as in light. Its non-desire is simply its not desiring anything out of God.[52]

When this happens, our desires can become the backbone of liturgy because they are stamped, like a coin, for liturgy. Desires, temperaments, dispositions, and actions will be accepted by God if done in total love for him, even if the world might never understand. "He has arranged all things to entice us into love. He coins our very desires into worship; and He lets us love Him, and glorify Him, and earn glory for ourselves by what would almost provoke a smile from an unbeliever, it looks so like a mere make-believe."[53]

52. Fénelon, *Maxims*, 4.
53. Faber, *All for Jesus*, 337–38.

5

Prayer

WE HAVE MENTIONED PRAYER several times so far, and it now needs a specific treatment of its own, because prayer is a special manifestation of this desire.

Do you pray well? . . . Prayer ought to be the desire of your heart. Permit me to ask you: when you pray, is it a real desire of your heart you offer to God? Do you really wish for the graces, for the good gifts which our Blessed Lord is willing to give you, and of which you are in so great need[?] Is nothing else nearer to your heart than his grace, than His love? Where is your heart when you pray? Is it all given to God? . . . This is what, in former days, was the desire of the saints, and of the just, under the old law; this is what was the desire of the Immaculate Heart of Mary, when, before the birth of our Saviour, she worshipped Him, longed for Him, and unceasingly implored His blessings. Do you ardently desire, do you long for the coming of your Lord within your own hearts? Do you desire His grace? Do you desire to receive the gifts of heaven? . . . Tell me honestly, is your prayer the conscientious, the sacred desire of your heart?[1]

Right desire is being trained in the simplest prayer of a child, and expected in the highest prayer, taught to us by the Lord himself. "What a prayer is that of our Lord's! who could understand it? Holy, sacred, Divine prayer! Yet we shall try to lisp something about it. Our Lord's prayer is a prayer of desire, a prayer of sacrifice, and a prayer of charity and goodness!"[2] The relationship may be named

1. De Ravignan, *Conferences on the Spiritual Life*, 20–21.
2. De Ravignan, *The Last Retreat*, 121.

from either end: call it *prayerful desire*, or *desirous prayer*. "It is desire which prays; for prayer is aspiration towards God."[3]

To aspire means to seek eagerly to attain something high or great, and in the case of prayerful desire, what the heart eagerly strives to attain is union with God himself: the desirous prayer ascends, and soars, and mounts up to God. The soul seeks her end, which is happiness, and so calls out to him who is her only happiness. Prayer calls out because love is at work. "God must be desired; for desire, as you know, is that tendency of the soul to expect, to call, to pray; and we know well that to pray is to wish. Desire, wish, and prayer are all the same, the sole end to be attained by love."[4] Desire is so much the heart of prayer that the terms are almost interchangeable. Prayer is a manifestation of desire; desire manifests itself as prayer. "To pray is to desire ardently, and desire, as you know, is that within us which expects, demands, calls for, and importunes."[5] Prayer exercises faith, hope, and love—especially love. "God desires to be loved as much as He is respected: and the Holy Spirit, who is the eternal love of the Father and the Son, inspires no prayer that is not altogether born of love, or does not lead to love. It should be love, or at least the desire of love that prompts the Christian to pray; love should be the final aim if not the subject of his prayer; and increase of love should be its fruit."[6]

You will be heard if you desire to be heard,[7] which is why continual prayer is possible: it is nourished upon the grace that God continually feeds to the soul in prayer. This continual prayer is sometimes treated as a technique only practiced by monks, but Paul directs all Christians to it: "Rejoice always, pray constantly" (1 Thess 5:16–17). "When all other actions are performed by grace obtained by prayer, and for the end proposed in prayer, then a person may be said to be in continual prayer, and much more if they be accompa-

---

3. De Ravignan, *Conferences on the Spiritual Life*, 195.

4. De Ravignan, *The Last Retreat*, 18.

5. Ibid., 15.

6. Grou, *The School of Jesus Christ*, 246.

7. Jean Grou, *The Christian Sanctified by the Lord's Prayer* (New York: Thomas Whitaker, 1885), 118.

nied with an actual elevation of the spirit to God."[8] What does the command "pray without ceasing" mean when reduced to practice? "It is desire, not words, which makes God hear us.... And a desire may last as long as we please; indeed, if we ought to pray always as Christ commanded, it ought to last always."[9]

> By prayer is manifestly meant the act of laying open before God the desire of thy heart for His aid to win humility, obedience, and all other good gifts for thy soul.... The Lord knows thy desire full well, nevertheless He wills that thou shouldst represent it to Him before He will completely satisfy it.... When thou art obliged to desist from representing thy desires to the Lord, either through fatigue, or the necessity of study, or by reason of other duties, thou shouldst at least hold Him fast in thy heart, and so in some sort "pray always." If thou canst not pray in act, thou canst still pray in intention. When the desire to pray is gone, thou art much to be pitied.[10]

Our authors speak about continual prayer in various ways, but it always seems to come down to this: "He always prays, who preserves a constant and strong desire of praying; for the very desire is prayer."[11] This is possible not only for Religious, but also for someone who is occupied in the world, because continual prayer is linked to a holy life with holy desires. "Why art thou distressed that thou canst not be always occupied in prayer? If thy life is good, if thou carefully abstainest from sin, if thou employest thy time usefully, if thou dost truly humble thyself in the sight of the Lord, and sigh after God and thy heavenly home, thou dost always pray; for a holy life and holy desires are a continual prayer before God."[12] Saint Catherine of Siena received such an instruction from the Lord himself: "Our Lord said to the virgin Catherine. 'The holy desire of the soul, that is to say, good-will, is a continual prayer, because it has

8. Baker, *Holy Wisdom*, 360.

9. Segneri, *The Manna of the Soul*, vol. 2, 433.

10. Segneri, *The Manna of the Soul*, vol. 1, 77.

11. Giovanni Bona, *The Principles of Christianity* (London: printed for C. Dilly, 1783), 71.

12. Blosius, *Spiritual Works of Louis of Blois*, 62–63.

the power of prayer. And, whatsoever man does for the love of God and of his neighbor, may be called prayer, since love is accounted as prayer.'"[13]

The soul is never in a state of *not* desiring something around it. An open eye will see *something*. The soul desires like the lungs breathe, and the only question is whether she is breathing noxious or healthful air. One can therefore use this natural disposition productively with conversion and by intention. Do all things in order of their last end, namely, with a sanctified intention. There is "no other manner of prayer but the internal exercise of the will in holy desires," and since the soul is naturally in a continual exercise of one desire or another, if, by practice, "we can so rectify our desires as to place them upon their only true and proper object, which is God, it will necessarily follow that the soul should be in continual prayer. *Si semper desideras, semper oras*, saith Augustine; if thou dost continually desire (God) thou dost continually pray."[14] When faced with a certain object, or assignment, or labor, or neighbor, a person should desire to find God therein, and thereby continually pray. Whatever is encountered in the world can become matter for eucharistic thanksgiving, so there is nothing in the world that cannot be incorporated into our regular oblation.

Progress in the spiritual life depends upon a different consciousness than we have of external things because this internal world is a closed garden in which bride meets bridegroom. This image from the Canticle of Solomon is frequently used. The union is known interiorly, and our interior is always with us, therefore "in every place and at all times we may know interiorly that all we are or desire is really in the presence of God, who is penetrating the most intimate secrets of our souls."[15] Christ has left his body (I mean the Church) with mysteries that cheer and inebriate, and he says to her:

"I am come into my garden, O my sister, my spouse, I have gathered my myrrh with my aromatical spices; I have eaten the honey-

13. Ibid., 223.
14. Baker, *Holy Wisdom*, 361–62.
15. Barbanson, *The Secret Paths of Divine Love*, 62.

comb with my honey; I have drunk my wine, my milk. Eat, O friends, and drink, and be inebriated, my dearly beloved" (Canticle 5:1). Which is to say: "By my Incarnation I come into the garden of my Church.... Therefore, O my friends, and my beloved, prepare the garden of your souls; for in them I desire to work other ... effects, you yourselves also working them, through my grace, to imitate my life."[16]

This hidden garden is the domain of prayer, where a harvest of desires is grown, and where the final utterance of every prayer is to ask Christ to come. "The word Amen is a prayer, or an expression of desire, 'God grant that it may be so.' Thus our Lord, the Amen, is the term of all our wishes, and his incarnation is the accomplishment of all our desires."[17]

Prayer is aspiration toward God, and if we do not yet pray, then we must pray to be stirred to pray by the Holy Spirit. Our parched souls need spiritual moisture, so the Holy Spirit acts like a divine gardener tending to his flora. He is constantly irrigating this interior world.

> As a gardener who waters a bed in his garden, and perceiving the water not presently to enter into it, stops a little to let it be imbibed by the earth, and goes no farther till it has sunk to the very bottom, and that the earth is well watered; in like manner, when the water of these holy affection and desires begins to enter into our soul, which is, to speak with the Psalmist, "like earth without water" (Ps. cxlii. 6); we must suspend the operation of our understanding, and think only of receiving these salutary waters, and enjoying this effusion of the will, till our heart being filled, we feel its wants no more.[18]

The liturgical feast of Pentecost can be thought of as rainfall to moisten our dry ground. "Do you see this arid barren piece of ground, thirsting for moisture, longing to become fertilized? then

16. De Ponte, *Meditations on the Mysteries of Our Holy Faith*, vol. 2, 10.

17. Saint-Jure, *Union with Our Lord Jesus*, 71.

18. Alphonsus Rodríguez (Alfonso), *The Practice of Christian and Religious Perfection*, vol. 1, 263–64.

when the grateful rain falls, how refreshed is the earth, how it expands! Thus it is that God takes care of our desires, and delights to prove to us in holy Scripture our need of them. We find in the Psalms, 'With desire have I desired.'"[19]

We hear an echo of this on our Lord's lips at the Last Supper: "With desire I have desired to eat this Passover with you" (Lk 22:15).[20] Now the Master asks for a return from his disciples: do you desire communion with me as I have desired it with you? If so, come to my house where the desire to pray will be roused.

We must take courage, and act with force, and when we cannot pray, we must excite the desire within us. The Apostles, before Pentecost, were full of imperfections; even after the Resurrection of their Divine Master, they still acted, alas! according to the impulses of nature, nevertheless there they were in the house together! With a good will, they desired ardently, they persevered in prayer, repeating incessantly, "Come, Holy Spirit, transform us, change us, regenerate the world;" and this is what drew down upon them all the graces of heaven. Let these dispositions be yours also; if you desire, in spite of dryness, temptations and disquietudes; if you beg of God His light, His grace, and all solid virtues, He will bless you, He will grant your prayer.[21]

Prayer is only conducted during the dark nights if desire rides perseverance. Prayer's aspirations for God are kindled by hope, performed in faith, and rejoiced in love, because the real goal is a loving union with Almighty God, and that can happen in a flash.

True prayer is simply another name for the love of God. Its excellence does not consist in the multitude of our words, for our Father knows what we need before we ask him. True prayer is prayer of the heart, and the heart prays only for what it desires. *To pray*, then, is *to desire or long for*, but to desire what God would have us desire. Those who ask, but not from the bottom of their

---

19. De Ravignan, *Conferences on the Spiritual Life*, 194–95.

20. King James translation: "Epithymia epethymesas" —with desire I have desired.

21. De Ravignan, *Conferences on the Spiritual Life*, 195.

hearts, are mistaken in thinking that they are praying. Even though they spend days in reciting prayers in meditation, or in forcing themselves in religious exercises, they do not truly pray even once if they really do not *desire and yearn for* the things they claim to be asking for.[22]

Prayer without desire is fruitless; prayer with desire is potent. The presence of fervorous desire makes a prayer efficacious. "We most commonly fail in the efficacy of our demands, because we want [lack] this *fervor in our desires*, and make our petitions tepidly."[23] Whence this tepidity? It happens when our affections are fastened to earthly things. "We prize them in our wills, though we slight them in our understandings; and, consequently, though we know in our judgment that our minds are to be raised up to higher objects, yet we do not seriously seek to be separated from them; whereas, if we verily and vigorously, humbly and heartily desired it, our prayers would soon return us happy fruit."[24] This proves abnegation to be the fee for efficacious prayer: we must accept the separation from lower objects if we are to ascend to higher ones. Mary Magdalene is offered as a New Testament witness to the suspension of attention to earthly things. Since she had placed all her desire inside of her Creator, no creature could give her comfort. She had a great longing to behold his body after his death; from this arose an inquietude that caused her to set out on foot to the sepulchre; and while her companions were contented by the angelic announcement, she remained at the graveside, where she manifested her fervor in tears. "In these four things I am to imitate this fervent woman, seeking our Lord with a desire *vehement, solicitous, constant, and devout,* resolving not to take any superfluous comfort in any creature, till I find out my Creator."[25]

Such powerful prayer is a gift to the Church from those communities of desire called Religious communities. Though they do not perform an active apostleship in the world, their prayer contributes

22. Fénelon, *The Complete Fénelon*, 87.
23. De Castañiza, *The Spiritual Conflict and Conquest*, 200.
24. Ibid.
25. De Ponte, *Meditations on the Mysteries of Our Holy Faith*, vol. 5, 41.

the special gift of "irresistible prayer." Elizabeth of the Trinity saw her cloistered life in that way. "I want to be an apostle with you, from the depths of my dear solitude in Carmel, I want to work for the glory of God, and for that I must be wholly filled with Him; then I will be all-powerful: one look, one desire [will] become an irresistible prayer that can obtain everything, since it is, so to speak, God whom we are offering to God."[26]

As we have said, God's descending desire summons man's ascending desire. God wishes for man's prayer to reach out to touch him, like the fingers of God and Adam that Michelangelo painted on the ceiling of the Sistine chapel. The union of love can jump the gap, like an electric spark, because each is charged with so much desire for the other. Every Christian is expected to aspire to perfection in divine love by the way of prayer, as Adam and Eve were intended to do, and which they were doing until desire was misdirected. The theological desire for union with God will keep in check all other passions for the world, which, again, is why desirous prayer stands upon the platform of abnegation. Worldliness takes the world without reference to God. It erases the divine horizon, and takes time and matter, and history and objects, and even other people, without reference to God. Worldliness takes all of creation as less than a sacramental gesture of love by God, and other than the matter for making a sacrificial oblation to God. Adam was not diverted from God in his paradisial state, and so it can be again for souls who are rescued and reborn. When worldliness is overcome, then all things can be put in order as steps that lead to God.

For, loving God only and purely for Himself, [Adam] had no strange affection to distract him, and the images of creatures, which either by his consideration of them, or operations about them, did adhere to his internal senses, did not at all divert his mind from God, because he contemplated them only in order to God [sic]; or rather he contemplated God alone in them, loving and serving Him only in all his reflections on them, or workings about them. So that creatures and all offices towards them served

26. Elizabeth of the Trinity, *Complete Works*, vol. 2, *Letters from Carmel* (Washington, DC: ICS Publications, 2014), 53.

as steps to raise Adam to a more sublime and more intimate union with God.[27]

The desire to ascend always requires casting off the freight that weighs us down in worldliness. Prayer changes the world around the Christian—it does not look the same, it is illumined by a different light, all things in it serve a different purpose. Even things that formerly tempted us to leave the passageway now become steps on a mystical Jacob's ladder.

Christ constructed this ladder not only for his use (to descend) but for our benefit (to ascend). "The same steps serve to mount and to descend. The same degrees by which the Word has descended to us on becoming man have served to elevate our nature to him by uniting it to His."[28] The same rungs on the ladder allowed the Word to descend to us, and allow us to ascend to him, making the Incarnation three mysteries wrapped up into one: love, glorification, and abnegation. First, the Incarnation is a mystery of love. "The strongest inclination of the person who loves is to desire and procure by all the means he can devise, union with the person beloved. Therefore the love that God bore to man caused him to desire, to seek, and to bring about this admirable union."[29] Second, the Incarnation is a mystery of glorification. "Human nature was in it raised to such a height of glory that there is no science nor power that can raise it higher."[30] The self-emptying of the Son of God was done out of love for mankind, that he may raise men and women up to the glory of divine life. Third, the Incarnation is a mystery of annihilation. "To elevate us to the height of infinite glory, it was necessary for him to humble, abase, and annihilate himself, making him a son of Adam the sinner."[31] This required Christ to join us on the first rung, the first step. The annihilation he made of himself was extreme humility; the annihilation we make of ourselves is abnegation. The movement is similar, but the matter is different: he gave

---

27. Baker, *Holy Wisdom*, 30.
28. Saint-Jure, *Knowledge and Love of God*, vol. 1, 284.
29. Saint-Jure, *Union with Our Lord Jesus*, 56.
30. Ibid.
31. Ibid., 60.

up glory rightfully his, we must give up self-esteem not rightfully ours.

The Trinity's desire to integrate the human race into its perichoresis of love caused the entire economy of salvation in the first covenant, from patriarchs to kings to prophets. The hunger of God for man had gone as far as it could; if something more were to happen it would have to come from a new covenant. Therefore, the first person of the Trinity sent the second person of the Trinity to become incarnate by the third person of the Trinity, and something began that was very new indeed. Christ in the flesh inaugurated communion with God such as it could not otherwise be known by man. Liturgy is a unique activity because Christ is unique, and the Church is the body of that Christ. It is the perichoresis of the Trinity, kenotically extending itself, to invite the synergistic ascent of man to deification (my definition of liturgy).[32] His desire for the children of Adam and Eve to commence the ascent that had been abandoned in Eden sets the whole wheel of salvation history spinning.

What are our feelings during this prayer? That is not always important. "It would be a delusion to fancy that we must feel a special attraction towards prayer; if we were ever thus borne on angels' wings, it would not be difficult to draw near unto the light, to grow in grace, to renounce ourselves. We must take courage, and act with force, and when we cannot pray, we must excite the desire within us."[33] The desire operates even during times less stimulating than when we feel like we are flying with the angels. The desire does not depend on a special sentiment. "We must not judge of meditation by the tender sentiments we have experienced, but by the profit we have derived from it, or at least by the sincere desire we have to do good and to practise virtue. When you leave meditation, however dry it may have been, with the desire, the resolution, to correct your faults and to do God's will, your time has not been lost."[34] Desire brings one to the altar of prayer; in turn, prayer creates desires and

32. Fagerberg, *On Liturgical Asceticism*, 9.
33. De Ravignan, *Conferences on the Spiritual Life*, 195.
34. Crasset, in Crasset and de Sales, *The Secret of Sanctity*, 172.

resolutions to do God's will. Prayer and desire stand in mutual support. Ask not what you have been feeling, ask what you have been doing—which demonstrates again that although affection is involved, desire belongs first to the will. "The actual feeling and consciousness of the divine Presence ought to keep the soul, together with all its faculties, constantly attached to God. This can be done by cultivating a strong and ardent desire which will enable it to possess him with a perpetual and simple tranquility of heart."[35]

We will not desire union with God, though, if we see him as a competitor for our worship. We cannot desire union with this God if we prefer a different god (idolatry), or want to be our own god (autolatry). "Now idolatry, if we are to believe the Apostle, is not confined to the worship of false gods. We can raise within ourselves many idols, and blindly offer sacrifice to them."[36] Abnegation consists of purifying our hearts of idols, overthrowing autolatry first of all, idolatry next, and desiring nothing but the glory of God. "Pride causes the sinner to make an idol of self, and put himself in God's place, since he prefers himself to God when his own interests, his satisfactions, his own will and desires are at stake."[37] God is a jealous God, the Scriptures tell us, not sharing his throne with anyone or anything else. Yahweh's jealousy does not rise from childish egotism. Jealousy means being zealous, watchful, *desirous* for the exclusive devotion required for covenant to operate properly. It is the same in a marriage: each partner desires exclusivity from the other in order for the covenant to stand firm. Jealousy is monogamy between God and his espoused people.

"He is a holy God; he is a jealous God" (Josh 24:19), and this conditions our prayer. "What better prayer can we make, than continually to desire the greater glory of God, to conform ourselves continually in all things to his Divine will, and to place all our joy

35. John of St. Samson, *Prayer, Aspiration and Contemplation* (New York: Alba House, 1975), 73.

36. Cécile Bruyère, *Spiritual Life and Prayer According to Holy Scripture and Monastic Tradition* (New York: Benziger Brothers, 1905), 361.

37. John Eudes, *Meditations on Various Subjects* (New York: P. J. Kenedy & Sons, 1947), 214.

and contentment in the joy and contentment of God?"[38] True prayer gives glory to God; idolatrous prayer gives glory to something without God, something other than God; autolatrous prayer gives glory to ourselves, which is a form of pride. True prayer is done within God, false prayer without God. The course correction needed is accomplished by abnegation, which is why denial of our own self-will and self-esteem is essential to this sort of prayer. "Remember that as God's will is always invariably fixed to desire and claim his glory, the shortest, easiest, and surest way of glorifying God is to will precisely all that he wills; and in proportion as we do this with more or less resignation, abandonment, and destruction of our own will, the glory we render to God will be greater or less."[39]

We may pray for our good, of course. We may pray to attain the reward accorded to God's saints. But there is a difference between a holy desire and a mercenary desire.

> You will observe, if you please, that there is a great deal of difference between a proper desire of reward and a mercenary habit of mind. The proper desire of recompense is one which looks principally to the glory of God, and to that glory refers its own reward....
>
> But a mercenary habit of mind is shown when we stop short voluntarily, deliberately, and maliciously at our own self-interest, neglecting and putting on one side the interests of God, and when we look forward only to the honours, satisfactions, and delights given to the faithful, and exclude, as it were, the tribute of glory and homage which they render for them to God.[40]

To make true prayer, our desire must be purified in its object, direction, intensity, and purpose. Perfect prayer will seek to glorify God at all times, in all requests, for every reason, during every event— even during trial and affliction. This is the test. Giving oneself over to God during such trials is the greatest audit of whether desire is

---

38. Alphonsus Rodríguez (Alfonso), *The Practice of Christian and Religious Perfection*, vol. 1, 344.

39. Saint-Jure, *Union with Our Lord Jesus*, 84.

40. Camus, *The Spirit of St. Francis de Sales*, 44.

true or mercenary. It is one of the reasons why God has allowed such trials of his greatest saints.

As we learn from John of the Cross, there are three signs that a spiritual man is walking in the night of purgation of the senses. First, he finds no comfort in the things of God, and none also in created things; second, his memory dwells upon God with a painful anxiety and carefulness; third, he is unable to meditate and make reflections, and to excite the imagination as before.[41] What else is there for the soul to do but persevere, whereby perseverance calms chaos and makes room for prayer? "There is nothing to be done but to be contented that she can just keep herself in peace, and to throw off depression and heaviness, without being troubled because she cannot produce such heroic acts towards God as she would wish. For the sincere and constant desire which she has of finding God and of pleasing him supplies for all that is wanting."[42] During aridity, dejection, and privation, the desire to please God must compensate for other spiritual acts the soul cannot produce. In this sense, desire is the soul's last witness. The desire to desire is proof of faith and love, wrapped up in hope. "When God gives us Consolation in Prayer, he gives us Marks of his Love; but when we meet with Driness and Desolation, and continue in it notwithstanding, we then give God Proofs of our Love and Fidelity to him.... Is a Servant idle when he waits in an Anti-Chamber for his Master's Orders?"[43]

Often desire produces great activity, but as often as not, desire is a response to a hesychasm (silence) and passivity God is requesting of the soul. "By desire, at least, dispose yourself to keep silence, and only break it in the exact degree in which the glory of God does not require it to be kept."[44] De Sales gives a famous illustration of this

---

41. John of the Cross, *The Obscure Night of the Soul*, in *The Complete Works of Saint John of the Cross*, vol. 1 (London: Longman, Green, Longman, Roberts & Green, 1864), 348–52.

42. Barbanson, *The Secret Paths of Divine Love*, 224.

43. François Fénelon, *Pious Thoughts Concerning the Knowledge and Love of God* (London: W. and J. Innys, 1720), 97–98. Capitalization and punctuation as in original.

44. Charles Gay, *The Christian Life and Virtues Considered in the Religious State*, vol. 1 (London: Burns & Oates, 1876), 388.

by imagining a statue placed in the niche of a gallery by some great prince. If that statue were somehow endowed with understanding so it could reason and talk, he imagines this conversation:

> O fair statue, tell me now, why art thou in that niche?—It would answer,—Because my master placed me there. And if one should reply,—But why stayest thou there without doing anything?— Because, would it say, my master did not place me here to do anything, but simply that I should be here motionless. But if one should urge it further, saying: But, poor statue, what art thou the better for remaining there in that sort? Well! would it say, I am not here for my own interest and service, but to obey and accomplish the will of my master and maker; and this suffices me. And if one should yet insist thus: Tell me then, statue, I pray, not seeing thy master how dost thou find contentment in contenting him? No, verily, would it confess; I see him not, for I have not eyes for seeing, as I have not feet for walking; but I am too contented to know that my dear master sees me here, and takes pleasure in seeing me here.[45]

The statue (and the man) desires to be where it is placed. Pleasing our Master is the purpose of prayer, even when our spiritual eyes seem blind, and our spiritual feet seem crippled. Only a deep desire to please God can account for this contentment in passive prayer.

Now perseverance is an act of the will and desire is an achievement of the will. Therefore, we can call this sort of prayer an achievement of wanting to will, willing to desire, desiring to pray. That fact holds quite a surprise for us. "I assure you on the part of God, that usually, indeed nearly always, when you think you are praying your worst, that is the very time when you are praying best. Why? Because on the one hand the will, and the firm desire to pray is a real prayer of the heart; and because, on the other hand, you pray then without any self-complacency, without any of those vain reflexions which spoil everything."[46] All the mystics give witness to the fact that God gradually withdraws the sensible consolations he

---

45. De Sales, *Treatise on the Love of God*, 220.
46. De Caussade, *Abandonment to Divine Providence*, 246.

granted at the outset in order to encourage the soul. Of course, his presence does not really withdraw; only our sense of the presence is diminished to the point of insensibility. The dark night arrives. At that point, "when you feel not in prayer that fervor you desire, and when you labour in vain to obtain an intimate union of your soul with God, exercise your will in conceiving an ardent desire thereof, and thereby you will supply and gain what you think you want."[47]

All that is left to us in moments when we do not feel like we are praying, or do not feel like praying, or feel like our prayers are failing, is to exercise our will in order to present God with our desire to pray. In a similar way, what we can do when we cannot weep, is to weep over the fact that we cannot weep. "Weep thou for compassion to see him weep, weep because thou art the cause of His weeping, and weep for thy sins that afflict His heart; and if this make me not weep, then weep because thou art so hard-hearted that thou canst not weep."[48] The dry state pushes the prayer down deeper—to the most internal desires of the heart. "Although these distractions and this aridity are painful, they do not prevent the constant desire to pray which remains in the depths of the heart, and it is in this desire that heartfelt prayer consists."[49]

The theologians of abnegation think this state is actually a grace from God, because dryness and powerlessness dismantle our haughty feelings of self-merit, and drive us solely to the sufferings of Jesus Christ, in whom we meritoriously participate. The dark night is the arrival of the cross, and the cross is the portal to the garden of the beloved. Although one might feel as if one is prevented from asking God for necessary helps, in fact "it does not prevent you wishing to ask for them, and you ought to know that with God, our desires are real prayers, according to St. Augustine. This made Bossuet say that a cry pent up in the depths of the heart was of the same value as a cry that reached the skies, because God sees our most secret desires, and even the first simple movement of the

47. Alphonsus Rodríguez (Alfonso), *The Practice of Christian and Religious Perfection*, vol. 1, 297.

48. De Ponte, *Meditations on the Mysteries of Our Holy Faith*, vol. 2, 172.

49. De Caussade, *Abandonment to Divine Providence*, 232.

heart."[50] Though we lack the spiritual gift to enunciate prayer like Isaiah, Jeremiah, or Paul, the pent up cries can reach the same heights. Aridity, involuntary distractions (voluntary distractions are another matter), the feeling of impotence, the lack of fervor—"none of these things prevent the desire to pray well, or to sigh and lament before God. His all-seeing eye detects the pure intention and preparation of heart, with all those acts that we should wish to have made; as He sees the fruits of the trees before the buds of springtime have formed on the branches; this is the beautiful comparison made by the Bishop of Meaux."[51] We are fortunate, indeed, to come before an omniscient God, whose foresight sees fruits that are still only buds in us, and whose hindsight sees the cross being imposed on a heart. "He is the Lord of your soul; let Him do what He wishes with His property."[52]

50. Ibid., 245.
51. Ibid.
52. Libermann, *Letters to Religious Sisters and Aspirants*, 49.

6

Unconscious Prayer

THE DESIRE GOD PLANTS in the soul takes root so far down that it operates hidden from our sensibilities. It can even operate hidden from our rational consciousness. "Souls with such great desires long for more than they know, for their mind cannot understand their cravings."[1] We don't know what to pray for, but the Spirit intercedes with sighs too deep for words (Rom 8:26) and we must scrutinize our prayers if we are to know what the Spirit desires.

> The heart in which the true love of God and true desire exist never ceases to pray. Love, hidden in the depths of the soul, prays without ceasing, even when the mind is drawn another way. God continually sees the desire that he has himself implanted in the soul. Though we may at times be unconscious of its existence, the heart is touched by it. Such a hidden desire in the soul ceaselessly draws God's mercies. It is that Spirit who, according to St. Paul, helps us in our weakness and intercedes for us "with sighs too deep for words."[2]

These spiritual authors are interested in theology, not psychology, but since the theological act of prayer happens in our soul (*psyche*) they have something to say about what goes on there. They ruminate about what happens under the surface of consciousness, because consciousness is a realm of the mind and they are looking at the depths of the heart. We can deduce some interior activities from what we see on the outside, but God looks with greater penetration: "I the Lord search the mind and test the heart, to give to

---

1. Francisco de Osuna, *The Third Spiritual Alphabet* (New York: Benziger Brothers, 1931), 228.
2. Fénelon, *The Complete Fénelon*, 87.

every man according to his ways, according to the fruits of his doings" (Jer 17:10). "As God sees all our desires, and as, according to St. Augustine, to desire always is to pray always, so in this consists our great prayer."[3] The heart is especially the home of the personal life, and to know the heart is to know the person in full, which is only possible for God. Even those who know us best (dear friends, children, spouses) do not know us entirely.

If God alone can search the heart in this way, we are advised not to judge anything before the appointed time (1 Cor 4:5). There is activity happening in the heart that is out of sight of external, empirical observation, and even out of sight of one's own internal, self-conscious observation.

> God upholds you insensibly as you experience yourself; and it is proved that this state is from God because of the peace that you possess in it apart from the senses, and because you would be vexed to be deprived of it. You only require patience, resignation, and abandonment, but these dispositions should not be felt. Remember that God sees in the depths of your heart all your most secret desires. This assurance should be sufficient for you.[4]

Expressing the heart's content by word and act are important for us if we would be whole and integral. To say one thing and yet harbor the opposite in the heart is at least hypocritical, maybe deceptive, and perhaps malevolent. We can dissemble before our fellow men by hiding the heart behind duplicitous speech, but we cannot hoodwink God. His eyes see what we attempt to disguise, his ears hear the desires of the heart that escape our ears.

An evil desire pierces heaven and stores up judgement, but a good desire also pierces heaven and is heard by the merciful ears of God. Furthermore, in his omniscience God even hears the desire while it is still being formed. "The moment we desire to form an act, it is already formed and held as accomplished, because God sees all our desires, even the first movement of the heart. Our desires, says Bossuet, are, with regard to God, what the voice is with regard to

3. De Caussade, *Abandonment to Divine Providence*, 229.
4. Ibid., 359.

men, and a cry from the depths of the heart, even unuttered, is of the same value as a cry sent up to Heaven."[5] Being creatures of time, we can only perceive along the unfolding of a temporal lifeline. Externally, we distinguish the child from the young man, the young man from the adult. Similarly, we distinguish the first desire from the resolve, and the resolve from the enactment. But as God's omniscience and foreknowledge knows the whole person (seeing the adult as he looks upon the child), so he knows the whole operation (seeing the enactment as he looks upon the first movement of the heart).

We make actions with our bodies; we also make actions with our hearts. We make both exterior acts and interior ones. Despite the latter being largely ignored by a society inattentive to the realm of the spiritual, the heart is incessantly active, therefore God has plenty to watch as he considers what a person thinks, what he loves, what he desires. These hidden desires are more numerous than the ones that finally direct our behavior, more active than the ones we abandon out of practicality, more powerful than the words we could say with our lips. Indeed, the desires flying under the radar of consciousness may be the more accurate gauge of our spiritual progress. When we have the sense that we have not made sufficient self-denial, we are sensing that we have not abandoned ourselves as much as we wish. This proves that the intention is present, only not fulfilled. If we feel sorrow that a desire has not been adequately achieved, it proves the yearning still exists. This is a realm in which God can anticipate us: he acts before we act, and desires before we desire. "Our Lord is so desirous of giving Himself to souls, the expansive force of His love is so great that, far from always waiting till the grace is asked of Him, He sometimes with ineffable sweetness anticipates the soul's action, even when that soul is far off from Him."[6]

Faith is required not only to know God, but also to know the true state of affairs within one's soul. If a person believes himself forsaken by God, yet still has a great desire to abandon himself to the

5. Ibid., 105–6.
6. Bruyère, *Spiritual Life and Prayer*, 37.

very One he feels forsaken by, then it is a sign that his faith recognizes he is never less friendless than he is at that moment.

> Does not the spiritual affliction which the fear of not being able to abandon yourself in all things, nor as well as you desire . . . prove the deep and hidden intention which is rooted in your heart, of practising this total abandonment and abnegation that are so meritorious? Does not God behold these desires, so deep and so hidden, and do they not speak for you to God more powerfully than any words you could utter? Yes, certainly, these desires are acts, and better acts than any others, for if you were allowed to practise abandonment in a manner that you could feel, you would find consolation, but would lose, at least somewhat, the salutary feeling of your misery, and would be again exposed to the imperceptible snares of self-love, and to its fatal satisfactions.[7]

On which does God train his eye: the sensation of regret about failed abnegations, or the continued desire to deny self-love? Which does God hear more loudly: our uttered words or our mute desires? Compare the situation to this. We sometimes struggle to say what we want to say—how is this possible? If we want to speak, and we are the ones who are going to speak, and we are preparing to speak, how can be we be struggling to speak? It is because we are searching for words adequate to the idea that already exists. The idea precedes the words, which is why we are dissatisfied with certain words, and continue to stammer until we find the right ones. Similarly, we sometimes struggle to pray as we want to pray—how is that possible? If we want to pray, and we are the ones who are going to pray, and we are preparing to pray, how can it be a struggle to pray? It is because vocal prayer wants to find the right words for the desire that initiated the prayer. God values the desire to pray as much as the act of prayer, values the mental praise as much as the vocal praise. The person who prays finds satisfaction in different kinds of expression.

---

7. De Caussade, *Abandonment to Divine Providence*, 373.

Sometimes thou wilt choose to pray by desires alone, or in very few words, repeating them often with sweetness and devotion; sometimes to pray in many and various words. It will be pleasant to thee, sometimes, to read thy prayers out of a book, sometimes to offer them to God without the aid of a book. Sometimes psalmody, sometimes another sort of contemplation may be most sweet to the taste of thy heart. In short, thou wilt be drawn to different practice at different times.[8]

God's eye is drawn to where love resides, therefore we can please him with interior acts. "Now the reality of the merit of devout desires, of mental praise, and of all interior as well as spoken acts of devotion is the loving side of this question. They need be nothing more than interior acts. Nothing more is necessary. They have touched God as such, and so have received their value and their merit."[9] God so loves us, and so longs for our love, that he has made it easy for our hearts to praise him. God does not need information from us in order to perceive our prayer.

Those who are unable to conceive how the heart can pray alone, without distinct acts, cannot understand either how a simple, general prayer can perfectly well include all particular prayers.... In this matter it is a common practice to treat God as though He were a man, and could not understand a prayer unless every detail of its requests were explained to Him.... O souls of little faith, and little knowledge of God, your intentions have reached Him before you have opened your mouth! No sooner are they in your heart than He sees them. Why torment yourselves by trying to explain them to Him? You desire every spiritual blessing for yourselves and for those whom you love; and is it possible that He who inspired you with those desires should not know that you have them?[10]

Once again, we find confirmation that God inspires, implants, and causes the desires for him that we are feeling. Love continues even when the mind is distracted.

8. Blosius, *Spiritual Works of Louis of Blois*, 64–65.
9. Faber, *All for Jesus*, 292.
10. Grou, *The School of Jesus Christ*, 233–34.

I can imagine God looking favorably even on our frustration in trying to put our prayer into words for the same reason the beloved looks approvingly at the suitor's attempts at bad poetry: because there is love behind the effort. The soul toils because she is not content with liturgizing God less than she wants to do. This pleases God. The desire to glorify God is the motivation for the spiritual journey. It operates even during the stunning example of suffering, during which more progress is often made than during times of fortune, because suffering can be "a symptom of cure not illness. 'But at these times I can neither pray nor have recourse to God.' No, perhaps not, at any rate not in a perceptible manner; but the heart prays without ceasing by hidden desires known only to God."[11] And it is even the motivation for undertaking a Christian death. "The amorous soul, perceiving that she cannot satiate the desire she has to praise her well-beloved while she lives in this world, and knowing that the praises which are given in heaven to the divine goodness are sung to an incomparably more delightful air,—O God! says she, how much to be praised are the praises which are poured forth by those blessed spirits before the throne of my heavenly king; how blessed are their blessings!"[12]

The Christian is prepared to die—can even be called eager to die, properly understood—because the soul knows the praises she can give in heaven will be greater than the praises she can give now. Our liturgy now is so imperfect, and we fervently desire to participate in a more perfect one. "He who loves cannot be satisfied if he does not feel that he loves as much as he is beloved," and when the soul sees that the transformation in this life cannot equal the perfection of the love with which God loves her, then that soul desires "the clear transformation of glory wherein it shall equal His love. For though in this high estate, which the soul reaches on earth, there exists a real union of the will, yet it cannot reach that perfection and strength of love which it is to reach in the union of glory."[13] The

11. De Caussade, *Abandonment to Divine Providence*, 221.

12. De Sales, *Treatise on the Love of God*, 190.

13. John of the Cross, *Ascent of Mount Carmel*, in *Complete Works*, vol. 2, 196–97.

union in faith will not satisfy the soul until it becomes a union in glory. This is a supernatural love, that exceeds natural love, and is stimulated not only by what it receives, but also by what it will be able to give. It is hardly even conscious of its own operations, so entirely fixed is it upon worshiping God.

> We hardly know whether to call [this love] a child of heaven or of earth. It is the love of adoration. It is a love too quiet for benevolence, too deep for complacency, too passive for condolence, too contemplative for gratitude; but which has grown up out of the loves of preference and desire, and is, besides, the perfection of all the other loves. It is too much possessed with God to be accurately conscious of the nature of its own operations. It finds no satisfaction except in worship.[14]

Ultimately, the desire we are discussing is a liturgical phenomenon. It is the creature's love-inspired desire to give thanks and glory to its Creator. It rises up from a soul that has been baptized into the love of the Holy Trinity, fed on the sacrament of love, experienced absolution for each failure of love, has been guided by Mary the Protectress of faith and love and hope, and comes to the last rites with eyes fixed on adding its will to the liturgy of heaven. "The Three divine Persons have one and the same desire, and one and the same will, and work in all things with perfect harmony, without any difference. . . . Even so I will endeavour to unite myself to God, and to make myself one thing with Him by love, having one and the same desire with His."[15]

Our desire is like the current in a stream, and though the river's surface may have flotsam floating upon it after our shipwreck in the world, so long as the desire moves forward under the gravity of grace, it will arrive at the divine ocean. God is mindful and attentive to this current. "He remembers his cries; He hearkens to his desire. Does the poor man recollect himself to pray: even before his heart has fully formed a desire, God has understood and graciously heard

---

14. Faber, *Creator and the Creature*, 217.

15. Louis de Ponte, *Meditations on the Mysteries of Our Holy Faith*, vol. 6 (London: Richardson and Son, 1854), 43.

it."[16] The kingdom of heaven belongs to the poor in spirit, and in the kingdom of heaven all desires will be granted, because a pure heart has desired one thing, one love, one God. Blessed are the pure in heart, who will one thing.

Because men are embodied souls (or ensouled bodies), they learn through the senses. Perceptions enter the mind through images, stimulate the imagination, take residence in memory, receive formation by both passive and active intellect, and then are put to use by reason. But in this case, we are not talking about an exterior perception, but an interior word, spoken by the Spirit of God. "We know, according to the Bible, that the Spirit of God dwells within us, works there, prays without ceasing, sorrows, desires and asks for what we ourselves do not know enough to ask for; urges us, inspires us, speaks to us in the silence, suggests all truth to us, and so unites us to himself that are no longer other than 'one spirit with God.'"[17] This is *spiritual desire*, i.e., desire caused by the Spirit. Here, faith is being taught in a different classroom. Doctors of theology—outside doctors—suppose that reasoning enlightens the mind, but "they do not count enough on the doctor within, who is the Holy Spirit, and who effects everything within us. He is the soul of our soul. We should not know how to form a thought nor a desire except though him. Alas, how great is our blindness! We act as though we were alone in this inner sanctuary. And on the contrary, God is there more intimately than are we ourselves."[18] Why can God know the desires formed in our inner sanctuary? Because he dwells there, too. Why can the desires formulated in this inner sanctuary reach the ear of God? Because he is enthroned there, too, and listens to them. We cannot form a desire except through this doctor within.

It is not quite accurate to use the word "unconscious" to describe this, though it comes close; perhaps we could say "beyond consciousness." The doctor within works covertly, inconspicuously, in secret. Many of the greater realities that make up love act in the same way, and come from the same place. Something goes on

---

16. Gay, *The Christian Life and Virtues*, vol. 2, 226.
17. Fénelon, *Christian Perfection*, 155.
18. Ibid.

beyond the conscious mind, unnoticed, until it returns to mind to be seen. We have "forgotten" it, we think, but it is not absent for that reason. It is just momentarily not attended to by the finite mind. For instance,

> a tender father does not always think distinctly of his son. A thousand objects take away his imagination and his mind. But these distractions never interrupt the paternal love. Whenever his son returns to his mind, he loves him, and he feels in the depths of his heart that he has not stopped loving him for a single moment, although he has stopped thinking of him. Such should be our love for our heavenly father, a simple love, without suspicion and without uneasiness.[19]

We should continually, constantly, be attending to the glory of God. This does not mean "always thinking of it with an actual and present intention, [which] would be almost impossible, almost beyond the condition of man." Rather it means the glory of God "is his most frequent thought, and that he recurs to it ever and again, as a man does to something he loves affectionately, and desires intensely."[20] Intensiveness of desire expresses itself in intentionality of mind, but the former may continue operating when the latter lapses. A stop to thinking does not put a stop to loving. This may be different with voluntary disturbances, but involuntary distractions "do not disturb love at all, since it exists in the will, and the will never has distractions when it does not want to have them. When we notice them, we let them fall, and we turn again to God. Thus, while the outer senses of the bride are slumbering, her heart watches, her love does not relax."[21] The interior garden has a life that goes on despite the noise and discordance that goes on outside its walls.

Within that garden, the Holy Spirit works in prayer. He not only makes us ask, but also asks in His own right in our prayers. How does the Paraclete speak? "In a language which is most mysterious,

19. Ibid., 55.
20. Faber, *All for Jesus*, 37.
21. Fénelon, *Christian Perfection*, 54–55.

secret, and unfathomable even by ourselves, and which is therefore described as 'unspeakable groanings,' because He asks 'for us' the contrary of what we ask."[22] We know the experience. We ask for something in particular; we believe it true and right; we think it would be great for us, and we ask in the way we should. Yet we do not obtain it. Just the opposite. Why?

> This is the reason: the Holy Spirit, seeing that the thing thou askest would be bad for thee, changed thy petition, so to speak, by substituting something which He knew to be profitable for thee.... It happens that thou sometimes prayest for something very earnestly, but that at the same time thou hast, almost unconsciously, a very good resignation to the Divine will, which makes thee desire whatever God chooses to send thee much more than the thing thou art asking of Him. Now this desire is the secret language of the Holy Ghost speaking in thee, for it is a desire which proceeds entirely from true love.[23]

The Divine will is opposite to our own, but a hidden, unfathomable, secret desire makes us resign to it instead of insisting on our own will.

On the one hand, doing God's will requires thinking of him, that is true. His will asks for a labor from us, either toward himself (piety) or toward others (charity), and then our intellect must engage in order to make choices to guide the labor. This is the sense in which we may say that we should always think of God. In her testimony during de Sales's beatification process, Jane Chantal wrote, "About fifteen years ago, I asked him if he ever, for long at a time, ceased to turn his thoughts to God; he replied: 'Sometimes, for about a quarter of an hour.' This answer, coming from a Prelate so occupied as he was with all kinds of varied and important business, filled me with admiration."[24] The mind must sometimes narrow its

---

22. Segneri, *The Manna of the Soul*, vol. 1, 363.

23. Ibid., 364.

24. Jane Chantal, in Francis de Sales and Jane de Chantal, *The Mystical Explanation of the Canticle of Canticles by St. Francis de Sales,* and *The Depositions of St. Jane Frances de Chantal in the Cause of the Canonisation of St. Francis de Sales* (in one volume) in *Library of St. Francis de Sales,* 154.

focus upon the task at hand, and direct the will outward to the assignment. It is good to think of God, to offer him the beginning of each action, and align each decision with his purpose. But on the other hand, "do not imagine that you have done nothing for Him if during the performance of the duty begun for Him you have not thought of Him: He knows your heart and your intentions. If you were asked for whom you were doing this action, would you not answer that you were doing it for God? Then have no fear: you have been laboring for Him even though some time has elapsed without your thinking of Him."[25] I am always married, but only sometimes think about it; one can always desire union with God, but only sometimes think about it.

We have already spoken of the *spiritual desire for communion*, and it becomes relevant here again. "The holy Council of Trent moreover, highly commends spiritual Communion, and zealously invites all the faithful to practise it; all truly pious souls have always observed this holy exercise. And what excuse can you give for not doing so? Is it want of time? It cannot be, seeing that a single act of desire and love, as quick as thought, is sufficient."[26] What comfort! A single act of desire, quick as a thought, as rapid as a flash of love, can be a communion with Christ. Spiritual communion is desire in operation.

> If we are deprived of Sacramental Communion, let us replace it, as far as we can, by spiritual communion, which we can make every moment; for we ought to have always a burning desire to receive the good God. Communion is to the soul like blowing a fire that is beginning to go out, but that has still plenty of hot embers; we blow, and the fire burns again. After the reception of the Sacraments, when we feel ourselves slacken in the love of God, let us have recourse at once to spiritual communion. . . . We can receive the good God only once a day; a soul on fire with love supplies for this by the desire to receive Him every moment.[27]

25. Crasset, in Crasset and de Sales, *The Secret of Sanctity*, 263.
26. Boudon, *Perpetual Adoration of Jesus*, 78.
27. John Vianney, *The Little Catechism of the Curé of Ars* (Rockford, IL: TAN Books and Publishers, Inc., 1987), 49.

We can receive the Savior sacramentally only once a day, "yet thou mayest receive Him spiritually every hour and moment. . . . For as often as thou desirest to receive thy loving Lord God thus spiritually into thy soul, thou shalt find Him ever ready to feast thee with His own sacred hands."[28] In fact, the authors speak of making spiritual communion with Christ at least "once in each day,"[29] or three times a day,[30] or "every hour,"[31] or one hundred times a day,[32] and mention is made of Blessed Agatha of the cross making "two hundred spiritual communions every day."[33] How can this be? Perhaps the parallel with continuous prayer is helpful. As we are invited to be both in continuous prayer and engage certain moments in prayer, so we are invited to be both in continuous desire for spiritual communion and find ourselves desiring it at certain moments.

We have also already spoken of the enclosed garden described in the Canticle, or Song of Solomon. Verse 2:9 says, "Behold, there he stands behind our wall, gazing in at the windows, looking through the lattice." We may imagine gaze meeting gaze in the Sacrament of Love. "To gaze—to gaze is all we desire. The fact, that so much is mystery to us, is no trouble. It is love. That is enough. We trust it. We would almost rather it was not made plainer."[34] Some mysteries thrive better in twilight than in bright sunshine.

> Behold, O my soul, thy loving Jesus, burning with the same love with which he loved thee when dying for thee on the Cross, is now concealed in the Most Blessed Sacrament under the sacred species; and what is he doing? *Looking through the lattices.* As an ardent lover, desirous to see you correspond to his love, from the Host, as from within closed lattices, whence he sees without being seen, he

28. De Castañiza, *The Spiritual Conflict and Conquest*, 189.

29. John Baptist Scaramelli, *The Directorium Asceticum; or, Guide to the Spiritual Life*, vol. 1 (New York: Benziger Bros., 1902), 657.

30. Alphonsus de Liguori, *Meditations for a Private Retreat of Eight Days*, in *Saint Alphonsus de Liguori: Selection* (Aeterna Press, Kindle edition, 2016), 2136.

31. De Castañiza, *The Spiritual Conflict and Conquest*, 189.

32. Scaramelli, *Directorium Asceticum*, vol. 1, 656.

33. De Liguori, *The Holy Eucharist*, 119, and repeated by Frederick Faber, *The Blessed Sacrament* (London: Burns Oates & Washbourne Ltd., 1861), 515.

34. Faber, *Creator and the Creature*, 112.

is looking at you, who are this morning about to feed upon his divine flesh; he observes your thoughts, what it is that you love, what you desire, what you seek for, and what offerings you are about to make him.[35]

When preparing for Communion, ask what you love, what you desire, what you seek. God knows. He already knows. He knows what we do not yet know. God's omniscience is not only a knowledge of distant, abstract, empyrean facts, it is also an omniscient knowledge of our innermost state.

The communion of saints is also involved with spiritual communion and sacramental Communion. When Saint Gertrude grieved at feeling ill-prepared to receive the sacramental body of Christ, she asked the Blessed Virgin and the saints if they would offer their worthiness on her behalf, "wherefore, our Lord said to her: 'Thou dost truly now appear to all the citizens of heaven adorned as thou didst desire to be.'"[36] The very desire itself, if it is heartfelt (felt in the heart), adorns one with the livery of sanctity. Christ made a similar remark to Saint Mechtildis, "When thou art about to receive Holy Communion, do thou desire and wish to the praise of My name, to have all the desire and all the love for Me with which any heart has ever been inflamed, and thus draw near to Me. For I shall regard and accept that love from thee, not as it is in thee, but as thou wishest it to be in thee."[37] We say to ourselves: "I wish I could love God more." Good. He is pleased with that. He will accept the love as we wish it could be, and then bring it to pass. He fills our desires as much as he can, both in heaven and on earth.

> Christ our Lord ... has in heaven all the Blessed sitting with Him at His table, to whom He makes a solemn banquet, in which the meat that is set before them is His own divinity and humanity, which they see clearly, and fill with it all their desires, and are inebriated with the wine of beatifying love.... [Now] I descend to ponder that this infinite God, who makes this banquet above in

35. De Liguori, *The Holy Eucharist*, 71.
36. Blosius, *Spiritual Works of Louis of Blois*, 247.
37. Ibid.

heaven, mindful of His children whom He has on earth, girds Himself much more to invite them, *putting Himself wholly with His divinity and humanity under these forms of bread and wine ...* that there with the eyes of faith we may behold Him present, and receiving Him within us, may fill our desires as much as here they may be filled.[38]

The sacramental reception of Jesus is miraculous and grand. "This I pray for, this I desire, that I may be wholly united to Thee, and may withdraw my heart from all created things, and by the Holy Communion, and often celebrating, may more and more learn to relish heavenly and eternal things."[39] But as magnificent as that miracle is, sometimes God can make even more effective use of the desire for spiritual communion.

> It is so useful, that I do not fear to say ... that it can produce the same graces as Sacramental Communion, and even greater; for though Sacramental Communion, in its nature, produces greater fruits, because, being a Sacrament, it works by its own virtue; yet a soul desirous of perfection, can make a spiritual Communion with so much humility, love, and devotion, that it deserves more grace than one who communicates sacramentally, but with less fervor and preparation.[40]

Vocal prayer and meditation require thoughts that are reverent and devout, and it is good to follow where they lead, but if one is unable to do it, do not lose confidence in prayers that embrace nothingness.

> If you have a pious thought so much the better. Be guided by it. If, on the contrary, you experience nothing, be content with remaining in your nothingness and poverty before God, ready to offer yourself and sacrifice yourself with Jesus to His Father. You may also give yourself to Mary, that she may offer you with Jesus to His

38. De Ponte, *Meditations on the Mysteries of Our Holy Faith*, vol. 6, 435.
39. Louis de Montfort, *True Devotion to Mary* (Bay Shore, NY: Montfort Publications, 1954), 263.
40. Boudon, *Perpetual Adoration of Jesus*, 77–78.

Father. This thought suffices and it is not even necessary that it be always present to your mind. It suffices that you have it at the bottom of your heart, in your desire and intention.[41]

If Jesus said his Father in heaven was pleased with the widow's mite, and with the Canaanite woman who asked even for crumbs, then he can be pleased even with the sort of prayers we sometimes offer up. Jesus told us that the kingdom of God is small as a mustard seed, that three measures of meal can be leavened by what the woman hid in it, that the one coin and the one sheep are more valuable than the nine and the ninety-nine. God likes small desires, too.

We conclude with two mysteries associated with the unconscious desires of the heart: predestination and prevenient grace.

What is at the bottom of the heart does not always rise to the level of the mind, but the cry from that deep place is answering a call from a high place. Prayer is a gift from God, so its supernatural character may overwhelm our finite understanding. "God is so good that he only awaits our desire to overwhelm us with this gift which is himself. The cry, he says in the Scriptures, will not yet be formed in your mouth, when I, who will see it before it is born in your heart, I will grant it before it is made. Thus it is our heart's prayer that God usually grants."[42] We have gone further and further back: from the spoken prayer, to the conceived prayer, to the desire to pray, and now we discover that the omniscient Holy One sees the cry before it is even born in the heart. File this under the mystery of predestination.

What can rouse a person from the pitiable state of being a slave to this world's vanities? He must pray for light; embrace abnegation; believe that all things work together for good to them that love God, even trials and crosses. Especially crosses. The person undergoing such a conversion must be filled with God's Spirit, and anyone without that Spirit is miserable.

Yet none are really without it save they who ask it not, or ask amiss. It is not with the lips, or external acts only, that we can win

41. Libermann, *Letters to Clergy and Religious* (Series 9), 286.
42. Fénelon, *Christian Perfection*, 70.

to us that Spirit of Life without Whom the best deeds are lifeless; but by the heart's desire, by a thorough prostration of self before God. He is so good, He waits but our hearty desire to fill us to overflowing with that gift which is Himself. He has said that the cry is not formed by the lips—scarce conceived by the heart—before He grants the prayer. But it is the heart's prayer which He grants.[43]

File this under the mystery of prevenient grace.

The cry does not live on the lips; the cry does not even live in the mind. Vocal prayer comes from the former, mental prayer from the latter. Vocal prayer is valuable because it awakens interior devotion, it forms a vent for interior devotion, and requires attention to the order, meaning, and end of the words.[44] Mental prayer is valuable because it is "the work of the three supreme faculties of the soul, in regard of that part which is pure spirit, and is called *mens*, from whence this prayer also is called mental."[45] Vocal prayer is important because it involves the body, and mental prayer is important because these three faculties of the soul exalt man over the beasts, but we should not be surprised at the end of this chapter to find that the desire of the soul is most important of all. "This, therefore, is what thou shouldst do. Say the words, and say them all, as is right; and if in the act of saying them thou art so weak as not to be able as yet thoroughly to change thy heart, at least desire to change it."[46] Desire *goes to* speech and thought, but desire *comes from* the place where love dwells. If one finds it difficult to let the heart express itself in words of love, follow Libermann's advice:

My reply is, "Why do you want to draw forth from your heart those words of love?" Leave them in your heart; Jesus is there; He will take them there himself.

Your present condition of soul demands that you remain before Jesus with interior love; it does not demand outward expression.

43. Fénelon, *Letters to Men*, 292–93.
44. Frederick Faber, *Growth in Holiness; or, The Progress of the Spiritual Life* (Baltimore: John Murphy & Co., 1855), 214.
45. Louis de Ponte, *Meditations on the Mysteries of Our Holy Faith*, vol. 1, 44–45.
46. Segneri, *The Manna of the Soul*, vol. 2, 477.

Incline always to Our Lord by the desires of your soul and do it with profound self-humiliation. Remain always like a victim before this sacrificing Priest.[47]

---

47. Libermann, *Letters to Clergy and Religious* (Series 7), 52–53.

7

Ejaculatory Prayer

WE HAVE SEEN DESIRE at work even during times of aridity, but if desire worked like a dewfall in the desert in the last chapter, in this chapter we will find desire working like an artesian fountain, gushing forth with the force of an internal pressure. This prayer is "unprocessed," so to speak, because of its immediate movement from man to God, from heart to heart, along the pathway of desire. "The more vigorously an arrow is shot from the bow the more swift is its flight. The more vehement and loving is an aspiration, the more truly is it a spiritual lightning-flash."[1] The Divine Pedagogue teaching this deep science is the Lord Jesus himself. He gives his disciples the treasures of his sacred humanity, his Mother, his ministry and Passion, his sacraments, and his Church. "See then! Jesus puts all these things into our hands as weapons of intercession. He fills our quiver full of these arrows, dipped in potent balms, to wound His Sacred Heart, which He uncovers to us for our aim. If aimed with devout intention, they must reach the mark, and if they reach it they must wound infallibly."[2] The thought that we can infallibly wound God is a miraculous promise made to desirous prayer, and its substance is ecstatic in form, and mysterious in content. "Behold the infinite wisdom and the hidden mysteries; Oh! the peace, the love, the silence of the divine bosom; Oh! the deep science God is teaching there; it is that which we call anagogic acts—ejaculatory prayer—Oh! how they set the heart on fire."[3] These prayers are "darts of love" shot at God. The acts of devout affection are "shot

---

1. Camus, *The Spirit of St. Francis de Sales*, 249.
2. Faber, *All for Jesus*, 140–41.
3. John of the Cross, *Spiritual Maxims* in *The Complete Works of Saint John of the Cross*, vol. 2 (London: Longman, Green, Longman, Roberts & Green, 1864), 567.

forth like arrows in order to strike at once the heart of God and inflame the heart of him who produces them."[4]

"Ejaculatory" is a favored term used, coming from the image of a javelin (*iaculum*) being thrown (*ex* + *iaclari*, throw, hurl, cast), but this prayer has other names, too, according to Cardinal Bona: aspiration, upward movement, and affections.

> They are called *aspirations or breathings*, because by them our souls breathe towards God, and God breathes favourably on our endeavours. And since, in aspiring towards God, we breathe nothing but God, therefore the fervour of charity is no less sustained in the soul by these breathings, than the bodily life is by its breathing of the air. Aspirations are called *upward movements*, because by them we are drawn away from things of earth, and raised to things above, and at length are carried up to a blessed union with God. They are called *ejaculatory prayers*, because, like darts or arrows, they pass swiftly into the Heart of God. Into His Heart they are cast as the object of their aim, that from Him we may obtain heavenly gifts. Lastly, they are called *affections*, as being affections of the heart, and desires or resolves of the will. An aspiration is nothing else than what it is defined to be by Gelenius, namely, a ready affection towards God as the highest Good.[5]

We will follow the Cardinal's division of terms when we gather descriptions below.

(1) *Aspirations or Breathings.* Desire emits prayers that "are sighs of love breathed out before God to ask his help and protection."[6] Respiration is the inhalation and exhalation the body must do in order to live; to fail in this is to expire. Similarly, "as the lungs and heart by their dilatation attract the air, so the soul attracts our Lord when she opens and expands with her desires and prayers."[7] Breathing is such a part of our bodily nature that we do it without thinking, and a similarity can be experienced in our spiritual nature. "As

---

4. Scaramelli, *The Directorium Asceticum*, vol. 1, 457.
5. Bona, *The Easy Way to God*, 34. Emphasis added.
6. Francis de Sales, *Letters to Persons in Religion* (New York: Benziger Brothers, 1909), 34.
7. Saint-Jure, *Union with Our Lord Jesus*, 42.

the action of continually repelling from our lungs the air that we draw into them, is made without any previous reflection or resolution to respire or draw breath; so these burning desires proceed so suddenly from the bottom of our hearts, that we sometimes make them, without having had beforehand so much time as to think of them, or to design or purpose with ourselves to produce them."[8] Aspirations and affections answer to the respirations of the body because between each breath our body takes we should "breathe out ... some holy affection, or some groaning of the spirit, or some short prayer of those which we call ejaculatory, spending the whole time, that is, between one respiration and another, in the pondering or understanding and spiritual taste of what we desire or ask, or of the thing for which we groan and sigh to God."[9]

Prayer has depth and height. At its depth, it comes from the heart, even from levels below consciousness; at its height, it can be applied to the highest stage of spiritual development (purgative, illuminative, and unitive). Prayer by way of aspirations and affections "is most accommodated to those that walk in the *unitive* way, aspiring and thirsting for actual union with Almighty God; and with this desire they labour to pray with the greatest continuance and frequency that they can: for prayer is as necessary for the perfect spiritual life of the soul as respiration is for the life of the body."[10]

(2) *Upward Movements.* The prayer of aspiration is not directed sideways or downward or inward: it is directed upward. The heart seeks its happiness, its home, and so follows the anagogic path. This is often communicated by using the metaphor of flame. Desires ascend, as flames rise. Our will and desire shoot forth an aspiration from an inflamed heart. There is a synergistic connection between God's constant love for us and our being further ignited with love, a connection made more by will than by intellect. "If a soul finds difficulty in disengaging from the world, let her content herself in

---

8. Alphonsus Rodríguez (Alfonso), *The Practice of Christian and Religious Perfection,* vol. 1, 341.

9. De Ponte, *Meditations on the Mysteries of Our Holy Faith,* vol. 1, 52.

10. Ibid., 52–53.

breathing forth heartily these or the like short words:— 'O my God, when shall I love You? when shall I embrace You?' Let her repeat them affectionately and perseverantly, and she shall sooner be inflamed with divine love than by the subtle consideration of the greatest secrets of heaven; for it is the will which unites us to God, not the understanding."[11] One does not disengage from the world out of Manichean tendencies, one disengages from the world insofar as it distracts us teleologically. Anything in the world that can assist us in our service of God, and be ordered to him, is a blessing. Anything that cannot is a curse, and one which ejaculatory prayers assist in breaking. Do not neglect ejaculatory prayers because "they are, so to speak, the heavenly side of distractions, thoughts of God that distract us from the world, and interfere with the quiet possession which the world has taken of our souls. Ejaculations are our doing for God what distractions do against Him. They have a specialty to evict distractions. There is no better practice for bringing them under our control."[12]

The upward movement can also be depicted by the metaphor of flight. And it is rapid flight! "These acts of the will are the spiritual wings of the soul to lift her up and unite her to her Beloved: they are short, sharp, and swift darts and desires, shot by our burning hearts, and reaching heaven in an instant."[13] Three advantages of them can be identified. Being short, they do not trouble the memory; being fervent, they rouse us to affection and devotion; being frequent, they still renew our attention to God's presence, and put us perpetually in mind of our duties.[14] These winged prayers are essential to the spiritual life. These are ardent sighs "sometimes breaking forth from the heart only, sometimes also from the mouth,"[15] but as often as not they do not require picture or speech, because they are "short but swift dartings of the soul into God, and

11. De Castañiza, *The Spiritual Conflict and Conquest*, 404–5.
12. Faber, *Growth in Holiness*, 373.
13. De Castañiza, *The Spiritual Conflict and Conquest*, 405.
14. Ibid., 405–6.
15. Benedict of Canfield (William Benedict Fitch), *The Holy Will of God: A Short Rule of Perfection* (London: Thomas Richardson and Sons, 1878), 36.

can be made by a simple mental glance cast towards Him."[16] Being arrows launched from the tautness of a bow, these prayers "penetrate even to God's heart in heaven, especially when they are accompanied with two wings—a true knowledge of the *content* our Lord takes in our practice of virtue; and a lively and longing *desire* to obtain it, for no other end than because it is pleasing to His Divine Majesty."[17]

De Sales was once asked what would involve more spiritual loss: omitting mental prayer or omitting aspirations? "He answered that the omission of mental prayer might be repaired during the day or night by frequent withdrawal of the mind into God and by aspirations to Him, but that mental prayer unaccompanied by aspirations was, in his estimation, like a bird with clipped wings."[18] Prayer not done out of desire for God is prayer in routine, in fear, in perfunctoriness. Prayer is upwardly mobile because God draws the prayer forth (he implanted the desire, as we have seen). So, de Sales concludes, "there is hardly any means of making up where this is lacking. Without it no one can lead a true contemplative life, and the active life will be but imperfect where it is omitted: without it rest is but indolence, labor but weariness; therefore I beseech you to adopt it heartily, and never let it go."[19]

(3) *Ejaculatory Prayers: Arrows.* It is a modest accomplishment to harbor a sporadic thought of God, but since we want a constant will for God, it is beneficial to regularly direct the will to God zealously. One can think without zeal; one cannot pray without zeal. Ejaculatory prayer springs from the tautness of the bow of desire.

> If ejaculatory prayers are to be really good, they must proceed from a soul that tends strongly toward God, and whose every desire goes directly toward Him, just as an arrow parts forcefully with the impulse of the bow, and wings its flight straight toward the target. As long as the bow, when bent, is held in restraint, the arrow

16. De Sales to Camus, *The Spirit of St. Francis de Sales,* 249.

17. De Castañiza, *The Spiritual Conflict and Conquest,* 110.

18. De Sales to Camus, *The Spirit of St. Francis de Sales,* 248.

19. Francis de Sales, *Introduction to the Devout Life* (New York: Vintage Spiritual Classics, 2002), 67.

remains immovable, though always directed toward the mark; but as soon as the hand which holds back the bow is removed, the arrow speeds away. It must be the same with our soul.[20]

The mind surveys countless subjects constantly, and God may be one among them, but having the attention pointed at the right target remains unsatisfactory until the prayer is released and speeds toward heaven.

The prayers are short and repetitive, which accounts for the charm and effectiveness of their frequency. "The brevity of these prayers is to be recompensed with their frequency,"[21] because they can be done even when there is not the opportunity to make other prayer.

> It would be well if every breath could be a loving sigh, and every moment be filled with the thought of God. If this cannot be, form a habit of recollecting yourself from time to time; the more frequently the better. Let the striking of the hour be a signal for recalling the presence of God. Accustom yourself to the easy and frequent use of ejaculatory prayers. We need but to love in order to pray and to sigh for God. These outpourings of the heart proceed from the Holy Spirit; they are a language of love readily understood by this God of love. We naturally think of what we love; hence we cannot say we love God if we rarely or never think of Him.[22]

Putting love in order requires correcting the misalignment of our desires (abnegation) until they are targeted upon our ultimate happiness. God is love; God's love incites our love; our arrows penetrate his heart and make a connection. "These passionate and flaming darts pierce the loving heart of God and compel him to pour himself out upon us. They enrapture the soul in him with an inexpressibly sweet and delightful ardor and impetuosity."[23] It is as if there were a cable attached to the javelin, and when it pierces the loving heart of God, electricity flows back along the cable to inflame the

20. Libermann, *Letters to Clergy and Religious*, (Series 8), 365.
21. De Ponte, *Meditations on the Mysteries of Our Holy Faith*, vol. 1, 70.
22. De Sales, in Crasset and de Sales, *The Secret of Sanctity*, 33.
23. John of St. Samson, *Prayer, Aspiration and Contemplation*, 72.

heart that cast it, so much so, that we can even speak of fiery arrows also coming in the reverse direction, aimed at us by God.

> Beside the many kinds of God's visits to the soul, in which He wounds it with love, there are certain secret touches of love, which, like a fiery arrow, pierce and penetrate the soul, and kindle it with the fire of love. These are properly called the wounds of love, and it is of these the soul is here speaking. These wounds inflame the will, and the soul becomes so enveloped with fire as to appear consumed thereby. They make it go forth out of itself, and be renewed, transformed into another mode of existence, like the phoenix from the fire. David, speaking of this, saith, "My heart hath been inflamed, and my reins have been changed; and I am brought to nothing, and I knew not." The desires and affections, called the reins by the Prophet, are all stirred and divinely changed in this burning of the heart, and the soul, through love, melts into nothing, knowing nothing but love.[24]

Love launches love; arrows fly from man to God, and God to man; desires meet desire. This is something that becomes possible after an Incarnation of God as a man. The ejaculatory prayer is likened to tender doves "because no voice so penetrates his divine ears as ardent desires. Not only does he desire to hear them, but they are an arrow that inflicts a wound of love, drawing blood and overcoming him who can only be conquered by love. . . . You must know that a sigh coming from the heart is a swift arrow aimed there by the bow of desire at the Lord who dwells in the heavens."[25]

As we have already mentioned, these types of prayer have the advantage of speed, which is a mark of the force of desire with which they are propelled heavenward. This speed provides another advantage. The ejaculatory prayers have "approached God's presence before the devil could have leisure to trouble him that made them, or to oppose any obstacle to them."[26] The javelins get through the enemy lines, and past the demons' opposition, frustrat-

---

24. John of the Cross, *Ascent of Mount Carmel*, in *Complete Works*, vol. 2, 22.
25. De Osuna, *The Third Spiritual Alphabet*, 225.
26. Alphonsus Rodríguez (Alfonso), *The Practice of Christian and Religious Perfection*, vol. 1, 341.

ing their desire to keep us disunited from God. The soul that is faithful to ejaculatory prayer comes nigh to the *semper orare* recommended by the gospel.

> Thus the soul is not only able to preserve a sense of the divine presence during the whole day, but to entertain herself sweetly with God—either in heart only, or with heart and mouth—and this without any manual or any mental work being able to distract her. The soul which is faithful to this practice of ejaculatory prayer may believe that she is coming nigh to the *semper orare* of the Gospel. She will find therein a great help for silencing the passions, repressing too great activity about external things, and overcoming spiritual idleness. In this way she will accustom herself to live in intimacy with God.[27]

(4) *Affections.* These brief acts—silent or spoken—put us in mind of God, which reminds us of both our own sins and his benefits. When pride has been shamed a man will not even look at the person he has offended, but when humility reigns a man will let God see his state, and not hesitate to look at God. "Open your heart before Our Lord and let Him see your needs. Having shown Him, as it were, the wounds of your soul, and its nakedness and poverty, be content with casting a longing glance toward Him. Preserve that desire in your heart and, from time to time during the day cast a glance at Jesus. All this must be done without many words, even interior words, and without violent efforts to produce those sentiments and desires."[28]

These are affections, in one way, and acts, in another. The affection is aided by uttering an expression of it. "The way to produce these aspirations is to form certain exclamations, questions and requests for love, union, perfection, etc. The soul should continue to do this with a most ardent desire according to the requirements of the subject with which it is occupied."[29] In our fractured state, choice and affection often conflict, evidenced by our sensation that

---

27. Bruyère, *Spiritual Life and Prayer*, 100.
28. Libermann, *Letters to Clergy and Religious* (Series 7), 107.
29. John of St. Samson, *Prayer, Aspiration and Contemplation*, 72.

we should not choose some of the objects for which we have affection, and by the fact that we might lack affection for some of the goods we know we should choose. But in our healed state, there is no contradiction in this antinomy of affection and choice, because we choose what we love, and love what we choose. Desire is the tautness of the bow; the ejaculatory prayer is the release of the arrow. The greater the desire, the higher the arrow flies and the more profound the affection for God. The desire must be strong enough to draw the bow, and our choice must be deliberate enough to release the shaft.

Ejaculatory prayer is an exercise, a discipline, an asceticism, to be done by steady repetition.

> Let us a hundred and a hundred times a day unite our life to Divine love by the practice of ejaculatory prayers, elevations of heart and spiritual retirements; for these holy exercises, casting and lifting our spirit continually into God, bear also up to him all our actions. And how could it be, I pray you, that a soul who at every moment darts up unto the Divine goodness, and who incessantly breathes words of love, in order to keep her heart always lodged in the bosom of her heavenly Father, should not be considered to do all her works in God and for God?[30]

Desire is housed in the will. Desiring God, we choose him; having chosen God, we desire him; then affection for God casts prayer heavenward. We elevate our hearts to God by an act of the will, which "consists in the ardent desires of the soul to unite itself to God, by the bands of perfect charity. It consists, [Bonaventure] says, in the deep sighs, which love prompts the soul to heave, in order to call her beloved to her, and in the tender and affectionate motions, which serve her as wings to fly up, and to make her approaches nearer and nearer unto him."[31]

This affection-saturated prayer has the advantage of accompanying us anywhere, at all times. We can carry it around with us, and

---

30. De Sales, *Treatise on the Love of God*, 419–20.
31. Alphonsus Rodríguez (Alfonso), *The Practice of Christian and Religious Perfection*, vol. 1, 341.

anything can set it loose. "Thus we may sigh for God's glory, send up to heaven one arrow-like word about the interests of Jesus in the streets of London, or breathe a little prayer for souls wherever we are. Without any constraint we may make scores of them in a day; and each one is more to God than a battle gained, or a scientific discovery, or a crystal palace, or a change of ministry, or a political revolution."[32] Something more important is happening in the soul of an ordinary person on the street than is happening in the political events whirling around him, because what happens in the soul is eternal and what happens in the temporal is temporary. Ejaculatory prayer is of inestimable value because it can be used "interiorly amidst all occupations. It keeps up the flame of desire, fosters the interior life, and when it becomes habitual is an unspeakable consolation."[33] It is therefore a splendid practice for persons who live in the secular world. The changes are interior, not exterior, and therefore "the merchant continues a merchant, the married remain married, the tradesman does not leave his shop, the exterior and visible qualities are still the same; but the interior—the thoughts, views, affections, desires and plans—become quite different."[34] A soul committed to Martha's service in the world cannot remain in mental prayer all day long. "You should not try it, but frequently raise the eyes of your mind to Him. Often repeat ejaculatory prayers, and if you lack the energy to do so, do it with your heart; merely sacrifice your whole being to God and do it wholeheartedly."[35]

Ejaculatory prayer is valuable to both those in Religious community, and to Christians in the world who keep regular times for prayer, because it prolongs throughout the day what was begun in vocal or mental prayer. Christ told his disciples to pray always, and not lose heart (Lk 18:1). That is, do not "fail either in the time assigned for prayer or in the fervour thereof, or in confidence, or, if possible, in the frequency thereof," and then the accompanying

32. Faber, *All for Jesus*, 206.

33. William Ullathorne, *Christian Patience: The Strength and Discipline of the Soul* (New York: Catholic Publication Society, 1886), 196–97.

34. Saint-Jure, *Union with Our Lord Jesus*, 353.

35. Libermann, *Letters to Clergy and Religious* (Series 7), 252.

ejaculatory prayers are "'the remainders of' those holy thoughts that we had in the morning, making to ourselves a feast, and preserving our devotion all the day."[36]

Would we benefit from some concrete examples of this aspirational, upward, ejaculatory, and affectionate prayer? Many of our authors provided them for the use of their readers.

De Sales says we need not be surprised to find ourselves using words from Scripture, because those utterances have special force, "such as the ejaculatory prayers of which the Psalms are so full, and the numerous loving invocations of Jesus which we find in the Song of Songs."[37] Abbess Bruyère observes the great importance that the Fathers attached to these frequent, short aspirations, and then directs us to the Psalms as giving numberless examples of such "javelins": "O God, come to my assistance," or "The mercies of the Lord I will sing for ever."[38] John Eudes often ends each of his meditations with an ejaculatory prayer for the reader to use. There are one hundred and five in *Meditations on Various Subjects*: "For to me, to live is Christ" (32); "We give Thee thanks for Thy great glory" (70); "Lord Jesus Christ, we are worth nothing" (111). There are twenty-eight in *The Priest*: "I will serve Thee, O Lord, I will serve Thee in holiness and justice before Thee, all the days of my life" (184); "Have mercy on me, O God, according to Thy great mercy" (187); "O most blessed Light divine / Shine within these hearts of Thine / And our inmost beings fill" (226). De Liguori gives ninety-one examples in his little book, *Visits to the Most Holy Sacrament*: "My Jesus, I will love Thee only; Thee only do I desire to please" (128); "Refuge of sinners, take pity on me" (133); "Jesus, my love, take all that I have; take full possession of me." De Ponte gives suggested prayers for each of the seven antiphons of evensong:

> O infinite "Wisdom," come to govern me in the way of heaven! O "Splendour of the Father," come to illuminate me with the splendour of Thy virtues! O "Son of Justice," come to give light and heat

36. De Ponte, *Meditations on the Mysteries of Our Holy Faith*, vol. 1, 70.
37. De Sales, *Introduction to the Devout Life*, 64.
38. Bruyère, *Spiritual Life and Prayer*, 99.

of life to him who is seated in the shadow of death! O "King of kings," descend to govern me! O "Master of nations," come to instruct me. O "Savior of the world," make haste to save me![39]

It is not as though one pauses from other preoccupations in order to desire God. This sounds foolish. "You say, for instance, 'I must remember God. Well! I remember now.' Or, 'I must make some ejaculatory prayers. Well! I make them now.' All this touches, as it were, only the surface of your mind, whereas it should penetrate to its very essence."[40] Cardinal Bona's entire book is an apology for this kind of prayer, as indicated in his subtitle—*The Easy Way to God: A Manual of Ejaculatory Prayer*—and although he gives examples in his other writings, he pauses in this book to survey the habits of repetition practiced by certain saints.

> The Blessed Clare of Monte Falco adored God with a thousand genuflexions every day, making each time an ejaculatory prayer.... Father Didacus Martinez, who is styled the Apostle of Peru, said sometimes: "Thanks be to God," six hundred times.... James Cerrutus, of the Society of Jesus ... every day poured forth innumerable acts of love, and thanksgivings. These sometimes amounted to as many as twenty-four thousand.... There were some persons under the guidance of the Father Gonsalao Sylveria, who implored the help of God by a short prayer ten thousand times a day.[41]

Hearing examples of such heroic prayer might overawe us to the point of not even attempting ejaculatory prayer, even if we remember that the saints often do actions on a scale, or in a degree, that is admirable but not imitable. It is appropriate, therefore, to register four warnings.

First, it is not a matter of computation. One cannot be sure that increase of number indicates spiritual progress. "The manias that afflict too many devout persons testify clearly enough how illusory

39. De Ponte, *Meditations on the Mysteries of Our Holy Faith*, vol. 2, 156.
40. Libermann, *Letters to Clergy and Religious* (Series 8), 365.
41. Bona, *The Easy Way to God*, 38–39.

is an overwhelming anxiety as to a mechanical matter of figures."[42] Second, we do not have to memorize a formula. "Sundry collections of ejaculatory prayer have been put forth, which are doubtless very useful, but I should advise you not to tie yourself to any formal words, but rather to speak with ear or mouth whatever springs forth from the love within you, which is sure to supply you with all abundance."[43] Third, it should never become a matter of routine; the very purpose of this kind of prayer is that it can be done free from formality. "It is a very good thing to bind one's self to the custom; but yet such prayers must not be made a matter of routine. They should rise from the heart rather than the lips, and are best when they consist of a simple turning of the soul towards God, unaccompanied by any words expressed or understood."[44] And fourth, continual prayer is a command to purify the heart continuously. The aspiration should produce self-denial. Being reminded of God is a good thing, but "it will not amend my ways, and I may remain self-seeking; and, although I shall be close to God, I shall not go to Him. This is just what happens to some people. They acquire the habit of the presence of God and of ejaculatory prayers; they are full of affectionate expressions and feelings towards God; and they are at least as full of themselves, and as infatuated with self-love. . . . O that self-seeking!"[45]

To conclude, it is the affectionate attention that matters. On the one hand, the state of prayer is a fundamental attitude, so the Church Fathers say it is better to "pray a little and well with attention, than to pray much after another manner; for God is not overcome with the multiplicity of our prayers, but with the weight and fervor of them."[46] On the other hand, can we call something that never manifests itself a reality? I may be in a fundamental attitude of affection, love, and fidelity to my wife, and still find it necessary (and joyful) to blurt out "I love you." The expression both comes

---

42. François Pollien, *The Interior Life Simplified and Reduced to its Fundamental Principle*, ed. Joseph Tissot (London: Burns Oates & Washbourne, Ltd., 1927), 312.

43. De Sales, *Introduction to the Devout Life*, 64.

44. Grou, *The Spiritual Maxims*, 102.

45. Pollien, *The Interior Life*, 324.

46. De Ponte, *Meditations on the Mysteries of Our Holy Faith*, vol. 1, 70.

from the sentiment, and helps to form the sentiment. That is why "the Fathers attached great importance to these frequent, short aspirations towards God as being well suited to form the spirit of prayer."[47]

We desire union with God, that is, we desire our perfection. Deification is humanity fully finished and consummated. Such union depends upon a combination of prayer and abnegation, which is why ejaculatory prayer has "ever been made much of by all who have been eminent for learning and sanctity. By it, as by a fire kindled in the heart, our sins are consumed and our vices destroyed. It takes from us all sticking to the earth, all that disfigures the soul, making it unlike God and hindering it from union with Him."[48] In other words, desire for God leads inevitably (if it is sincere desire) to imitation of God. The prayer leads to the practice of virtues. Bona gives his list of what is accomplished by kindling this fire in the heart: "temptations are overcome and virtues are acquired; the soul's powers are perfected, the understanding is imbued with heavenly light, supernatural acts are exercised, the intention is purified, the affections are elevated, the will is inflamed, the mind is disposed for contemplation, and the whole man is transfused into God."[49] Although the expressions, by thought or on the lips, pass away in a moment, "their fruit endures permanently, and the prayer is continued by the continuation of a good desire, founded in charity. A good desire prays always, for the affection of a sincere love lifts up its voice continually before God."[50]

This is equally true of our sacramental life. We ask God, with earnest desire, to enkindle our love for him, and ejaculatory prayer is very useful for this.

> Then offer and dedicate thyself humbly and wholly, with heart and affection, to the divine pleasure, and retain an ever-ready and inflamed desire to please God and follow His blessed will. And when this holy desire and affection shall be thoroughly enkindled

---

47. Bruyère, *Spiritual Life and Prayer*, 99.
48. Bona, *The Easy Way to God*, 39–40.
49. Ibid., 40.
50. Ibid., 33–34.

in thy soul, thou wilt seem to move thy Lord God also to be so much enamoured with thee, as to desire thou shouldst freely open thy heart to Him, that He may the next morning enter in unto thee, feast with thee, and take His full delight in thee. Then do thou also declare thy mutual desire to receive Him with these kind of ejaculatory prayers:—O heavenly and divine Manna, when will that wished-for hour come when I shall, to Thine own content, receive Thee into my soul?[51]

Ejaculatory prayers can follow meditation as remainders of the morning's holy thoughts, and they can prepare for Communion when self-oblation invites God to enter into the heart. They are an accompaniment to, extension of, and preparation for liturgy, not a replacement for it.

Launching a dart of desire is described as both a choice (release the arrow) and a reflex (breathe out) because, although they are made briefly, they have lasting effects. The sound of a vocal aspiration fades immediately, but the desire, the affection, and the sincere love that spoke it remain, and deepen by it having been spoken. So even when the words are no longer spoken by the throat, the heart might continue speaking the desire.

Aspiration as such is a loving, ardent transport of mind and heart which elevates the soul above itself and all created things, and seeks to be intimately united with God in the ardor of its loving desire. This desire, thus expressed, surpasses all sensible and comprehensible love. Under the impetus of the Spirit of God, and with its own cooperation, the soul arrives at divine union by a sudden transformation of the spirit in God. . . . Although aspirations are composed of only a few words, they lift the soul up entirely into God, and do not permit any sensible division between the two (i.e., *God and the soul*).[52]

Follow the grace of the Holy Spirit, who, himself, is directing desires to their proper end. Ignore the sensation that you are responsible for these prayers: it is God who has planted the desire that is stretch-

51. De Castañiza, *Spiritual Conflict*, 185.
52. John of St. Samson, *Prayer, Aspiration and Contemplation*, 68.

ing the bow. It is God who is training you to lift up your eyes to him. The risen Savior asked Mary Magdalene why she was weeping when he met her on Easter morning. Why? Did he not know the cause of her sorrow? "It was not to find out that He questioned her, since all things are most clear and manifest to Him [*Heb.* 4:13]. But this dear Saviour of our souls posed such and similar questions to elicit ejaculatory prayers and acts of love and union."[53]

Ejaculatory prayer does in practice what one knows in theory. "This practice consists in doing and suffering, out of pure love for God, everything every day perfectly, in walking in His presence, in often piercing the Heart of my Spouse with ejaculatory prayers, in keeping my heart ever attentive to His inspirations."[54] The ancient world was infatuated with the idea of a flying carpet, "but winged aspirations, all on fire, are a far better kind of golden carpet, for in a moment they bear off the devout soul into heaven, and carry her even to the throne of the Godhead."[55] This is a spiritual practice— our spirit's and the Holy Spirit's.

Such a desire can run the length of every day of life we weave on the time allotted us. It can entangle itself in every thought and action. "The faithful soul should have the custom of applying herself to these frequently, in all places, and at all times. She should thus raise up her will to God, and her heart, day and night, at home and abroad, sitting and walking, in every affair, every action, every occupation."[56] Do not lament to think you lack training or qualification. This desirous prayer has only one teacher.

> There are many who cannot meditate, but few who cannot send forth loving sighs.... [These sighs] are the prayer of souls wounded by the love of God, and aspiring to union with Him; they can no longer speak; their love is poured forth in sighs....
> Now, though this prayer is the final disposition for union with God, and the occupation of those who can no longer meditate, yet

---

53. Francis de Sales, *The Sermons of St. Francis de Sales for Advent and Christmas* (Rockfort, IL: TAN Books and Publishers, Inc., 1987), 5.

54. Alacoque, *Letters*, Kindle edition, letter 142.

55. Bona, *The Easy Way to God*, 32.

56. Ibid., 33.

all souls can practise it: it constitutes what we call ejaculatory prayers, which are loving darts which speed from our heart to the very heart of God.

It is also a prayer that knows neither art nor method; it is taught by love.[57]

It is not taught by books. In fact, "if you perceive the looking in your book to hinder your mind, whereby you are the less able to reach God and to be united to him, lay aside your book ... for I would that your devotion should be free to you, and that you should follow the grace of the Holy Ghost without confusion or anxiety."[58] The Holy Spirit is love; that is why he is the teacher of prayer.

57. Crasset, in Crasset and de Sales, *The Secret of Sanctity*, 202–3.
58. Blosius (Louis of Blois) *Mirror for Monks* (London: C.J. Stewart, 1872), 39–40.

8

Desiring and
the Theological Virtues

DOES FAITH DESIRE? Does hope desire? Does love desire? Is desire faithful, hopeful, loving? What would the theological virtues of faith, hope, and love desire? Does desire draw from, or contribute to, these three infused theological virtues? All does seem to be connected, but what is the nature of the connection? Hints have arisen thus far, but it is time to address the relationship directly. We shall take each in turn.

Faith

Faith stands at the beginning for a Christian who seeks spiritual growth by the practice of the virtues. In order to begin practicing the virtues, they must be sought; in order to be sought, they must be desired; and this desire God asks from us. He is "delighted that they do ask of Him. Which delight He manifests by the repetition of these three words, which in a manner signify the same. Ask—seek—knock: as if He said, behold how much I desire that you ask of me, ask me, ask me, ask me."[1] Door-knocking is the vocation of faith, a response to God, and an enactment of prayer.

> Before the desire for perfection can become strong and constant the soul must spend a long time knocking at the door by means of deep sighs, humiliations and prayers. After that, the good God, who has given it the grace and the desire to importune him thus, will open the door and receive it into his embraces according to its capacity and disposition. And in proportion as the soul feels itself drawn and touched, to that extent does it advance in a sincere and

---

1. De Ponte, *Meditations on the Mysteries of Our Holy Faith*, vol. 6, 351.

firm desire for God. Now it looks for occasions to exercise its loving desire.[2]

People often complain that they do not know how to pray, but "experience has taught me that persons of good will who speak in this way know better than others how to pray, because their prayer is more simple and humble, but, on account of its simplicity it escapes their observation. To pray like this is to remain by faith in the presence of God, with a hidden, but constant desire to receive His grace according to our needs."[3] In prayer, faith does not seek understanding (as is the famous definition of theology), it seeks to remain in the presence of God.

Faith is the slight tug felt by the fish when the divine fisherman twitches his line. We sinners think we are doing something, when actually we are responding to God's appeal to knock upon the door leading to the interior garden. Desire gives daring to faith, and grace causes undaunted desire, as Jesus makes clear in his parables of the friend at midnight (Lk 11:5–8) and the persistent widow (Lk 18:1–8). The permission God gives to the faithful soul to annoy him, bother him, pester him, is just the kind of thing that love would do. Faith acts with a force of desire that is a sort of holy importunity that harasses heaven. "Is your heart really desirous? Yes, it is; but does this desire pursue you, does it animate you? Do you weary Heaven with your importunities? Do you suffer? Do you weep? Do you persevere?"[4] Faith is a confidence, a perseverance, a fidelity, which

resides partly in the understanding, and partly in the will. In the understanding, inasmuch as the suppliant believes most firmly that God, impelled thereto by His sovereign goodness, and bound as He is by His oft-repeated promises, will assuredly grant the graces for which we ask. In the will, because, adhering to a belief so solidly grounded, this power undoubtingly and unhesitatingly trusts . . . that these favours will be obtained; and encouraged and

---

2. John of St. Samson, *Prayer, Aspiration and Contemplation*, 192–93.
3. De Caussade, *Abandonment to Divine Providence*, 229.
4. De Ravignan, *Conferences on the Spiritual Life*, 22.

animated by such hope, prays with fervour of spirit, with great earnestness, and with a sort of holy importunity.[5]

Faith knocks because it desires to meet the inhabitant of the house. When John Vianney was asked "What is faith?" he answered, "Faith is when one speaks to God as to a man."[6]

Faith does seek truth, which it grasps by divine light, but the truth it seeks is not merely information. Faith is a kind of knowledge ("what is *the faith?*"), but there is a particular reason for wanting to know. "We only desire to know, in order that we may increase our love. To love is better than to know. Indeed it is itself a higher knowledge."[7] Faith is a keen longing to live the divine life (deification). It is a desire to know God, by meeting God, and by living in God that is the onset of deification. "It seems not only that the soul understands and produces acts of divine knowledge, but that it has become deiform."[8] Faith is man's side of desire meeting desire; from God's side, it is grace. If a person feels a keen longing to live the divine life, he may be assured that

> the longing manifestly comes from God, and is itself the beginning of that which it seeks. . . . For God does not plant such a desire in a Christian heart, to leave it unfruitful; if you are eager in the pursuit of this blessing, God is the inspirer of your eagerness; if you do all in your power to obtain it, God is stirring you up, and giving you courage and perseverance. Therefore you will obtain what you ask, provided you go on asking, and faint not. Could God reject a soul that desires to be all His own, and that only desires this so far as He gives it the good will?[9]

This desire is only the beginning—we do not want that fact to be overlooked in this book—but beginning is sufficient to allow God to start the redemption he has planned. The reason God's grace

5. Scaramelli, *The Directorium Asceticum*, vol. 1, 387.

6. John Vianney, quoted in Joseph Vianney, *The Blessed John Vianney, Cure D'Ars, Patron of Parish Priests* (New York: Benziger Brothers, 1906), 187.

7. Faber, *The Precious Blood*, 148.

8. Barbanson, *The Secret Paths of Divine Love*, 201.

9. Grou, *The Spiritual Maxims*, 228–29.

gives this desire is so he can satisfy it. He is only awaiting faith's trigger.

> We besiege the crucifix to obtain a little humility and meekness, and we have not the courage to repress our impatience or to humble our self-love. Then see what happens! God hears the desire, and even accepts the prayer: grace goes forth from the Sacred Heart of our Divine Lord; for every Christian prayer has the power to open His Heart. . . . Purify, then, your soul, at least, by a serious repentance, and a sincere and actual desire to give glory to God, by corresponding with the grace you solicit.[10]

On the one hand, faithful prayer opens the heart of God. On the other hand, the heart of God is already open in a way that draws forth our prayer. This is the mystery of the grace-faith unity. The spirit of faith is a gift from God, yet we must pray for it. To put the question bluntly:

> By what means can we obtain this spirit of faith? Since it is as much the gift of God as faith itself, does it depend upon ourselves to secure it?
>
> Yes, it depends upon you; and you will infallibly obtain it by prayer. In faith itself you possess the germ of it: ask God fervently, urgently, and perseveringly to develop it and make it active. But in order to ask for it thus you must know its importance and its value; you must desire to possess it, and neglect nothing that can prevail upon God to grant it to you.[11]

Lacordaire calls this antinomy *an imperfect circle*: faith is necessary for prayer, and it is necessary to pray for faith. "It is prayer, gentlemen, which re-establishes our intercourse with God, which recalls us to His action, which does violence to Him without inuring His liberty, and which is consequently the mother of faith."[12] The world is full of these imperfect circles, "but see how God

---

10. Gay, *The Christian Life and Virtues*, vol. 1, 286.

11. Grou, *The School of Jesus Christ*, 358.

12. Jean-Baptiste Henri Lacordaire, *Conferences of the Rev. Pere Lacordaire, Delivered in the Cathedral of Notre Dame, in Paris* (New York: P. O'Shea, Publisher, 1853), 201.

escapes from this. To pray, I admit that faith is necessary, at least a faith begun; but do you know what a faith begun is? Faith begun is doubt; doubt is the commencement of faith as fear is the beginning of love."[13] Lacordaire does not mean doubt as being skeptical about God, he means a sincere doubt that makes a person skeptical of his own doubt in God!

> Perhaps after all, mean and imperfect being that I am, I am the work of a Providence who governs me and who watches over me! Perhaps that blood which but just now flowed upon the altar is the blood of a God who has saved me! Perhaps I may be able to obtain to the knowledge, the love of this God! Perhaps! that doubt, gentlemen, is that which is the beginning of faith, and that faith begun, you will not easily root it out of your heart; God has made it fast there with the diamond. This is faith in its vague state: which will pass on to the state of conviction if you desire it, which will not proceed if you do not desire it; which lends itself to all, to affirming God or to denying him, to loving or to hating him.[14]

The divine gardener has planted faith, and we water it with our desire; if we do not, it will never grow into conviction. Even in the state of doubt, one can exercise faith: it is exercised in the form of desire. And it seems the union of fear and desire is a liturgical one. "The union of fear and desire is a beautiful worship, modestly befitting the creature, and reaching with venturous reverence to the perfections of the Most High. To have no fear of God is to be, not only without love of Him, but without knowledge of Him also. To be without the desire of God would be almost worse than to rise against Him through despair of reaching him, as the reprobate do in their hopeless land. God is jealous of this desire."[15] Faith will proceed from its vague state into a state of fidelity—if you desire it. It will not proceed if you do not. Desire moves faith forward into the liturgical realm that is a portent of beatitude.

Faith takes a person's gaze off the world's vanities, and fixes it

---

13. Ibid.
14. Ibid., 201–2.
15. Faber, *Spiritual Conferences*, 121.

upon God so the person can gaze upon the world in the right light. As we said in chapter three, the desire and the act merge in a simplicity that makes the desire equal to an act. "The simple desire to act and to throw itself into God without any express words will be an assurance to the soul that it has its gaze fixed on God. This inclination is very simple, so simple that the soul doesn't seem to have it. Thus the desire to act and the expressed act will be one and the same thing for it."[16] The faithful ones (*fideles*) remain true to God; an unfaithful one (*infidel*) commits infidelity in the covenant. "Be faithful then dear confrere. Be faithful to all the graces and favors God bestows upon you. Nurture those noble desires in your soul. Pray unceasingly for their fulfillment and act in practice as if you already possessed all those graces, that is, act as the greatest saints have done."[17]

Hope

Hope has a number of connotations in the secular orbit: wish, expectancy, dream, optimism. It has different connotations in the theological orbit: it is a lively desire that leads to abnegation. "Hope is therefore not a feeble desire for eternal life, as some may imagine, but it is a desire, lively and animated, which detaches us from all other things by uniting us entirely to this great object, which inspires us with the will and desire to sell all and give all, in order to obtain this precious treasure."[18] Hope does not reside merely inside a person; it stretches forth, as a connecting rod. "You are thus obliged to unite yourself to God by hope, that is to say; to regard God as your sovereign good, and to seek to possess him in preference to all other things."[19] Hope requires one to prefer the enjoyment of God to all the goods of the world, which means desiring God more than all the goods of the world. It can begin already, hopefully (we mean: in a hopeful manner). "By hope, we expect the

16. John of St. Samson, *Prayer, Aspiration and Contemplation*, 101.
17. Libermann, *Letters to Clergy and Religious* (Series 8), 28.
18. John Eudes, *Man's Contract with God in Baptism* (Philadelphia: Peter F. Cunningham, 1859), 54–55.
19. Eudes, *Man's Contract With God*, 53.

fulfilment of these promises: we hope that we shall be rewarded for all our good actions, for all our good thoughts, for all our good desires; for God takes into account even our good desires. What more do we want to make us happy?"[20]

Hope does possess an element of expectation because a distance still separates us from our beloved until he comes. *Parousia* means "presence," and we await Christ's presence, his Parousia. The sensation of distance is due to two factors: first, the temporal nature of our pathway (our natural finitude), and, second, our aloofness toward God (our unnatural fallenness). The former is still under the control of God's providential design; the latter is a self-imposed exile to be overcome. No natural hope will soothe us in either our finite or exilic state, since we were made for God, and a supernatural hope will be required to direct us to him. "Hope is the interior cry of our Baptism, and, as it were, the active consciousness that Baptism gives us of our incomparable destinies. It is the hunger and thirst [desire] of our supernatural being, the regular movement of those supernatural wings which God also gives to our soul the moment that he justifies it."[21] When we have a clear view of the distance that separates us from God, then "we are more fully conscious of our exile, and have a more ardent desire to see it ended. Now, in a heart that is faithful to God this desire and this consciousness are the same thing as a more perfect hope."[22] When love aspires, it hopes; a heart faithful to God is under the rule of a more perfect hope.

We have repeatedly connected desire to aspiration. De Sales pauses a moment to distinguish between hoping and aspiring (*esperer et aspirer*), noting that "we hope for those things which we expect to get by another's assistance, and we aspire unto those things which we think to reach by means that lie in our own power."[23] Does this put the word "aspiration" off limits because we never attain God by our own power, only by his grace and mercy? It would, except God's mercy wants us to cooperate with his favor,

20. John Vianney, *The Little Catechism*, 7–8.
21. Gay, *The Christian Life and Virtues*, vol. 1, 261.
22. Ibid., 262.
23. De Sales, *Treatise on the Love of God*, 108.

and "our hope is thence in some sort mingled with aspiring, so that we do not altogether hope without aspiring, nor do we ever aspire without entirely hoping. . . . Hope by aspiration becomes a courageous desire, and aspiration is changed by hope into a humble claim."[24] De Sales concludes, then, that as soon as *faith* has shown us our sovereign good, we have loved it; if it is absent, we have *hoped* for it; if we believe it will bestow itself on us, then we *love* and desire it yet more ardently. This is how the three theological virtues commingle. "Now by this progress love has turned its desire into hope, seeking[,] and expectation, so that hope is an expectant and aspiring love; and because the sovereign good which hope expects is God, and because also she expects it from God himself, to whom and by whom she hopes and aspires, this holy virtue of hope, abutting everywhere on God, is by consequence a divine or theological virtue."[25]

It is much safer to place our hope in God's faithfulness toward us, instead of in our faithfulness toward God. He is more stable than we are. He is stronger than we are. Desire for God yields hope in God's faithfulness.

> Well, then, since you desire to be entirely God's, why do you fear from your weakness, in which you are to put no sort of trust? Do you not hope in God? Ah! He who trusteth in him, shall he ever be confounded? No, sir, he shall never be. I beseech you, sir, to quell all the objections which might arise in your mind. You need make no other answer to them save that you desire to be faithful on all occasions, and that you hope God will make you so.[26]

Hoping God will make us hopeful is like desiring to desire: if we do not have it yet, at least we want it.

Hope returns us to humility: "it would be absurd to hope for the reward which is promised to the humble without being humble, or at least without the desire to be humble."[27] Why isn't this desire to

---

24. Ibid.
25. Ibid.
26. De Sales, *Letters to Persons in the World*, 208.
27. De Bergamo, *Humility of Heart*, 146.

be humble as easy as it sounds? Because it means self-mortification and self-denial; it means giving more glory to God than collecting esteem for ourselves; it means overcoming passions. The power of hope is required in order to get over these hurdles. The Christian who possesses both grace and charity will exult in abnegation, because

> then he loves what he ought to love, he hates what he ought to hate, he desires what God wills that he should desire, he flies from what displeases God, he is saddened by offences done against God, he rejoices and takes delight in the things which are pleasing to God. Then his zeal fills him with anger and indignation against all that detracts from the honour due to God; he hopes in God and not in the creature, he fears nothing save to offend God, he is fearless in God's service.[28]

Desire-in-the-form-of-hope is awakened and increased by revelation. We hope for many goods known to our human nature, or for some imagined, inflated version of natural goods. But when God reveals our true teleology, then we desire goods we would never have imagined on our own—goods like eternal life, and adopted sonship, and being deified. The famous patristic illustration of deification is iron in fire. The nature of iron is cool, but when placed in fire it receives the form of fire, even though it does not cease to be iron. Likewise, the soul remains itself, "but whereas it before was cold, now it burns; whereas it before was dark, now it shines with light; whereas it before was hard, now it has become soft. The essence of God has so flowed into its essence, that we may say the soul has, as it were, the same tint or color."[29] Who could have hoped to be the same tint or color as God?! It is not natural, it is supernatural; it would not be espied by a natural hope, only a supernatural one. But that is what we are in for, and nothing less. "For if likeness is a cause of love, how much am I bound to love Him who created me to His own image and likeness? If 'every beast loveth its like' (Sirach 13:15), and everything desires to be joined with that in which it beholds its

---

28. Camus, *The Spirit of St. Francis de Sales*, 322.
29. Blosius, *A Book of Spiritual Instruction: Institutio Spiritualis*, 94–95.

own likeness, how shall not I love Almighty God, and rejoice to join myself with Him, since with so great love He hath made me like to Himself?"[30] God left a sleeping kernel of that desire even in fallen man, until a revelation could awaken it; God left an ember of that desire even in fallen man, until the breath of revelation could inflame it. Reason understands it, but reason could not have conceived it. "What! reason has not in itself the means of uniting to God, and yet it desires to be united to God! But why does reason desire this? What obliges, what urges reason so to desire, since it does not possess the faculties which justify that ambition?"[31]

We could speak about the same deification if we changed the illustration to speak about iron becoming magnetized. Here is a description of a person making acts of faith and love on the day before Communion, preparing to receive the Lord spiritually.

> He set his heart and desire towards Christ our Lord, and there with that act of love and desire, he would make an interior act with his heart to bring Christ right inside himself by way of love. Just as the magnet attracts iron to itself, so the act of love made by this soul drew its God to itself, to its heart, by force of love, until it placed him right within its entrails and heart, deep inside itself. So it was that he used to feel immediately that Christ had come and was with him, feeling his presence within himself.[32]

Every part of divine revelation speaks to the heart's hopeful desire, which is a steppingstone to love. The entirety of salvation history addresses the hopes of the heart. "In this life charity does not, and never can, exclude hope. As long as we do not possess the thing we love, we desire to do so; and not only desire it, but hope for it, in virtue of God's promises; and we count it a duty to hope for it, by reason of the express command He lays on all His children."[33] It feels comfortable to say we are commanded to believe, and com-

30. De Ponte, *Meditations on the Mysteries of Our Holy Faith*, vol. 6, 94.

31. Jean-Baptiste Henri Lacordaire, *God and Man. Conferences Delivered at Notre Dame in Paris* (London: Chapman and Hall, 1872), 31.

32. Alonso Rodríguez (Alfonso), *Autobiography*, 85–86.

33. Grou, *The Spiritual Maxims*, 224.

manded to love, and here we discover that we are equally commanded to hope.

Love

"Love can refuse nothing that love desires, nor desire anything that love refuses."[34]

What really, finally, is the engine of desire? Love, of course. It is the shortest way. "We must love [God] to reach Him. Love is the shortest way; it is that which makes us not only walk, but run and fly towards our end."[35] Love is an even closer synonym for desire than the other two words, perhaps because faith and hope are not absent from love. They permit and equip it.

Hear now the prayers of a soul that indeed desires really to love Thee. I desire to love Thee with all my strength, I desire to obey Thee in all that Thou willest, without self-interest, without consolations, without reward. I wish to serve Thee through love, only to please Thee, only to content Thy heart, which is so passionately enamoured of me. My reward will be to love Thee. O beloved Son of the eternal Father, take possession of my liberty, of my will, of all that I possess, and of my entire self, and give me Thyself. I love Thee, I seek after Thee, I sigh after Thee; I desire Thee, I desire Thee, I desire Thee![36]

That is the exclamation of a lover.

Faith keeps *love* informed and confident; *hope* keeps love attentive and persevering. Love and desire are the offspring of one and the same faculty, namely, willing the good of God's glory.[37] There is only one sort of saint: one who desires God supremely. No one will be sanctified without this desirous love, since salvation is the saint following Jesus to his theocentric demeanor. In conversion, a sinner's love is turned from egocentric to ecstatic: from being curved

34. De Caussade, *Abandonment to Divine Providence*, 86.
35. De Ravignan, *The Last Retreat*, 18–19.
36. De Liguori, *The Holy Eucharist*, 142.
37. Camus, *The Spirit of St. Francis de Sales*, 69.

in upon ourselves to being placed on a liturgical trajectory to God. Love can only love what is deserving of love. "Let us, then, with all the affection of our heart, love Him on this model, producing often toward Him nets of love, of choice, of complacence, of contrition and of desire."[38] Love desires, and every act of purified desire is an act of pure love. Blessed are the pure of heart. "As soon as you have the desire to love Him, you may rest assured that you truly love Him. Every act of desire of that sort is an act of love; hence you are not to be pitied when you are in a state of spiritual dryness. All you have to do in such moments is to remain humbly at the feet of Jesus."[39]

The desire to love comes from the soul, but since we are embodied souls, we can often help it with a bodily gesture. "Father St. Jure recommends making an agreement with the Lord every morning. Each time you make a certain sign, such as placing your hand on your heart or raising your eyes toward heaven or toward the crucifix, you desire by that sign to make an act of love, to see God loved by all, of offering of yourself, or other similar desires."[40] But the bodily practices are a means, only. Someone who doesn't go beyond gestures of piety and religion "simply will not understand what we are talking about. He may be quite faithful to external practices, but, until he has gone beyond their ultimate purpose, which is to inflame his heart with such a desire to praise God that he doesn't know how to praise him sufficiently, he will not attain the interior practices. This desire belongs to what the mystics call a *constantly active* love."[41]

In addition to acts of the body, there are the classically named interior acts: acts of faith, acts of hope, acts of love, acts of contrition. To these, we suggest adding one more: acts of desire. All of these can be expressed exteriorly, but because they are interior none of these can really be seen. Yet lack of expression does not compro-

---

38. Saint-Jure, *The Spiritual Man*, 233.

39. Francis Libermann, *Letters to People in the World*, Spiritan Series 6, vol. 2 (Pittsburgh: Duquesne University Press, 1963), 217–18.

40. De Liguori, *Alphonsus de Liguori: Selected Writings*, 285.

41. John of St. Samson, *Prayer, Aspiration and Contemplation*, 157.

mise the act. Consider the act of love: it "consists in a motion of the will towards God. The tenderness, the sweetness, the inflamed sentiments, the tears which follow upon this spiritual act of the will, are merely accidents of charity, failing which, its substance remains unimpaired."[42]

Love desires union, and is characterized by its search for beatitude, which is what propels it to go faster and faster toward the Beloved. Love is how we experience the quality of infinity during our stay in the finite. "You see everything our Heavenly Father does is for love. He vouchsafes to long for our love. He makes us so that we can only be happy in loving Him; and then, looking compassionately on our intense desire to love Him more, He does all that we will let Him do to enable us to love Him more and more worthily and fervently. Thus all is love from first to last: there is no other measure; there is no other principle."[43]

God looks kindly on the faithful soul living in hope under this desire for union, therefore it should "not be disquieted if it perhaps rarely feels itself intimately united with God, to whom it aspires; for God receives its good will and holy desires with the same complacency as if it languished with love, and were perfectly united to Him."[44] The point of the entire collection of quotes in this book has been to notice that God is pleased by the desire-seed even before love is fully grown. "God doesn't even wait for you to take the first step. When you desire his love he leaps ahead and presents himself to you bringing with him the graces and gifts you most need. God waits for just a word from you to show you how near he is, how ready he is to hear and comfort you."[45] We are talking about the speed of heaven here—the speed of angelic messengers, the agility of resurrected bodies, and actually the alacrity of God himself: cheerful, willing, eager, prompt, brisk, even sprightly. "Consider how God our Lord exceedingly *delights* in being *served* with *zeal* and

42. John Baptist Scaramelli, *The Directorium Asceticum; or, Guide to the Spiritual Life*, vol. 4 (New York: Benziger Bros., 1902), 223.

43. Faber, *All for Jesus*, 170–71.

44. Blosius, *Spiritual Works of Louis of Blois*, 58–59.

45. De Liguori, *Alphonsus de Liguori: Selected Writings*, 277.

readiness, for as He is essentially alacrity itself, and as all the works He does and the rewards He gives us are done with great joy and fervour, rejoicing to do us good, most justly does He command me to serve Him."[46] No one has any reason to doubt that God loves him, since "He looks upon the most dreadful sinners in the world lovingly when they have the least true desire to be converted to Him. Tell me, do you not intend to belong to God? Do you not desire to serve Him faithfully? And who gave you this desire, this intention, unless Himself in His loving regard for you?"[47]

We have already spent a chapter exploring the theme that God implants desire; if charity is an expression of desire, then we may expect him to have implanted charity, too. Indeed, it is the fire he said he came to cast upon the earth.[48]

> Love or charity is a gift from God; we begin to possess it when God puts the desire of it into our hearts. This desire is, as it were, the first spark; and it is for us to convert it by our co-operation into a fire that shall flame within us. Jesus Christ declares that he is come *to cast fire upon the earth, and that he wills that it were already kindled* (Lk 12:49)!
>
> Since God desires that we should love Him He is always ready to give us the power of loving Him, if we on our side desire it too; so let us ask perpetually, repeatedly, and perseveringly for that precious gift; let all our prayers have that end in view, and all our holy aspirations aim at it.[49]

Love, the desire to love, and the power to love, all come from the source of love himself. He authored the universe with threads of love running throughout it: love of self, love of neighbor, and a nat-

---

46. De Ponte, *Meditations on the Mysteries of Our Holy Faith*, vol. 1, 273.

47. Huguet, *The Consoling Thoughts of St. Francis de Sales*, 56.

48. Luke 12:49 is often interpreted as a prophecy of harsh judgment, but these authors describe the fire as divine love. For example, Eudes, *The Sacred Heart of Jesus*; Libermann, *Instructions for Missionaries*; Grou, *The Interior of Jesus and Mary*; John of Ávila, *Audi, Filia*; de Sales, *Treatise on the Love of God*; de Liguori, *Way of Salvation and of Perfection* and *The Holy Eucharist*; Saint-Jure, *A Treatise on the Knowledge and Love of our Lord Jesus Christ*.

49. Grou, *The School of Jesus Christ*, 61–62.

ural love for God that is quickened by desire. Grace perfects nature, and divine charity perfects natural love, which is the very reason why God endowed our nature with it. "God has endowed human nature with a certain love for self which man is incapable of suppressing or opposing. God has willed it to such an extent, that He has set it up as the standard for charity towards our neighbor: 'Love thy neighbor as thyself.' Sanctifying grace quickens this natural propensity by adding to it an ardent desire for God, so that we tend entirely towards Him."[50]

Once granted, faith, hope, and love stir a desire to abandon self to the glory of God, and there are two chief ways of exercising this meritorious abandonment.

> The first is, to say to God, "Lord I hate and detest my sins and imperfections, and I will make every effort to correct myself with the help of Your divine grace. . . ." The second way is to say, "My God, I desire to please You, I desire my own salvation and sanctification, the gift of prayer, of mortification, and of all virtues. I ask them of You, and I will exert all my powers to acquire them, whenever You show me an occasion of doing so; nevertheless in this as in all other things I prefer Your holy will to my own wishes, I only desire to possess that degree of grace and virtue that You are pleased to bestow on me. . . ." These acts, made with the whole heart, are the fruit of that pure charity which, according to the Doctors of the Church, is as efficacious as baptism and martyrdom for blotting out all our sins.[51]

Conclusion: Perichoresis

There seems to be a perichoretic relationship between faith, hope, and love, which revolve around a nucleus of desire. Hope is "the practical radiation of *faith*. . . . While time lasts, *love* cannot be conceived without hope. . . . For love to *aspire* is to hope."[52] The whole saving apparatus of the Church exists to communicate these truths and bring them to life, and can be heard in the cry of the Scriptures, of the Fathers, and of the Saints. "This desire is the breathing of the

---

50. Libermann, *Living with God*, 46.
51. De Caussade, *Abandonment to Divine Providence*, 240–41.
52. Gay, *The Christian Life and Virtues*, vol. 1, 261–62.

Christian soul, the natural and indispensable fruit of his faith, the exercise of his hope, the witness of his love; for God is truth, and love lives upon light."[53] When God's holy will becomes the measure of our desires, then a unity is formed among these theological virtues. Their combination bursts forth in ejaculatory prayer during times of exhilaration, but the peace the combination gives during times of arid desolation make those dark nights of even greater value. "An hour thus passed before God, although accompanied by dryness and distraction, obtains perfectly the desired end. The soul has been exercised in union with God since it did nothing the whole time save to tend towards Him by faith, hope and charity, not formulating the acts of these virtues in a sensible manner, but virtually by a continuous turning towards God. Being faithful in performing this mental prayer the soul strengthens its supernatural life and acquires facility in it."[54]

Love. Hope. Faith (I mean it as a verb: do faith). Do so without limit, because all three are specially designed to progress toward a perfection without limit. Most of us, most of the time, are far too easily pleased, and desire's assignment is to agitate, disconcert, stir up, and unnerve us. Praying for perfection is a sign of spiritual progress.

> I repeat what I said before, that we do not value this mere desire at its proper price. If we did, we should make more use of it; for we always use what we esteem. . . . It is true that we seldom fulfil what we desire; for it is as of old, the spirit is willing, but the flesh is weak. Nevertheless, what we do accomplish, bears some proportion to what we desire, and especially to the vehemence of our desire. These are great reasons for fostering this supernatural desire the most we can.[55]

The perfection we desire is not after the pattern of Abraham or Moses, or even the Cherubim or Seraphim. It is the perfection of Christ, which consisted principally in three things: being without

53. Ibid., 363.
54. Libermann, *Living With God*, 197.
55. Faber, *Growth in Holiness*, 38–39.

sin, embracing all the virtues, and possessing these perfections with the highest excellence.[56] God is perfect; he wants his works to be perfect. Since God is perfect in himself, he has a desire that all his works be perfect, which caused Christ to tell his disciples to be perfect as their heavenly Father is perfect. "That is to say, 'Content not yourselves with a mean purity and sanctity . . . but take you an infinite pattern of infinite perfection, by which, after His example, you may procure the greatest perfection which is possible for you, and let this pattern be your heavenly Father, to the end that, like true and legitimate sons, you may aspire to be very like Him, in these three things which His infinite perfection comprehends.'"[57]

It is an ersatz humility to refuse this invitation to perfection, and insults the God who became flesh to make it possible. What the God-Man has, he wants us to have; what he is, he wants us to be. Our desires are too weak, the object of our desires is too small.

What is it that you desire, you who aim at perfection? Give yourselves full scope. Your wishes need have no measure, no limit. . . . The present is ever filled with infinite treasure, it contains more than you have capacity to hold. Faith is the measure. Believe, and it will be done to you accordingly. Love is also the measure. The more the heart loves, the more it desires; and the more it desires, so much the more will it receive. The will of God is at each moment before us like an immense, inexhaustible ocean that no human heart can fathom; but [since] none can receive from it more than he has capacity to contain, it is necessary to enlarge his capacity by faith, confidence, and love.[58]

---

56. De Ponte, *Meditations on the Mysteries of Our Holy Faith,* vol. 3 (London: Richardson and Son, 1853), 154.
57. Ibid., 154–55.
58. De Caussade, *Abandonment to Divine Providence,* 19–20.

9

Grace and Desire

HERE WE WILL CONSIDER the conundrum of grace and free will.
Traditionally there are four positions to avoid, two regarding God
and two regarding man. God's role should be seen neither as coer-
cive nor contingent (he does not override our free will, and divine
ability to act is not dependent on our permission), and man's role
should be seen neither as quiescent nor determinative (our free will
is not inactive, and our action does not decide divine action). Holding all these dimensions in balance has caused no end of trouble in
scholarly treatments of grace and free will. The theology of desire
may have something to contribute because it pitches the issue in a
different key. Our part is not to *cooperate in the labor* of salvation.
God does all the labor! He redeems, he saves, it is his blood that
washes clean, it is his power that has torn down the gates of Hades.
We do not co-create our redemption, and therefore the relationship
between grace and free will is not a question of apportionment of
labor, or an assignment of ratio. However, we do *cooperate with the
gift*, if not its production, and we take part in God's gift by intense
desire. "Do you suppose that those graces which are destined for so
many others, are not for you? Do you wish for them? Our Lord
offers them to you, He awaits but one desire of your will,—the disposition of your heart,—to pour them down on you."[1]

God's part is grace; man's part is desire. God energizes, man synergizes. The sequence of cause-effect that we normally experience in
temporality does not quite apply. God does not dwell afar, waiting
for a signal. His desire for us is the foundation of our affectionate
desire for him. And our responsive desire is caused by a sufficient

---

1. De Ravignan, *The Last Retreat*, 54.

knowledge of our sin in the face of God's majesty, and *that* knowledge can only be provided by a supernatural light that God constantly offers. Understanding and power are related, which is why "the psalmist so often repeats, *The Lord is my light* against ignorance; *The Lord is my salvation* against the want of power. By the one we are taught what we are to desire, and we are enabled by the other to bring our desires about; but they both depend on grace."[2]

Two *wills* become one—that is the lesson of the theology of desire. We cannot say that two *works* become one (the work done by God and the work done by man), because the work God does is infinitely more valuable and necessary than any virtue we perform. We do not unite our virtues with his, our efforts with his, our merits with his, because we are on the receiving end of each of these. When Camus asked, "What! Are we to talk of our merits and graces as if He needed them, and were not Himself absolute merit and infinite goodness and perfection?" De Sales replied, "but what then is merit, but a work pleasing to God, and a work done in His grace, and by His help, and for His love—a work which He rewards with increase of grace and glory?"[3] A work pleases God when it is congruent with his will, so we unite our will with his in order that the reign of God may be established in our hearts. Salvation is common desire (by God and man) for the kingdom of God.

> There is no doubt that God, for His part, wills it and desires it ardently. If we too desire and will it the thing cannot fail to take place; for it only depends on these two wills, and as soon as they work together the result is certain. God's share in the work is always ready, and always given or offered to us: enlightenment, inspiration, graces both general and particular, and help both within and without. What He expects from us is a strong determination to be altogether His, to obey Him in everything and to refuse Him nothing.[4]

2. Lewis [Luis] de Granada, *The Sinner's Guide* (Philadelphia: Henry McGrath, 1845), 111.

3. Camus, *The Spirit of St. Francis de Sales*, 142.

4. Grou, *The School of Jesus Christ*, 160.

When God desires the increase of his glory, and we desire the increase of God's glory, and God is more greatly glorified, then two wills have met and become one. "For the will of such a soul is so transformed into the will of God that we can no longer say there are two wills, but one, namely, the will of God alone. Thus it seeks only the divine will in its actions."[5] This is true not only in times of consolation, it is also true at the foot of the cross: the soul still desires only the will of God even during periods of abandonment, poverty, agony and death.

On the one hand, it is all God. "We ought to say to God: 'I can do nothing of myself. I can only give You my desire to love You. Here it is! O my God, uphold me and do all Yourself.'"[6] Theologians of abnegation have plenty to say about our nothingness before the Lord. Everyone should ponder "that I was created of nothing, and that of myself I am 'nothing;' that I merit nothing, and that presently I shall be turned into nothing if God do not continually preserve me; neither should I be able to do anything if God did not continually aid me."[7] When Margaret Mary Alacoque yielded to a slight movement of vanity in speaking of herself, she recalls that "as soon as we were alone, [God] called me to account in the following manner, saying with a look of severity: 'What hast thou to boast of, O dust and ashes, since of thyself thou art but nothingness and misery!'"[8] Confessing nothingness is simply the confession that God is God, and we are not. God "will admit no rival,"[9] and "all is not too much for him."[10] Confessing our nothingness is the most fundamental act of religion, the repudiation of idolatry, the basis of spirituality, the animation of liturgy, and the structure of the sacraments. "All religion is founded upon the mortification of self-will, which if it lives religion dies, and if religion is to live self-will

5. John of St. Samson, *Prayer, Aspiration and Contemplation*, 161.

6. John Vianney, *Thoughts of the Curé of Ars* (Charlotte, NC: TAN Books and Publishers, Inc., 1984), Kindle edition, 10.

7. De Ponte, *Meditations on the Mysteries of Our Holy Faith*, vol. 1, 106.

8. Margaret Mary Alacoque, *The Autobiography of Saint Margaret Mary* (Charlotte, NC: TAN Books and Publishers, Inc., 2012), Kindle edition, chap. 62.

9. de Bernières-Louvigny, *The Interior Christian*, 88.

10. Fénelon, *Christian Perfection*, 31, 67, and 119. He liked to repeat the thought.

must die."[11] It is the confession that unites liturgy with spirituality. "He is pleased only with souls that are reduced to nothingness, souls that are all in Him and find everything in Him, since they are nothing in themselves."[12] All depends on God, to the point that even when we concern ourselves with our own salvation, it is because God has planted the good thought.

> Perhaps you will say: If I do not think of myself and my spiritual needs and my salvation, who else will think of them? Do you originate your thoughts of them? Is it not God who puts good thoughts and good desires into your heart? . . .
>
> Is it He, or is it your own self-love that makes you neglect Him and think only of yourself? Even the thoughts and desires of which you are yourself the object are only given to you by Him that you may be led, little by little, to the state of perfection in which you will think more of Him than of yourself.[13]

On the other hand, something depends on us. Although not done by us, it cannot be done without us. One heresy emphasizes man's activity in a way that detracts from God's grace, another heresy emphasizes God's grace in a way that excludes man's responsibility. Segneri takes both to task in light of Christ's statement in John 15:5: "I am the vine, you are the branches. He who abides in me, and I in him, he it is that bears much fruit, for apart from me you can do nothing." The fact that "the branch cannot bear fruit *unless* it is in the vine" most assuredly does not mean "therefore it cannot bear fruit *when* it is in the vine."[14] God has capacitated our desire for cooperation. "This fire which Jesus Christ came to bring, and which He desires to kindle, will not kindle in my heart, or at least will not abide and take root there, if I do not myself wish that it should kindle; if I do not try to entertain it, try to augment its ardour by my co-operation."[15] The heart that the Holy Spirit tries to set on fire is living, not dead, and the reaction of a living person

---

11. De Ponte, *Meditations on the Mysteries of Our Holy Faith*, vol. 1, 299.
12. Alacoque, *Letters*, Kindle edition, letter 106.
13. Grou, *The School of Jesus Christ*, 241–42.
14. Segneri, *The Manna of the Soul*, vol. 2, 397.
15. Grou, *Meditations upon the Love of God*, 3.

is different from the reaction of a cadaver. The Holy Spirit can move the sun and moon, the waters and air, without resistance, but the living heart is not like a material creature because it is endowed with will. The Spirit must therefore approach the living heart on the level of desire, and tease it forward. The flame requires matter to feed on, and this matter must be fed into the flame voluntarily by the living soul. The flame lit by the Holy Spirit must be augmented (enlarged by addition) by the matter from a person's earthly existence, willful desire, efforts at virtue. Rodríguez says that advancing in virtue requires *both* sincerely desiring and strenuously endeavoring, and refers to a pithy answer given by Thomas Aquinas to a sister who asked about her salvation.

> She asks him, "How she could save her soul?" He answered, "By willing it;" if you desire it, you will be saved, if you desire it, you will make progress in virtue, you will render yourself perfect. All then depends on our willing it, *i.e.*, on our willing it seriously and effectually, and on exerting ourselves with all possible diligence to secure our salvation. For Almighty God is always ready to assist us; but if our own will is wanting, all the exertions of our superiors are unavailing.[16]

The desire is so very necessary because we cannot advance spiritually unless we hunger and thirst to do so. Such a disposition is best "for obtaining from God the perfection we aim at. St. Ambrose says, that the Lord is so well pleased with the man who feels this longing desire, that he fills his soul with graces and favours."[17]

God is well pleased. We are speaking less about a mechanical interaction, and more about a loving Father whom we can please. We are speaking less according to the physics of cause and effect, and more according to a personal gratification. The connection of grace and free will is not automated, conditioned, or machine-like, it is an affectionate reciprocity. God's personal delight is involved,

---

16. Alphonsus Rodríguez (Alfonso), *The Practice of Christian and Religious Perfection,* vol. 1, 11.

17. Ibid., 13.

which conditions how we speak about prayer's energy. One way of praying is to "walk in the presence of God, like one friend with another" so that "for the greater part of the day he goes along in the presence of his God the two by themselves, without any process of the reason."[18] Another is to have fervent and loving talks with God, another is to ask fervently for something while the soul gazes as its God, another is either vocal or mental, another is to combine prayer with mortification, and another is this: "in a moment the soul is alone with its God, its heart full of fervent desire. Such is the force of this desire of the heart through which he makes his request to God, that it seems as if someone were compelling his beloved God to give him what he asks."[19] Compelling God! The desire has such personal energy that it almost translates into force: a force of love that draws God into the soul.

The world cannot understand this because it operates under a rubric of liberty versus coercion, where the increase of power by one decreases the power of the other. Then the contribution made by free will looks like it comes about by thievery from the value of grace. However, when one frames the question within the activity of love, we can speak of a kind of force—a force that God permits because he has created it. We do not force God; his own nature is in force. "His bounty, charity, and mercy, force Him to favour us; for He Himself imprints and infuses that spirit into us by which we do Him violence."[20] Such is the surrender made in covenants of love. It does not feel improper to say a child compels his parents, a spouse compels her beloved, a friend compels his friend. Love compels God and man to the same trysting place (*compellere*: to drive together, drive to one place), and thus love's response gives desire an irresistibility that compels without coercing. Neither God's freedom, nor man's freedom, is repressed. The goodness of God is a fountain from which his benefits flow, the first being "the great inclination which the goodness of God has to communicate itself,

18. Alonso Rodríguez (Alfonso), *Autobiography*, 89.
19. Ibid., 90.
20. De Ponte, *Meditations on the Mysteries of Our Holy Faith*, vol. 5, 73–74.

and to do good to others."[21] What moves grace our direction? God's goodness: his inclination to communicate himself. What moves our desire in his direction? God's goodness: his kindness to a sinner.

Far from being crushed, man's freedom is elevated. Indeed, it takes on the flavor of omnipotence. "If you never desire anything but what God desires, you will always attain the object of your desires, because God's holy will can never fail of being entirely performed."[22] A person no longer feels a friction between his own will and the will of God. The just man actually "always does *his own will*, because he has placed his will in the will of God, and of His divine Spirit; in doing, therefore, the will of God, he does his own will, because his own will is no other than the will of God. For which reason St. Bonaventura says, that those who are conformed to the divine will, are as Gods, omnipotent, to do what they will."[23] The faithful person can do what he wills (which is quite different from doing whatever he wants), because he wills what he does. Freedom will be preserved. "As their desires are the same as those of God, they cannot fail to have all that they want, since God desires nothing in vain."[24] The righteous always get their way, because they want the way of God. God's omnipotent will is the will with which the person of *faith* and *hope* has united himself, because he is in *love* with God. The heart always receives its desire, because it wants what God wants to give. Obey God and your will will never be contradicted. It will go with the grain of reality, not against it. Wisdom orders all things sweetly, so in the potency of God's will "we find delight in willing it, which is proper to His divine wisdom and omnipotence."[25]

The heart prays for what it desires, and the heart now desires only what God would have it desire. Prayer is a meeting of wills, the contact of hearts, and a conformity of desires, which holds the

21. De Ponte, *Meditations on the Mysteries of Our Holy Faith*, vol. 6, 74.

22. Alphonsus Rodríguez (Alfonso), *The Practice of Christian and Religious Perfection,* vol. 1, 410.

23. De Ponte, *Meditations on the Mysteries of Our Holy Faith*, vol. 5, 230.

24. Claude de la Colombière, *Sermons*, vol. 1, *Christian Conduct* (DeKalb, IL: NIU Press, 2014), 133.

25. De Ponte, *Meditations on the Mysteries of Our Holy Faith*, vol. 6, 306.

secret to the puzzling idea that we can "compel God." What feels like compelling comes from placing our will in tandem with God's (*tandem* means to follow), resulting in gladness on God's part and delectation on ours. Every lover knows captivation yields sweetness.

> My heart is no longer free—I have given it to the King of kings, and it is mine to dispose of no more. I hear in my heart the voice of my Beloved: "My bride, you refuse all earthly honour to follow Me; like Me, you shall meet with sorrow and the cross.... Yet what sweetness and joy I will make you taste in your tribulations! The part I have chosen for you is by far the better one, nor should I have kept it for you had I not loved you dearly.... I covet your heart, I love it, and have chosen it for My own! I long for the day when you will be wholly Mine! Guard well your heart for Me!"[26]

We will fall short in understanding the working of grace if we do not start with the sort of phrases just quoted. Why does God pursue human beings? He covets their hearts. God is the one being who can covet without the desire becoming immoderate or disordered. It is a trait the saints try to copy.

This also solves the problem of how the desire is both ours and implanted by God. By slow steps the desire in us changes from being extraneous to being personal. The gift becomes a possession with which we are equipped. The heart *might*, *may*, and finally *can* turn its eyes to heaven. Divine cupidity causes a return attraction: the soul now chases the God who has been chasing her. God causes an effect which is co-caused, and this creates the liturgical life typified by the Canticle of Canticles. We live in a new country.

> [Christ] made of His life our life, of His destiny our destiny, of His Father our Father, of His God our God. These are those "best ointments" which make the Bride run after the Bridegroom (Cant. 1:2), and to unite herself to Him, in order to espouse His actions when she had espoused His Person. To this soul thus subjugated and ravished with love the altar becomes her country—or better still, as it

26. Elizabeth of the Trinity, *Reminiscences* (New York: Benziger Brothers, 1914), 27–28.

were, her nuptial dwelling. She lives only to die, because this death, united to that of Christ, appeases, attracts, rejoices, glorifies God.[27]

Go from your country, God said to the father of faith. Like Abraham, we are called out of the land of our fallen father, Adam, to take up residence in the land of a new altar.

A good will is necessary: it is necessary to will the good. We cannot assure ourselves of having it, so we must beg God for it. Most of all, do not be afraid, because wrong fear asphyxiates desire.

> Make the attempt, Christian soul, and you will see if I speak truly. If you tell me that it is not in your power to enter on this path of prayer, I answer, on God's behalf, that He is ready to second your good will, and to bring you into it. . . . This very request would be the beginning of it; and how should God refuse you what He inspires you to ask? If few persons possess it, it is because few desire it, and those who do ask it, for the most part, fear to obtain it. God reads the heart; He sees whether we respond to the feelings which He breathes into it, and always hearkens to those who do so respond.[28]

People who reproach God for rejecting their prayers are people who have been praying lukewarmly, or egocentrically, or disorderedly. They have been praying with the intention of directing God's will, instead of letting theirs be directed by him. Such persons claim to ask for a good will, but at some point God will show them (on judgment day, if not sooner) that "if they had it not, they themselves only were to blame. I repeat, that a soul which co-operates to the best of its power with present grace, must infallibly obtain greater graces from moment to moment; and if it carries on this co-operation steadily, it will certainly attain to all the holiness which God expects of it."[29]

In the cooperative exchange, God is not reacting to a contribution we make of our share of the labor; God is replying to the desire that has responded to his. We can never contribute our share of the

27. Charles Gay, *The Christian Life and Virtues*, vol. 2, 81.
28. Grou, *The Spiritual Maxims*, 97.
29. Ibid.

labor, but our desire for God can conform to God's desire for us, and so yield to it. Usually, the exchange of love has a simultaneity that confounds the past-present formulation of cause-effect. God's desire causes our desire with a synchronicity, wherein his is the forming love, ours is the formed love. His is the prototype, ours is the icon. "This is the love that Jesus Christ is ready to give me, if I desire it of Him, and ask Him for it sincerely; it is impossible that He should give me any other love, because He really has none other to give."[30] The theme of this book has been God welcoming a heart that so much as *desires to desire* to offer itself up in oblation. "Finally, my Dear Jesus, I place myself entirely in Thy hands. I abandon myself so completely to Thy good pleasure that I no longer desire to have any other will or desire, save to let Thee will, desire and choose for me, in this and in everything else."[31] The act of giving oneself to God is not part of a negotiation, or a concession we bring to the table. We do not parley with God from opposing sides of a dispute, asking how little we can get by with. Here are the actual questions: "How must we then give ourselves to God? Does not this step depend more upon His grace than upon ourselves? Is not this gift an act of the most mature and ardent love, and is it in our power to perform such an act?"[32] Here is the actual answer: "it is in your power if you sincerely desire to do it, because on God's part all is ready. He desires nothing so much as the possession of our hearts, if we, on our part, are only ready and willing to come to Him with confiding trust."[33] Does this desire do anything to us? Yes. It leads to offering prayer, keeping commandments, practicing virtues, abnegating self-love, annihilating self-will, spiritual communion, assisting at Mass, receiving sacraments, loving neighbors, ministering charity, and embracing humility.

Divinely inspired desire leaves certain marks behind, and although we cannot pretend to give an exhaustive list, we will men-

---

30. Grou, *Meditations upon the Love of God*, 115.
31. Eudes, *Meditations on Various Subjects*, 172.
32. Jean Grou, *Self-Consecration: or the Gift of One's Self to God* (New York: E. & J. B. Young & Co., 1887), 105.
33. Ibid.

tion four: patience, perseverance, progress, and perfection. We will group them into two pairs.

Patient perseverance is a first pair. We would probably arrange a different timetable from the one God has chosen for us if we were the foreman of our own spiritual development, but his providence is wiser, therefore we must be patient and persevere. Patience is prolonged endurance. God is always more patient than we are, and if our will conforms to his, then patience with his schedule must be practiced. We must persevere in patience, not demanding more, or more speed, from God than he judges wise. "Success will come when it is the will of God. To desire detachment, love of contempt, is well, and we ought to do so, but we must not desire them except insomuch as God is willing to bestow them on us, and not to a greater degree than He Himself wills. Let us labour, it is our lot; but victory depends on God; He gives it if He wills, and when He wills."[34] Humility requires patience to ripen; patience requires humility to survive. Patience brings joy if practiced over a whole lifetime, and in this life, patience is attached to perseverance. A number of virtues are interconnected. "Obedience leads to perseverance; humility leads to perseverance; devotion also greatly conduces to perseverance; but, to speak correctly, patience does not engender perseverance, but contains it. Finally, how shall we describe patience? It is itself a species of perseverance."[35] The soul that is filled with contemplative love of God has no greater joy than meditating upon Him, and having learned that all earthly joys are vain and empty, "she only desires that which God willeth: she loves what He loveth: that alone which is displeasing to Him is hateful to her. So entirely is her heart in conformity with God's holy Will, that she longs far more ardently that it should be accomplished than that any desire of her own should be fulfilled. Thus does she dwell always in perfect peace, abandoning herself wholly to God, and submitting joyfully to whatever His Providence may appoint."[36] Provi-

34. De Ravignan, *The Last Retreat*, 106.
35. Segneri, *The Manna of the Soul*, vol. 1, 114.
36. Louis Tronson, *Examination of Conscience upon Special Subjects* (London: Rivingtons, 1870), 17–18.

dence is the disposition and order of all the means God appoints to attain his ends, and since we should desire his end, not ours, we should be patient under his government.

This brings us to the second pair of marks found upon the desirous heart: progress and perfection. Strive to progress toward the perfection God has determined is best for you. "Our whole ambition should be to attain the degree of perfection that has been appointed for us, since it has not been given to everybody to reach the same height."[37] Do not cease to advance, for to do so is to fall back. This adage is repeated regularly. Although we are to be patient with what God gives us, it is also necessary "to co-operate with divine grace by an ardent desire of advancing, nor ever to think one has so far advanced as to imagine he must not still make greater progress, because not to wish to advance, is to fall back. But such is the nature of human desire, if it be true desire, that it is always on fire, and never rests until it obtain what it desires."[38] We witness desire's cooperation with grace when it longs to make as much headway toward perfection as is possible in this life, under obedience to what God has predestined. Even if this life does not allow an infallible certainty of being in a state of grace "yet there are signs that give a moral probability of it, and the surest mark we can have is to feel in our hearts an ardent desire of daily perfecting ourselves more and more in virtue."[39] Do not crave more than God intends to give. Do not compare yourself to anyone else. Do not envy. God makes no comparisons; he deals individually.

Under the laws of nature, a stone returns to earth, water returns to its lowest point, and fire returns to heaven. But if our desires are brought to a boil, they forget their own nature and leap up.

And thus, as water put over the fire, when it is very hot, seems to forget its own nature, which is heavy and tends downwards, and

---

37. Jean-Baptiste Saint-Jure, in Jean-Baptiste Saint-Jure and Claude de la Colombière, *Trustful Surrender to Divine Providence: The Secret of Peace and Happiness* (Rockford, IL: TAN Books and Publishers, Inc., 1983), 17.

38. Bona, *A Treatise of Spiritual Life*, 293.

39. Alphonsus Rodríguez (Alfonso), *The Practice of Christian and Religious Perfection*, vol. 1, 20–21.

leaps up, imitating the lightness and nature of the fire that affects it, so the soul, inflamed with this heavenly fire, rises above itself, and striving to ascend with the spirit from earth to heaven, from whence this flame comes, boils with most ardent desire for God, and rushes with violent impulses to embrace Him, stretching up its arms on high to try to reach Him Whom it loves so much; and as it can neither reach Him, nor cease to desire Him, it faints with its longing, unfulfilled desire, and says with the bride in the Song of Songs, "Tell my Beloved that I am sick of [with] love." (Cant. 5: 8)[40]

Love returns to love. The love God has implanted tries to return to him, incessantly. That is what causes ceaseless prayer. Progress toward perfection is advancement in trying to please God more and more. "St. Bernard says, that there is no more certain mark of God being present in a man's heart, than the desire of still increasing in grace."[41]

Are we graced? The surest marks one can feel are patience, perseverance, and progress toward perfection. This is not as easy as it sounds to the ear of the world. "Oh, how few there are who pray! How few there are who desire what is truly good! Crosses, external and internal humiliation, the renunciation of our own wills, the death of self, and the establishment of God's throne upon the ruins of self-love—these are indeed good. If we do not desire these, we are not truly praying."[42] Abnegation is a fee levied, and as an ingredient of desire, it thickens its practice. A desire untranslated into practice is a chimera, and unlikely ever to be realized. "Always remember that the desire of humility is not enough; it is not difficult to desire it, but to practise, to accept, to go in quest of humiliation is another thing."[43] Humility will feel like humiliation so long as there is an ounce of vainglory remaining. Abnegation must guide the desire

40. Luis de Granada, *Counsels on Holiness of Life: Being the First Part of The Sinner's Guide* (London: Rivingtons, 1869), 139.

41. Alphonsus Rodríguez (Alfonso), *The Practice of Christian and Religious Perfection*, vol. 1, 19–20.

42. Fénelon, *The Complete Fénelon*, 87.

43. De Ravignan, *The Last Retreat*, 106.

along a straight, but very narrow path. The perfection sought is for God's glory alone, and not for any esteem from the world. "Entertain and increase the desire of living for God alone. For this purpose open the eyes of your soul and realize that you possess nothing of yourself, but that all holiness and all grace reside in Jesus. Have always a quiet and peaceful recourse to His divine bounty, for you have a very real desire to live for Him alone, but your desire is not yet translated into practice."[44] The interior face of desire is a heart yearning for God, the exterior face of desire is a practice.

In order for the desire to be translated into practice, one must die to self and live for Christ. The signpost of perfect love, planted in the midst of the world, in the middle of history, is the Cross. Whereas progress patiently advances toward love, any progress toward perfection will mean advancing toward the cross to embrace it. The cross is the tool the Holy Spirit uses to cut a person free from worldliness, and is the only tool that can cut worldly restraints. The application of this salvific implement exacts a price from the person on whom it performs its liberation. Remember that the solution to the grace and free will conundrum occurs when the person wills what God wills. God wills to set us free: that is, he wills to apply the cross to us.

> He reigns sovereignly in the soul of one who leads a hidden life, who, making no reservation of his own wishes, at least with full consciousness, apart from the will of God, desires only what He desires, and desires Him alone in all things. Such a one performs external acts when God requires it of him, but without leaving His sole beloved All, abiding ever hidden with Jesus in God alone, and seeking no share in creatures.[45]

It might involve physical suffering, but not necessarily; it most certainly will involve spiritual martyrdom. "Spiritual writers tell us that though the desire of certain souls to please God by their sufferings is acceptable to him, still more pleasing to him is the union of certain others with his will, so that their will is neither to rejoice nor

---

44. Libermann, *Letters to People in the World*, 275.
45. Boudon, *The Hidden Life of Jesus*, 107.

to suffer, but to hold themselves completely amenable to his will, and they desire only that his holy will be fulfilled."[46]

The will cannot stop willing. This is its natural work. But it must be corrected from a false end to a true object, an unsuitable goal to a proper ambition, a penultimate objective to its final purpose, which is a welfare designed by God Almighty. "Thy good pleasure is my sole desire. Do with me what Thou wilt.... I surrender myself entirely into the hands of God, my Eternal Father, who dost desire my welfare more than I do myself, who alone knows what is best for me and alone can obtain it for me."[47] Then patient perseverance leads toward perfection because desire is embracing its object. It occurs in faith now, in glory later. This is certainly applicable to the life of the sacraments. "What things can be more purely divine than these Sacraments? Yet see how sensible they are to human touch! ... They do not need our active cooperation, so much as our permission. They require obstacles to be removed, but not assistance to be conferred."[48]

46. Alphonsus de Liguori, *Uniformity with God's Will* (Rockford, IL: TAN Books and Publishers, Inc., 1977), 15.

47. John Eudes, *The Sacred Heart of Jesus* (New York: P. J. Kenedy & Sons, 1946), 56.

48. Faber, *The Precious Blood*, 118.

10

Practical Desire

I DO NOT WANT TO LEAVE the impression that the desire being described is restricted to saints, or those who have made tremendous advance in the spiritual life, and is therefore beyond the faculty of most of us. We are uplifted by reading accounts of great desire in great souls, and we look to them for inspiration and guidance, but should not feel abashed or discouraged at the less spectacular desires that fill the mundane. There is a practical, ordinary expression of desire that we should acknowledge. "Do not be ashamed of the ordinary, needful actions which lead us on in the Love of God."[1] Consider, also, "that holiness does not consist in doing great things, but in doing thy works perfectly.... Dost thou not see that holiness is not to be sought in the works, but in the worker? The work which falls to thy share may be ignoble, may be trivial, may be of little importance; yet do not doubt that it will suffice to sanctify thee, provided it is done with the greatest possible perfection."[2]

This chapter asks what the *praxis* of desire looks like. It requires time, and time is a gift given by God. The *saeculum* (age) consists of time, into which the eternal can make its way. Here desire brings a breath of awe to the commonplace, and that is why we should be submissive to God even in the desires that seem to lack luster. Do not be discouraged, because there are recommended exercises. "Here is the practical conduct I should like you to follow: preserve in your heart the desire of belonging entirely to Jesus. Constantly aim at that goal, but, while tending toward it, expect everything at all times from His divine goodness and not from your own efforts

---

1. De Sales, *Introduction to the Devout Life*, 241.
2. Segneri, *The Manna of the Soul*, vol. 1, 184.

nor even from your violent prayers."[3] The few give witness by their success, while the many give witness by their effort.

Practical desire is desire that can be rehearsed in little, ordinary moments. *Rehersen* means to repeat, to go over something again and again as a preparation. Behind that stands the word *rehercier*, which literally means to rake over the ground, or turn over the soil. Rehearsing tills the soil of the soul in preparation for piety, and rehearsing our desire prepares the heart for devotion. "Be faithful then dear confrere. Be faithful to all the graces and favors God bestows upon you. Nurture those noble desires in your soul. Pray unceasingly for their fulfillment and *act in practice as if you already possessed* all those graces."[4] Acting "as if" is an important component of desire, until we possess the thing we desire. So do not be put off by feeling like an imposter when you fail to act as the greatest saints have done. Instead, mimic them in the fervency of their prayer. The prayer cannot be a sham if God has commanded us to make it. Our Lord himself teaches us this.

> This preparation of the heart consists in an ardent desire to possess him. This is why holy church makes us remember during this season the holy patriarchs who sighed for the coming of the Messiah, who, for that reason, is called in the Holy Scriptures the Desired, or the Desire of all peoples. We stir these desires in ourselves in prayer, when we open our hearts in the presence of God, and when we beg him to come to take possession of us. Jesus Christ himself has taught us this manner of prayer, when he commanded us to ask of his Father that his Kingdom come, meaning that he reign tranquilly within us, and that we be bound by love to his laws and to his Gospel.[5]

Desire is preparation of the heart—a kind of interior rehearsal of the Kingdom's reign.

We are talking about practicable desire, so here is a piece of prac-

3. Libermann, *Letters to Clergy and Religious* (Series 7), 107.
4. Libermann, *Letters to Clergy and Religious* (Series 8), 28. Emphasis added.
5. François Fénelon, *Spiritual Letters of François De Salignac De La Mothe-Fénelon* [*to Countess Gramont*] (Cornwall-on-Hudson, NY: Idlewild Press, 1945), 65–66.

tical advice: you won't necessarily feel the desire. Do not be surprised if the desire is not perceptible through bodily senses or through observation of the mind. God's power will be required to bring the desire to practice. "You need not be astonished that your desire to belong to God is neither ardent nor very sensible; this is neither necessary nor possible. Try merely to make [your spiritual exercises] sustained, continual and practical. If you want to have them reduced to practice, you must expect this from God alone, beg Him for it with perfect sincerity and aim to preserve them always in your heart."[6]

The practical is acquired through training and action, not theory and speculation. Desire is acquired by habit, not hypothesizing, and therefore it can be practiced in the valley as well as on the mountaintop. One needn't climb the mountain with a prophet, or the ivory tower with a professor in order to find a practice place. There are small, daily opportunities.

> Persevere in thoroughly conquering yourself in these small daily contradictions you receive; make the bulk of your desires about this; know that God wishes nothing from you at present but that. Busy not yourself then in doing anything else: do not sow your desires in another's garden, but cultivate well your own. Do not desire not to be what you are, but desire to be very well what you are; occupy your thoughts in making that perfect, and in bearing the crosses, little or great, which you will meet. And, believe me, this is the great truth, and the least understood in spiritual conduct.[7]

The garden plot one inhabits is plenty large for combating vices, practicing virtues, and cultivating desires. And there will be time to practice every day, so no need to hurry. "The Wise Man says of the virtuous woman, 'Her hands hold the distaff' [Prov 31:19]. I could say much about these words. Your spindle is a mass of good desires; spin every day a little; carry out the thread of your wishes into execution, and you will do much. But beware of hurry; that would lead

---

6. Libermann, *Letters to Clergy and Religious* (Series 8), 367.
7. De Sales, *Letters to Persons in the World*, 319.

you to make knots in your thread, and spoil your work. Let us go on quietly; however slowly we advance, we shall make great progress really."[8]

The good desires should be spun every day, quietly, and without vexation. The desires can be simple, both in the sense of having few parts, and in the sense of not being many numerically. The perfection we seek cannot be fully attained in this world.

> We can mortify the flesh, but not to the absolute exclusion of all rebellious passion; we shall often still be liable to distractions, and so must we then be troubled, restless, disappointed, despairing? Certainly not. Must we entertain a host of desires? No! Our gratitude may be very simply expressed. We may wish that we had the Seraphim's fervour, therewith fitly to serve and worship God; but we must not waste time in mere longings, as though in this world we could attain real perfection, and then grow irritable because we do not succeed.[9]

This is why all desire must be framed within *Thy kingdom come*. Our eyes are fixed on heaven, but we are still drudging here below, and should think practically about the present day's march. "To advance well we must apply ourselves to make good way in the road nearest to us, and to do the first day's journey. We must not busy ourselves with wanting to do the last, but remember that we are to do and work out the first."[10] The devil has already had his way if someone's vainglory fixes on the last day of the journey to such an extent that the first day's campaign is never mounted. A paradox has been revealed: our eyes should be fixed both on the horizon and the next step, both on tomorrow and today, both on the ultimate end and the present path.

It was earlier suggested that *praxis* in the mundane requires time, and now we learn the reason why: because this desire unfolds across each person's entire history. It needs time. Start by giving the first day's journey the time it needs, and then add months and years, and

8. De Sales, *A Selection from the Spiritual Letters of S. Francis De Sales*, 84.
9. Ibid., 331–32.
10. De Sales, *Letters to Persons in the World*, 10.

even the whole lifetime. The desire must not be spasmodic, coming into existence one moment, then disappearing with no lasting effect. It must accrue from day to day, which is a feat of perseverance. A person must desire long and steadily if a character is to develop. Then the desire can focus on particulars, even while it is aware of the whole. It would be a serious mistake to think that one can disregard particular crosses out of contempt of their small size.

> What I wish to say, then, is, that it is of great importance for our spiritual advancement, to take to heart, for some time, some one thing in particular; and it must be precisely what we find ourselves [to] stand most in need of. And in prayer we must chiefly insist upon this, and beg it of God with fervour several times, several days, nay, even several months; making this our chief business, having it continually before our eyes, and lodging it in the very bottom of our hearts, till we come at last to obtain it. . . . St. Thomas, speaking of prayer, says, that the more the desire unites itself to one thing in particular, the more perfect and efficacious it is.[11]

This is simply a description of how a successful journey happens. If one changed one's destination every other day, one would never get nearer to the original destination. Likewise, if one neglected to make that first day's march, one would never get any further along.

"God does not give good desires without giving the means to accomplish them."[12] So take delays and detours in the journey as part of God's plan, and remain firm.

> Courage then, my good child, you will see we shall get on; for this dear and sweet Saviour of our souls has not given us these inflamed desires of serving him, without giving us the chance of doing so; without doubt he only defers the time for accomplishing your desires in order to choose a more suitable one; for you see, my dearest daughter, this amorous heart of our Redeemer measures and adapts all the events of this world unto the good of the souls which, without reserve, are willing to serve his divine love.

11. Alphonsus Rodríguez (Alfonso), *The Practice of Christian and Religious Perfection*, vol. 1, 274.

12. De Sales, *Letters to Persons in the World*, 354. Title of letter 37.

This good time then which you desire will come on the day which this sovereign providence has named in the secret of his mercy.[13]

This is why it was so important to emphasize the union of two wills. Both are required for progress, and while God is ready to give promptly, the receiver may not be as ready to receive (especially when the gift is packaged with the cross), so God takes all the time necessary to prepare his children.

> We murmur and accuse God of not keeping His promises. But our God is a Father of kindness who prefers to put up with our complaints and criticisms rather than stop them by gifts which would be fatal to us. . . . It would be hating you, not loving you, to take away your cross before giving you the virtues you lack. If God found some desire in you for these virtues He would give you them without delay, and it would be unnecessary for you to ask for the other things.[14]

If God found a desire for his Kingdom, he would cause that Kingdom to arrive on the doorstep of the soul this very minute. But the cultivation of the recipient involves his conversion from egocentricity to theocentricity, which means putting down rebellion and picking up obedience. Then we would "so love to obey that we have an insatiable desire to be commanded, so that all that we do may be done from obedience; and this is the obedience of the perfect, which I desire for you. It is a pure gift from God."[15]

The first reason to obey God is because he is God. After that we can also obey because it is to our benefit. Our salvation glorifies God, which is why he saves us. The twin purposes of liturgy are the glorification of God and the sanctification of man—and the former is the reason for the latter, the latter adds to the former. That is why we may desire both God's glory and our salvation in unison.

13. Ibid.
14. De la Colombière, in Saint-Jure and de la Colombière, *Trustful Surrender*, 120.
15. Francis de Sales, *The Spiritual Conferences* (New York: Benziger Brothers, 1909), 166.

God calls you to all these holy works; hear him and obey. Consider that you can never take too much pains nor practise too much patience in the pursuit of so great a good. How happy will you be if at the end of your days you can say with Our Lord: *I have finished and perfected the work thou gavest me to do!* Desire it, effect it; think of this, pray for this; and God, who has given you the will to desire it, will give you strength to execute it.[16]

What one man should do to glorify God is different from what another man should do. The service one man makes to God is different from the service another will make. Glorifying and serving God should be everyone's utmost desire, but the *means* of serving God can be malleable, according to his will. Providence provides varying procedures to shift our desire from the world to God, lest we become overly attached to any single method. "We must absolutely, invariably, and inviolably desire only God. But the means of serving Him should be the object of a very feeble desire on our part, so that if one means be taken from us we shall not be greatly affected thereby."[17] Calm reflection of a lifetime seen in retrospect will reveal inflection points where God changed the soul's tack. Perhaps the change was from contemplative to active, or vice-versa; or from solitude to community, or vice-versa; or from peace to suffering, or vice-versa. We can only be zealous and firm in prayer when we surrender to God's will. "[T]he reason why we obtain so little from God is because we do not ask much. We are too limited in our desires, and too languid in our prayers."[18]

Meager desire yields lethargic prayer, a state most unsuitable to any devotion. Practical desire is not a technique, it is an expression of affection. "You wish that God should give you the immense treasures that cost the blood of His Son, and you ask them as if they were worth little or nothing. Great favors ought to be asked with great affection; there should be some proportion between the vehemence of the desire, the ardor of the supplication, and the excel-

---

16. De Sales, *Letters to Persons in Religion*, 37–38.
17. De Sales, *Maxims and Counsels*, 177.
18. Croiset, *Devotion to the Sacred Heart*, 91.

lence of the thing desired and supplicated."[19] Tepidity and negligence in prayer proves one is not in a condition to receive God's favors yet. Cool prayer, i.e., prayer without affection, tries to barter with God, or cajole him, and God easily sees through these maneuvers. Such maneuvers are insulting to a love covenant. The coolness of prayer shows that a person "has no real desire to obtain what he asks, that his prayers are mere words, and that he cares little whether they be heard or not, since, if he did, he would certainly make them with greater fervor. Therefore, let us strive to animate all our prayers with an ardent affection; let them be as burning incense."[20] If making passionate requests of God sounds intimidating, consider the fact that all friendships and loves require this importunity if they are to exist truthfully.

Practicality connotes being useful, in the sense of being suitable and ready to be put into effect. Such practicality is inappropriately applied to God if it implies making him useful to us. But we may speak of a practicality of desire in the sense that it is useful to devotion and religion. "It is not sufficient then, that you feel in yourself these good desires, but you must endeavour that these desires become efficacious, and that they be put in execution. For action is the true proof or trial of virtue."[21] If one's actions do not correspond with one's resolutions, it means the resolutions were not true desires in the first place. One should then imitate the blacksmith who puts a piece of iron back into the fire when it fails to forge the first time. "Put, therefore, these imperfect desires again into the fire of prayer, and there endeavour to render them efficacious, and do not give over till your actions are conformable to your purposes, and till there remains nothing which can render you wavering or inconstant in their execution."[22] Desire will produce practical results if the fire of prayer forges the exact instrument necessary for growth in grace. For this to happen, we may need to have our desires improved by God, the first step being abandonment of our selfish desires.

19. Saint-Jure, *The Spiritual Man*, 304.
20. Ibid., 302.
21. Alphonsus Rodríguez (Alfonso) *The Practice of Christian and Religious Perfection*, vol. 1, 283.
22. Ibid.

Humility and self-renunciation make us pliant under the action of the Master's grace, but "that pliability, which makes the soul a faithful instrument in God's hands, comes only to a soul whose first desires and hopes have been overthrown."[23] Libermann takes a familiar image from Jeremiah and Isaiah.

> You should remain in the Lord's presence like clay before the potter. The workman does what he pleases with it: he beats it, presses it, and beats it again to make it supple. The clay offers no resistance; it leaves the potter perfect liberty to do with it what he wishes. The potter fashions a vase and it often happens that when it is half-finished he breaks it up and reduces it to a shapeless mass. He then starts anew to make of it the particular vase he wants. The more the clay has been battered and crushed, the easier it is for the potter to achieve his purpose.[24]

The desire has, all along, been to put ourselves in God's hand. Now that you have done so, "allow God full liberty to handle you."[25] How are sick souls cured of self-love and self-interest?

> They must be turned to the love of God; they must be made to understand that, if they are zealous for the interests of God, He will have a special care for theirs; that if they prefer the Will of God to anything else, they should desire above all that it should be fulfilled; and with such a desire their salvation runs no risk. If they live in love, it is quite certain that they will die in love; and that wherever they carry the love of God with them, there they will find Paradise.[26]

When hearts are really turned to God they find the familiar intercourse that Adam and Eve enjoyed in Paradise. Practical desire is effective in the presence of God. "If God were to take all else from us, He will never deprive us of Himself so long as we desire Him."[27]

23. Libermann, *Letters to Religious Sisters and Aspirants*, 131.
24. Libermann, *Letters to Clergy and Religious* (Series 9), 116.
25. Ibid.
26. Grou, *Meditations upon the Love of God*, 94–95.
27. De Sales, *A Selection from the Spiritual Letters of S. Francis De Sales*, 105.

What will satisfy practical desire? Not increased information, not completed projects, not successful campaigns. Only one thing.

> Entertain me no more with any knowledge of Thee, or with Thy communications, or impressions of Thy grandeur, for these do but increase my longing, and the pain of Thy absence, for Thy presence alone can satisfy my will and desire. The will cannot be satisfied with anything less than the Vision of God, and therefore the soul prays that He may be pleased to give Himself to it perfectly in truth, in the consummation of love.[28]

Rehearsing for heaven involves preparing for the beatitude that will be felt by standing constantly in the presence of God. As there is no vicissitude in heaven, and saints enjoy the same enjoyment of God constantly,

> even so, on earth, those who have attained a perfect conformity to the divine will, and who establish their own contentment in that of God, never suffer themselves to be disquieted or any ways discontented at the inconstancy of things, and the divers accidents of this life. Their will is so totally subjected to that of God, that the very assurance they have, that all things come as sent by him, and that his holy will is accomplished in whatever adversity happens to them, makes them, by preferring his will to their own, look upon all their tribulations and sufferings as so many joys; and all their griefs and sorrows as so much sweetness and consolation.[29]

We have a glimpse of that kingdom of heaven on earth, with its paradise of delights, since we resemble in some degree the blessed in heaven who perpetually enjoy God.

Practical desire is not a strategy to escape from suffering or tribulation or adversity; it fastens itself upon God in suffering, tribulation, and adversity. God does not answer our desire for prosperity, he answers our desire for love, and answers it by coming himself. The exercise of the presence of God is an exercise of love. What does

28. John of the Cross, *Ascent of Mount Carmel*, in *Complete Works*, vol. 2, 39.

29. Alphonsus Rodríguez (Alfonso), *The Practice of Christian and Religious Perfection*, vol. 1, 398.

God do when he sees this practical desire in a soul? "God, on His side, seeing before Him a soul that desires to have Him always present ... delights in its faithfulness, He redoubles His grace, He visits it frequently, He constantly makes Himself felt within it; not only has it the knowledge of His Presence, but it has the taste of it, it experiences the delights thereof. He enters into familiar communion with it, and admits it into intimate union with Him."[30] The presence of God is what we are after—not theoretically, but actually. Desire is experienced as true, beautiful, and good when it experiences God's presence (also known as Paradise). This can occur in every state of life. It is the goal of the active and contemplative life, of sacramental gift and liturgical oblation, of interior and exterior actions, because we are attentive to what we desire. "To watch oneself is to be attentive to God. It is to have him always present. It is to withdraw into oneself. It is not to be weakened or distracted willingly among his creatures.... It is to expand, as the Prophet said, one's heart in the presence of God. It is to find him in one's self. It is to seek him by the fervor of one's desires."[31]

This vigilance is a spiritual exercise that need not, and should not, be confined to certain times or places. It can, and should, be constant—indeed, the watchfulness is a form of the constant prayer desired by the heart. "During the day let the principal interior occupation be what is called simple interior waiting, silent, peaceful, and entirely resigned; and do not think that this is idleness, waste of time, or in any way useless, because, as a beggar who waits the whole day long at a rich man's gate, or at the church door, is by no means idle but much occupied interiorly with his own misery, his wants and continual necessities; so, in the same way, a soul in this simple waiting before God is very much occupied interiorly...."[32] Desire is a form of expectation, and the beggar who waits at the gate occupies a state of hopeful expectation. The person waiting on his interior is unseen by the world, uncredited by the world, but all angels' eyes are upon him. Any time, and at all times, this desirous

30. Grou, *Meditations upon the Love of God*, 56.
31. Fénelon, *Spiritual Letters [to Countess Gramont]*, 62.
32. De Caussade, *Abandonment to Divine Providence*, 199.

state is in simple waiting before God, making the following acts: "of faith in the presence of God, of adoration before this great God whose infinite power and mercy it acknowledges; of self-distrust; of profound humility in thinking itself incapable of anything; of desire for the holy operations of God, of hope since one does not wait for what one does not expect to receive; and of abandonment to divine Providence in regard to all His gifts or operations."[33] Although these acts may not be sensible, specified, or even accurately performed,

> yet they are none the less there, at the bottom of the heart; and God, at least, sees them in our desires, and in our state of preparation. Now, as you are aware, our wishes and desires, even if only begun to be formed, are to God what the voice is to our fellow men. He hears them, in fact, far more clearly than men hear our voices, and it is enough for Him that we form these desires; for, as the Psalmist says He knows even the mere intention and disposition of our hearts from the first moment that they begin to turn, and to move towards Him.[34]

There is a difference between *placing* ourselves in the presence of God, and *keeping* ourselves there. To do the former, it is necessary "to recall our minds from every other object, and make it attentive to this presence actually;" to do the latter, we must make acts toward God by understanding or will, "whether by looking at him, or looking at some other thing for love of him; or looking at nothing, but speaking to him; or, neither looking nor speaking, but simply staying where he has put us."[35] Practically desiring (I do not mean "almost desiring;" I mean desiring in practicable way) can go on wherever God has put a person because the desire can be lifted up to heaven from anywhere that person has been put. The hour has now come when one will desire the Father neither on this mountain nor in Jerusalem (a reference to Jn 4:21), but in every household, every workplace, on every street corner. The activity of

33. Ibid.
34. Ibid., 199–200.
35. De Sales, *Letters to Persons in the World*, 332–33.

the temple has flooded the world in anticipation of a city without a temple (a reference to Rev 21:22).

Thinking again of his illustration of the king who put up a statue in its niche (we quoted it in chapter 5), de Sales repeats it in a letter to Madame de Chantal, saying the king has placed each of us in such a niche, namely, a situation especially suited to our abilities, a special area for service. Because the master has put the statue where he did, the statue does not move, does not want to move, does not ask for transfer to a more esteemed location. De Sales imagines a question and answer dialogue with the statue:

> Why don't you move?
>> Because he wants me to remain immovable.
> What use are you there, what do you gain by being so?
>> It is not for my profit that I am here, it is to serve and obey my master.
> But you do not see him.
>> No, but he sees me, and takes pleasure in seeing me where he has put me.
> But would you not like to have movement, to go nearer to him?
>> Certainly not, except when he might command me.
> Don't you want anything then?
>> No; for I am where my master has placed me.[36]

De Sales concludes with the exclamation, "My God! daughter, what a good prayer it is, and good way to keep in the presence of God."[37]

The soul desires to love, so she loves to desire. What is the first request of the Bride in the Song of Songs? "Let him kiss me with the kisses of his mouth!" Practice for Paradise. No kiss except the one from the infinite God will be sweet enough to satisfy the bride's desire. "The infinite good makes desire reign in possession and possession in desire, finding a way to satiate desire by a holy presence."[38]

---

36. Ibid., 333. This is the entire text of the passage; I have only inserted line breaks to emphasize a format of question and answer.

37. Ibid.

38. De Sales, *Treatise on the Love of God*, 178.

11

The End of Desire

THE PUN IN THE TITLE is intentional. It is meant to refer to both a conclusion and a cessation. Death is the end of desire, as in its conclusion, purpose, and completion; death is also the end of desire, as in its termination, discontinuance, and cessation. We only desire what we do not possess; when we come into possession, it is the end of desire. So desire belongs to the realm of pilgrimage that ends at death, at which time desire will be no longer applicable, and no longer necessary. Death is the gate to what desire hoped for. "The true lover desires to be with his beloved. We cannot see God while we remain here on earth, hence the saints have yearned for death so that they might go and behold their beloved Lord, face to face. 'Oh, that I might die and behold thy beautiful face!' sighed St. Augustine. And St. Paul: '*Having a desire to be dissolved and to be with Christ*'" (Phil 1:23).[1]

Death is the gateway to heaven: therefore desire entirely changes our attitude toward the gate. We have been told what to expect on the other side of death, and it is what we have desired all along, so the meaning of death is changed for the desirous person. The Kingdom we have been waiting for is just around the corner, moments away. Wait, there is more. The Kingdom is coming for us, and "we ask for it every day in the 'Our Father.' We must all ask that God's 'kingdom come.' So we must all wish for it, since prayer is only the heart's desire, and since that kingdom can only come for us through our death."[2]

The Kingdom comes, and the keeper of Hades surrenders his

---

1. Alphonsus de Liguori, *Uniformity with God's Will* (Rockford, IL: TAN Books and Publishers, Inc., 1977), 28.
2. Fénelon, *Christian Perfection*, 105.

keys, the thief turns into a messenger, the terror becomes a door-way, the face of death has changed ever since Christ stared it down at the tomb outside Jerusalem. The soul that desires righteousness is no longer panicked at the face of death, because she seeks the Lord, and death is servant to that desire. Joy attracts, and clarified joy (joy that has been cleansed of impurities) attracts all the more forcefully. "The desire which precedes enjoyment, sharpens and intensifies the feeling of it, and by how much the desire was more urgent and pow-erful, by so much more agreeable and delicious is the possession of the thing desired. Oh! my dear Theotimus, what pleasure will man's heart take in seeing the face of the Divinity, a face so much desired, yea a face the only desire of our souls?"[3]

Death is not frightening if one's fear is of the Lord. The fear of the Lord is the beginning of wisdom (Ps 111:10), and such wisdom is also "a just cause for glory to all those who are penetrated by it. It is a source of joy, and a crown of gladness. Yes; the fear of the Lord does indeed bring joy to the heart of the just."[4] *Gaudete!* The soul of a just person will be crowned. "How beautiful the sight if we could see with the eyes of some sublime intelligence, how this desire of God is the whole beauty and the whole order of His vast creation, drawing onwards to Himself.... It is this desire which saves and justifies, which crowns and glorifies. It is this love which is height-ened and made more exquisite by the tremulousness of holy fear."[5]

Eager desire for the one waiting on the other side of the door changes how we go through the door. Most of the world thinks the important thing is to manage the business of this life, and only worry about the soul as an after-thought. Salvation of the soul is treated as a final clean-up, a last-minute improvement, a snatching of sacraments before dying. "Of course this is something, and God, in His goodness and mercy, accepts even this little measure of good will.... But it is certainly not God's idea of what a human life should be, or what a good death is. A death of this kind of a stum-

3. De Sales, *Treatise on the Love of God*, 140.
4. Ambrose de Lombez, *A Treatise on the Joy of the Christian Soul* (London: S. Anselm's Society, 1894), 155.
5. Faber, *Creator and the Creature*, 216.

bling into, not the opening of, a door into eternity. To stumble into a house is not a mode of entrance that is very becoming."[6] Christianity, to the contrary, thinks one "makes death," and how one does so is an important accomplishment. Death is the great, decisive moment of salvation or damnation: "to every one the *end* comes, and with the end comes that decisive moment on which depends a happy or a wretched eternity."[7] Eternity is contingent on a temporal moment. "In the space of a few hours will be given me, either Life eternal, or death for evermore."[8] Death changes the perspective on life retrospectively: "At the hour of death, all the glory of everything that is worldly vanishes away, applause, amusements, pomps, and grandeur. Great secret of death! which makes us see that which the lovers of the world do not see. Fortunes which have been envied, the grandest dignities, the proudest triumphs, lose all their splendor when they are reviewed from the bed of death."[9] There are no practice runs, and no do-overs: "Only one trial is accorded thee."[10] There are no do-overs of any of the moments leading up to it, either. Every moment is pregnant, waiting to give birth to something eternal.

The preacher says in Ecclesiastes 11:3, "If a tree falls to the south or to the north, in the place where the tree falls, there it will lie." The tree lies where it falls, as does a life, so pay attention to which way you are leaning now.

> Consider that thou art this tree of the parable here spoken of. If when cut down thou fallest to the south, thou shalt keep to the south; if to the north, to the north thou shalt keep. Thou shalt have no hope of ever changing thy position. Either for ever a king upon a throne, or for ever a slave in a dungeon; either for ever in joy, or for ever in sorrow; either for ever glorious, or for ever

6. Edward Leen, *What is Education?* (New York: Sheed and Ward, 1944), 276–77.

7. Liguori, *Way of Salvation and of Perfection*, 197.

8. Luis de Granada, *Considerations on the Mysteries of the Faith* (London: Joseph Masters, 1862), 75.

9. Alphonsus de Liguori, *Preparation for Death* (Philadelphia: J.B. Lippincott & Co., 1869), 17.

10. Martin von Cochem, *The Four Last Things: Death, Judgment, Hell, Heaven* (New York: Benziger Brothers, 1899), 31.

infamous.... If thou art all anxious to know on which side thou
shalt fall, thou canst easily ascertain. See to which side thou art
now leaning.[11]

Our soul's desire is a tendency (*tendentia*: inclination, leaning)
either toward God or away from God. The prospect of falling with
finality, conclusively and decisively, without further chances to
repent, should make us correct our leanings now. How? Follow a
gardener's advice: "This is the way to train a weak sapling. If you
desire to make it grow straight when it leans to the left, you must
bend it further to the right than is absolutely necessary."[12] That is
why the ascetical tradition often says one should refrain even from
what is permitted. Asceticism is virtue practiced with supereroga-
tion—beyond the obligations of the law. "Wouldst thou as in duty
bound root out some hatred from thy heart? Practise some acts of
love which are not of obligation, as for instance, to pray for him
who has offended thee, to speak well of him, to treat him kindly,
even to do him some little service unobserved."[13] Overcompensate
when straightening the sapling so it corrects its bend and grows
straight.

Death tests the sincerity of desire. More times than we like to
admit we find ourselves *saying*, with words in the mouth, that we
would like to serve God, to be devout, to be holy *if* "one could serve
God, please others, and satisfy oneself at the same time"; *if* one
could "find as much readiness, as much pleasure to fast, to pray, to
read books of piety as I find at gambling and at the theatre"; *if* "that
could be done without difficulty, without care, without pressure."[14]
A person often has enough desire to wish he was forced to practice
the good, but not enough desire actually to welcome it. Are such
desires seriously formed? "Do we really dare make this feeble excuse
at death, when our Judge criticizes us for our negligence? I really
would have wanted, if I could have? What are you saying, if you
could have? And what was there then of impossibility in the practice

11. Segneri, *The Manna of the Soul*, vol. 1, 7–8.
12. Ibid., 35.
13. Ibid., 34.
14. De la Colombière, *Sermons*, 93.

of the most perfect piety? Has there never been either a male or female saint in your state or temperament?"[15]

Death will concentrate desire, the way a magnifying glass concentrates light to the point of a burning ray. We should go into it with the predominant and abiding desire of an entire lifetime. As we can only die once, we can only live once.

> We die only once, and from thence we conclude, that we must die in a proper state, because there is no longer a possibility of returning, to repair, by a second death, the evil of the first. In like manner, we only once exist, such and such moments: we cannot return upon our steps, and, by commencing a new road, repair the errors and faults of our first path; in like manner, every moment of our life which we sacrifice becomes a point fixed for eternity; that moment lost, shall change no more: it shall eternally be the same; it will be recalled to us, such as we had passed it, and will be marked with that ineffable stamp.[16]

We know (in the back of our minds, anyway) that this end is waiting, and we should purposefully direct ourselves toward it. "The great business of our whole life is to secure this happy eternity; and else can secure it but a good death. This is the necessary gate, through which we must pass to eternal life: if we think of arriving at it by any other way, we shall miss the road. A good death, then, must be the study and business of our whole life: our whole life ought to be a preparation for it."[17]

Desire for God changes the experience of death for the believer, and gives it a different condition. The soul is calm. Even the intensified contrition that death can force upon a soul can be met with peace. "As thou now dost truly desire and try to please Him and art now sorry to have offended Him, be sure that at thy departure from this world He will receive thee not harshly but with loving-kindness. . . . There thou wilt be certain of salvation and future hap-

15. Ibid., 94.

16. John-Baptist Massillon, *Sermons by John-Baptist Massillon, Complete in One Volume* (London: Printed for Thomas Tegg, 1839), 104.

17. Richard Challoner, *Considerations Upon Christian Truths and Christian Duties* (Philadelphia: Eugene Cummisky, 1874), 12.

piness, and thou wilt be there gladly rather than here in this world."[18] The more intense the desire for the new aeon, the gladder the departure from the old. The more severe the remorse over lost opportunities to glorify God, the happier the entrance to an eternity spent in this occupation.

Desire can change death from an experience suffered into an action performed. Here are two actions, among many. First, "death is the best penance which we could do. Our sins will be purged more purely and wiped out more effectively by our death than by all our penances. It will also be as sweet for men of goodwill as it will be bitter for the wicked."[19] Second, death can be turned into an act of sacrifice. The lifetime of a desire to serve God should be concentrated by death to enkindle a martyr's sacrifice.

> I desire the grace granted to so many martyrs, to die for Thy love. But if I am unworthy of so great a grace, grant at least, my Lord, that I may sacrifice my life to Thee, together with my entire will, by accepting the death which Thou sendest me. Lord, I desire this grace; I desire to die with the intention of honoring and pleasing Thee thereby: and from this moment I sacrifice my life to Thee; and I offer Thee my death, when or wheresoever it may take place.[20]

Desire, we have said, is a will, a longing, an intention, and an aspiration for an object. The higher the object, the greater the desire; the nearer the object, the more intense the desire. Its intensity draws from the personal Parousia about to happen: Christ is coming for a soul.

In its finality, death can be considered a judgment—an unavoidable judgment—because the concluding moment draws the curtain on a soul's struggle. This life is occupied with the struggle against self-love, from which springs the three temptations identified by Saint John: the lust of the flesh, the lust of the eyes, and the pride of life (1 Jn 2:16). They function as temptations because our inclina-

---

18. Blosius, *Comfort for the Fainthearted*, 93.
19. Fénelon, *Christian Perfection*, 104–5.
20. De Liguori, *The Holy Eucharist*, 162.

tion is to delight ourselves in the temptation, and "this rises from the condition of our nature, which so earnestly loves good that it is subject to be enticed by anything that has a show of good, and temptation's hook is ever baited with this kind of bait."[21] It may be what the world calls honor, or some sensual attraction, or some worldly gain. These temptations will be extinguished after the flesh dies, and the light of the eye goes out, and opportunities for advancing self-esteem are no more, but one struggles until one's death date with a simultaneous wish to give in to them, and to be rid of them. They are accompanied by the devil's collateral temptation to postpone the existential decision until later, hence the interior vacillation we feel. It will last until death, and it will not get any easier at death.

> That soul wishes and does not wish. It feels that God ought to be obeyed, that the inspirations of grace ought to be followed, but the heart sinks, the hands fall inertly, and it remains just where it was. No resolution, no generous determination is taken. There are sacrifices to be made in the heart, in daily life, in old established habits, but that soul says; "I cannot:" it stands wavering, and finally draws back. How long will this paralyzing condition last? Till when? Until death, perhaps! My children, delay does not remove obstacles, it diminishes no difficulties.[22]

The harassment of temptation would go on forever if a stop were not put to it. Death forces desire's choice, and death is a servant of God in this sense. The reason the spiritual tradition counsels attentiveness to death is so one will not delay dealing with this paralysis. The terminus conditions the route a life takes. The Bride awaits the return of her Bridegroom while she is in a state of fragility. She lives on a desire for purity, the way the Israelites lived on manna in the wilderness.

> Will she ever offend her Spouse? Perhaps; though sincere, she is so frail! though she lives, she is so tempted! But if she forgets herself,

21. De Sales, *Treatise on the Love of God*, 154.
22. De Ravignan, *Conferences on the Spiritual Life*, 137.

if she turns aside, if she falls, hardly is the fault perceived, but
drowned in so many tears, that she appears afterwards to be still
more beautiful than if she had never wept.

All contributes to render her pure, and she takes care to make
all work together for this end. Purity attracts her, a universal
purity, a Divine purity; she feels that here no excess is possible,
and she will never attain to that purity which she has desired. She
lives, then, on desire, on aspiration; her peace is her labour.[23]

Desire allows a premortal taste of the postmortal state. Death draws
a terminal line, but a desire living on aspiration can already begin to
borrow now from the beatitude promised then. It is as though
desire makes a small opening in the dam wherein the soul tastes
some of heaven's sweet water even though currently swimming in a
saltwater sea.

What most concerns a thing is its end. The philosophers knew
this. Aristotle called the end the *first of principles*, because it regulates all.

"Look at an archer," says he, "and observe how the movements of
his eyes, his arms, his whole body, tend only to his desired end.
The end is the cause of causes, because it puts causes in action,
and, as the first mover, it gives them their bent, and because all
employ themselves for it." So, the efficacious intention and resolution one has to attain an end, necessarily include the use of all
suitable means. This we see in a sick person, who refuses no rem-
edy which is likely to restore his health. Hence the search for, and
the application of, means always bear proportion to the affection
with which an end is desired.[24]

We might conclude that a soul is *pulled* into heaven, not *pushed* in.
Desire beckoning is more powerful than morality pushing. Mount
Zion is scaled according to the affection one has for it. The expedi-
ents, methods, and practices of the spiritual life are done in proportion to the desire one has for the end, which is union with God. Of
course, certain arrangements will have to be made in the order of

23. Gay, *The Christian Life and Virtues*, vol. 2, 277–78.
24. Saint-Jure, *The Spiritual Man*, 195.

spiritual tasks, and they will vary for different souls according to God's providence. The order comes from a sort of spiritual prudence. But in all these tasks, and in all these arrangements, the end is the organizing principle. The end of desire (on the other side of death) will give direction to the present work (on this side of death).

There is another name for what lies on the other side of death: perfection, meaning a state of being finished, complete, full, lacking in no way. The soul lives in expectation of its own perfection, and "how happy are they who, living in expectation, do not grow weary of waiting!"[25] The sinner is imperfect; the *converted sinner* lives in hope for perfection on the other side of death. "We cannot be all we wish on this side the grave. But we can get on towards it, by means of love."[26] God is pleased with success, but he is also pleased with striving. "Let him not imagine that he is not pleasing to God because he is not yet perfect, for he is highly acceptable to God if only from his heart he desires and with all diligence strives to become more perfect; and happy will he be if, engaged in this kind of combat, he goes out of this life."[27] Most of us are overtaken by death too soon for our perfection to be fulfilled. We live in Zeno's paradox, which said that we can never cross a boundary because the distance to it can always be divided in half, the further half never being traversed. In order to cross death's boundary, we must desire something on the other side of it. "You will say to God, 'Thine eyes did see my imperfect being,' and yet 'in Thy book all are written.' Who are meant by 'all'? Certainly all those in whom is found the true desire of advance. For if those who are truly desiring to advance are overtaken by death, what is wanting in them will be made perfect."[28]

Advance without ceasing, because God will reward the high-water mark of the love we gave him up until the point of death, and miraculously change our concupiscence from earthly to heavenly.

25. Francis de Sales, *The Sermons of St. Francis de Sales on Our Lady*, Kindle edition (Charlotte, NC: TAN Books, 2013), 123.

26. Faber, *All for Jesus*, 316.

27. Blosius, *A Book of Spiritual Instruction: Institutio Spiritualis*, 20.

28. Blosius, *Comfort for the Fainthearted*, 38.

O glorious constraints of this heavenly concupiscence! It is a love which makes us not only desire God, but desire Him supremely above all things. It makes us desire Him only, Him always, and Him intensely; and it allures us with untyrannical exclusiveness to seek Him in all things here, and to long for Him as being Himself our sole sufficient and magnificent Hereafter. By this love both high and low are saved; and without it was none ever saved that was saved. . . . [A]nd the death-bed patient who has never known a higher love will be saved by this alone.[29]

Children run on the dry sidewalk to build up speed when they want to slide on the ice where they cannot run. Run through this life, and go past the finish line with all the desire you can build up. "We read of a very holy Jesuit, that he revealed to his companions that he had been detained for some time in purgatory, because in his death the desire of God had not been sufficiently prominent."[30] The present desire will affect the future reward. If the spiritual beginner exercises his soul daily, strives to join himself to God through internal conversations and loving desires, perseveres in self-denial and mortification, and is never discouraged by his frequent falls and innumerable distractions, then

he will certainly arrive at perfection and mystical union, if not in this life at least in death. And even if he should not arrive at it then, most certainly he will arrive at it after the death of the body.

For in eternity he will enjoy that perfect union in greater or less degree, according to the greater or less intensity of the desire with which he sought it here below. God will bestow upon us an eternal reward for our good desires, even though in this pilgrimage we never attain to what we desire.[31]

Be like the archer who aims higher than the target to counteract the influence of gravity on the arrow's flight. Or be like the archer who tries "to draw with a strong hand the bow of good desire, that no moment may pass by in which he does not gain God more perfectly.

29. Faber, *Creator and the Creatures*, 216.
30. Faber, *Spiritual Conferences*, 121.
31. Blosius, *A Book of Spiritual Instruction: Institutio Spiritualis*, 90–91.

For God will reward for ever the true desires of his soul, even if what he desires he should never obtain in this life."[32]

The reward may not come until later, but tardiness cannot discourage a desire that is true. It will come soon enough, says the soul, because it will come when God chooses.

> Let us remain in expectation regarding the attainment, sooner or later, of our goal, leaving that to Divine Providence, who will take care to console us, as He did St. Simeon, at the time He has destined to do so. And even if this should be only at the hour of our death, that ought to be enough for us, provided that we fulfill our duty by always doing what lies in our power to do. We will always have soon enough what we desire when we have it when it pleases God to give it to us.[33]

Philosophy is love of wisdom (*philos sophia*) and the Christians were called true philosophers, because "true wisdom consists in knowing how to order the whole conduct of our life to the attainment of our last end."[34] Christians know the noble design that is holding the universe together, in both life and death.

> The design itself is so noble and the end so divine, that a soul cannot begin to aspire unto it too soon, nor take too much pains to procure it. Yea, the very desire and serious pursuance of so heavenly a design brings so great blessings to the soul, and puts her in so secure a way of salvation, though she should never perfectly attain unto it in this life, that there is none so old nor so overgrown with ill habits but ought to attempt, and with perseverance pursue it, being assured that at least after death he shall for his good desire and endeavours be rewarded with the crown due to contemplatives. For it is enough for a soul to be in the way, and to correspond to such enablements as she hath received; and then in what degree of spirit soever she dies, she dies according to the will and ordination of God.[35]

32. Blosius, *Comfort for the Fainthearted*, 71.
33. De Sales, *Sermons on Our Lady*, Kindle edition, 123–24.
34. Segneri, *The Manna of the Soul*, vol. 1, 18.
35. Baker, *Holy Wisdom*, 51.

The only knowledge that could order the whole conduct of life would be a knowledge of our last end, and how to attain it. God is our last end; he has revealed to his children how to attain eternal life. "If wisdom is God, as St. Austin says, the true philosopher, that is, he who loves wisdom, is he who loves God; and as wisdom is personally attached to the Son of God, it follows that the true philosopher is properly he who loves the Son of God. Hence, by a philosopher, the Holy Fathers understand a Christian."[36] The philosopher's stone that could change lead into gold is as nothing compared to the philosopher's stone that Christianity offers by Peter as rock of the Church: "The true philosopher's stone is submission to the order of God, which changes into pure gold all their occupations, all their weariness, all their sufferings."[37] Crosses are turned into glory, love works for another's welfare without envy, abnegation denies self the right to rule, the ministry of Christ is shared with members of his body. "If we can perform our actions in this manner—if we can find this treasure hidden in the fields, this treasure so exposed, and yet so hid at the same time; how rich should we become, and how soon should we be perfect? This is truly the philosopher's stone, which changes iron and brass into gold; because how mean soever any action is of itself, it renders it very precious."[38]

We do not know well enough what we really desire, so we beg God to "tear me away from myself, and I will be fully yours. What do I have to do on earth? What can I desire in this valley of tears, in which evil seems to triumph and in which good is so imperfect? . . . I love nothing that I see. I do not want to love myself at all. My only desire is to love your coming."[39] Turning egocentricity into theocentricity is a miracle of the Holy Spirit, and it begins with abnegation. Then, after death, a person shall be rewarded with the crown of life. "It is called the crown of life, to distinguish it from crowns

36. Saint-Jure, *Knowledge and Love of God*, vol. 1, 84.
37. De Caussade, *Abandonment to Divine Providence*, 13–14.
38. Alphonsus Rodríguez (Alfonso), *The Practice of Christian and Religious Perfection*, vol. 1, 128.
39. Fénelon, *The Complete Fénelon*, 231.

bestowed by men, which wither and die," and it has been promised by God a thousand and a thousand times:

> All Scripture is full of it. . . . If the Lord gave thee but one glimpse of the crown which He has prepared for thee, how great would be thy courage, thy alacrity, thy joy! But He, for thy own greater profit, does not choose to show it; He wishes thee to trust in Him. Indeed, how canst thou ask to see it, when it has not yet been made? It is for thyself to make it. According to the measure of thy sufferings, shall be thy crown. . . . "He promised it in return;" for this crown is not a gift, it is a recompense.[40]

In the Canticle is a song of the Marriage Feast that John of the Cross overhears. The Bride is occupied—we might even say preoccupied—with love, and goes to an appointed place. "There Thou wilt show me / What my soul desired."[41] The soul is always desiring, but does not always know what. The magnificence of the crown could not fit into the size of the desire, so the desire had to be confounded and go to a higher place. John interprets.

> This desire or aim of the soul is equality in love with God, the object of natural and supernatural desire. He who loves cannot be satisfied if he does not feel that he loves as much as he is beloved. And when the soul sees that in the transformation in God, such as is possible in this life . . . it cannot equal the perfection of that love wherewith God loves it, it desires the clear transformation of glory.[42]

The reason we desire the clear transformation of heaven is because on this side of death we cannot love God as much as we want to love him, liturgize God as much as we want to glorify him, offer as much as we want to sacrifice. How different death is for the one who desires Christ's Parousia from one who is indifferent to Christ's presence. The former joins Christ's victory with acts of praise and desire.

40. Segneri, *The Manna of the Soul*, vol. 1, 26.
41. John of the Cross, *A Spiritual Canticle* in *The Complete Works of Saint John of the Cross*, vol. 2 (London: Longman, Green, Longman, Roberts & Green, 1864), 11.
42. Ibid., 196.

Now look what these acts of Praise and Desire will do for you. They will take the world out of your hearts, and make its pleasures look small and dull to you. . . . All things seem easy which are for Jesus, all things welcome which are steps to Him. . . . "Oh, but how sweet to see for the first time the Sacred Humanity of Jesus!" This is what Praise and Desire bring us to.[43]

Even death is welcome, since it is the last step here, and the first step toward seeing the Sacred Humanity of the one we have earnestly desired.

43. Faber, *All for Jesus*, 315–16.

Appendix:
The First to Live the Christian Life

ONE DOES NOT KNOW where prejudices come from. That's why they are called prejudices: they are "pre-judgments," assessments made ahead of the facts, evaluations concluded before experience with the situation.[1] Therefore I cannot tell you where my prejudice against post-Reformation Catholic spiritual writers came from. It did not come from a study I had made of something lacking in Lallemant; I was not confused over details in de Sales; I had not set Bérulle and Barbanson and Blosius side by side for comparison; and yet none of the Latin spiritual writers exerted any pull on me. I have read some patristic authors, east and west; I have read eastern Orthodox authors, ancient and modern; I have read some western medieval authors, scholastic and monastic; and, naturally, I have been forced to read more than a few modern theologians for my academic duties. But the Catholic spiritual writers from 1500 to 1900 seemed to me fussy, dramatic, and overly severe while they obsessed over the cross, suffering, and mortification. They felt like a literary version of baroque architecture, and held no charm for me.

However, they have been infiltrating my thoughts for the past decade. It began when Fénelon smuggled himself into my office in a box of books a friend gave to me; the letters of Libermann seemed like they could have arrived in the post that morning; St-Sulpice was a landscape as foreign as the moon, but Olier waved me in; and after that, it was a matter of friends introducing me to other friends. I had been fishing from one side of the boat and had been told to cast my net on the other side, and I've barely been able to pull in my haul. Academic study consists of throwing nets according to what one plans to catch: historians cast a net across a time period, and systematicians do it across themes. I am fishing in this sea with a net

1. This was delivered as the Kenrick Lecture at Kenrick-Glennon Seminary in Shrewsbury, Missouri, October 2023.

I am calling *theologians of abnegation*, because it identifies a flavor I detect in this writing. Like Jean Grou, these authors speak of *renunciation*: "This very necessary renunciation, of which the fruits are so sweet and the reward so great, is the great stumbling-block of the Gospel."[2] Like John Croiset they speak of *mortification*: "Mortification is so necessary for the perfect love of Jesus Christ, that it is the first lesson that Jesus Christ himself gives to those who wish to be his disciples."[3] Like Jean Baptiste Saint-Jure they speak of *self-denial* and *nothingness*: "Behold what self-denial effects in a man! This is why it is called 'annihilation,' a state of nothingness."[4] And they speak incessantly about crosses, like St Margaret Mary Alacoque, who says our self-will and self-love will hate crosses, but their acceptance is necessary because "the cross is the throne of the true lovers of Jesus Christ."[5]

These authors take seriously the self-denial that Jesus imposes as a condition for being his follower, according to Mark 8:34, Matthew 16:24, and Luke 9:23. "If any man would come after me, let him *deny himself* and take up his cross daily and follow me." Abnegation is central to the gospel Christ proclaimed. Jean-Jacques Olier says the reason "our Lord put abnegation in his gospel as the first step we must take in the Christian life" is that "self-centeredness, being filled with the self, blocks Jesus Christ and the fullness of his divine life from entering us."[6] Libermann insists that abnegation is not our idea, but the Lord's. "It is not I who preach abnegation, it is our Lord himself who has set down the conditions under which he will receive us as his followers.... No doctrine has ever found more

---

2. Jean Grou, *The School of Jesus Christ* (London: Burns Oates & Washbourne, Ltd., 1932) 34.

3. John Croiset, *Devotion to the Sacred Heart of Jesus* (London: Burns & Lambert, 1863), 77–78.

4. Jean Baptiste Saint-Jure, *The Religious: A Treatise on the Vows and Virtues of the Religious State*, vol. 1 (New York: P. O'Shea, 1882), 573.

5. Margaret Mary Alacoque, *The Letters of St Margaret Mary Alacoque: Apostle of the Sacred Heart*, Kindle edition (Charlotte, NC: TAN Books, 2012), letter 16.

6. Jean-Jacques Olier, *Introduction to the Christian Life and Virtues*, in *Bérulle and the French School*, ed. William M. Thompson (New York: Paulist Press, 1989), 262–63.

forceful expressions in the Gospels.... The words of our Savior allow of no quibbling."[7]

The vocabulary surrounding abnegation sounds harsh to our modern ears: *mortification, nothingness, resignation, humiliation, abjection, abandonment, self-detachment,* and *hating the world.* But I think it sounds harsh because we hear it against a limited horizon of morality or psychology, and I propose abnegation must be understood against a more transcendent horizon. That horizon, I submit, is the act of liturgizing a God whose infinite justice and love demands our total worship. "God will have no Sharers,"[8] says Giovanni Bona. And Louis de Granada describes the purified soul as having "but one love, and one desire; so that, whatsoever she loves, it is for the sake of one alone, and this one she loves in all things."[9] Liturgy is an act of love toward the One alone, which puts all other loves in right order. Pure love removes all nourishment from self-love. Worldliness and self-love fade away in the light of Mount Tabor on the liturgical summit because "when our eyes are once cleared up by this heavenly brightness, we discover a new light, which represents things quite different from what they appear to us at first."[10]

So I have made the name of my net more precise by referring to *theologians of liturgical abnegation.* The language of abnegation is founded on liturgy because liturgical abnegation is an act of true adoration, as Abbess Bruyère explains:

The true adorer follows his Master even unto the entire abnegation of himself, practicing to the letter all that our Lord Jesus tells him.... [N]o one can pretend to be an adorer in spirit and in truth if he has not resolutely broken with all idolatry.... To be true adorers we must have destroyed all these idols, we must have

---

7. Francis Libermann, *Instructions for Missionaries* (https://dsc.duq.edu/cgi/viewcontent.cgi?article=1021&context=spiritan-rc), 133.

8. Giovanni Bona, *Manductio ad Coelum: or, a Guide to Eternity* (London: printed for Henry Brome, 1672), 4.

9. Lewis [Luis] de Granada, *The Sinner's Guide* (Philadelphia: Henry McGrath, 1845), 123–24.

10. Ibid., 95.

entirely purified our hearts of them, and have established within ourselves the dwelling place of God.[11]

Idolatry is a problem because, Bona says, we "set up as many Idols as there are Creatures which we love with an inordinate Affection,"[12] and we love many things inordinately. Religion is a virtue because it renders God his due. When asked to whom *latria* should be given, justice answers that only the Uncreated should be worshipped, not a creature. But there is something more serious than worshiping an image (*eidon-latria*), and that is worshiping ourselves: *auto-latria*. Autolatry is more secret and more serious than idolatry because the false god dwells within, and must be cured by self-abnegation if we are to live in this world aright (that is, righteously). Abnegation withdraws our esteem from the created world—and it denies self-esteem outright—because we discover we want to give all reverence to the Creator.

Liturgical abnegation is a conversion of self-glorification into a desire for God's glory alone.

Abnegation simply means the removal of any hindrances to our union with God. But of what does this abnegation consist? The answer to that question would require a lifetime for an individual to discover, and so far two millennia of scholarship has not finished with the question, so I will turn to a cheat sheet from Jean Grou. Here is his descriptive list: abnegation *renounces glory,* to the point of embracing poverty, privation, labor, mortification, suffering, and humiliation; it *renounces repose,* to the point of enduring fatigue, annoyance, contradiction, and calumny; it *renounces reputation,* to the point of being mocked, outraged, and treated as a fool without uttering a word of self-justification; it *renounces a favorable view by the world* and accepts being an object of malediction in the sight of God; it *embraces a humility* that acknowledges the guilt of human sin; and it *renounces sweet consolations* from God, to the point of bitterness, bereavement, and acceptance of death.

---

11. Cécile Bruyère, *Spiritual Life and Prayer According to Holy Scripture and Monastic Tradition* (New York: Benziger Brothers, 1905), 360–61.
12. Giovanni Bona, *Manductio ad Coelum,* 4.

Oh, wait a minute. My mistake. I have been reading from chapter 41 of Jean Grou's book *The Interior of Jesus and Mary*, which is titled "Of the Abnegation of Jesus Christ."[13] He is describing the life of abnegation that Jesus lived. Jesus practiced abnegation! Jesus's life of servanthood, obedience, and redemption was abnegation in action. This idea is startling only if we confine abnegation to sin, and do not associate it with liturgy. The sinner has reason for self-denial, but the liturgist has greater reason for self-denial. Christian abnegation is liturgical, not morbid. It is part and parcel with a purified glorification of the Father by the gracing of the Son and inspiration of the Holy Spirit.

So I put before you, for consideration today, that if the Christian life is one of abnegation, humility, surrender, and denying self and world, then we may say *Jesus is the first one to live that Christian life.* John Eudes says "the Christian life is a continuation of the life of Jesus upon earth" the way "the life of the arm is a continuation and extension of the life of the head."[14] Jesus lived in self-abnegation for the glorification of his Father and the sanctification of man (those are the two purposes of liturgy), and Grou says "he requires nothing of us which he has not practiced in the highest perfection."[15] It allows Charles Gay to be blunt, and refer to Jesus as *the first Christian*: "God and man will go on penetrating one another more and more, uniting the one to the other always still more, and approaching incessantly that ineffable union of which Jesus, the first Christian, says, 'I and my Father are One' (John 10:30)."[16] Louis Bourdaloue says we define a Christian by the characteristics that Jesus exhibited. First he said, "I am not of this world" (Jn 8), and second he said, "I am from above" (Jn 8).[17] These very characteris-

---

13. Jean Grou, *The Interior of Jesus and Mary*, vol. 1 (New York: Benziger Brothers, 1893), 311–21.

14. Quoted in Charles Lebrun, *The Spiritual Teaching of St John Eudes* (London: Sands & Co., 1934), 100.

15. Grou, *Interior of Jesus and Mary*, vol. 1, 311–312.

16. Charles Gay, *The Christian Life and Virtues Considered in the Religious State*, vol. 1 (London: Burnes & Oates, 1878), 51.

17. Louis Bourdaloue, *Sermons, and Moral Discourses, on the Important Duties of Christianity*, vol. 1 (Dublin: James Duffy, 1843), 178.

tics also delineate the Christian: "What, think ye, is a Christian? First, a man, by his profession, separated from the world. Secondly: a man, by his profession, consecrated to God."[18] Jesus asks his disciples if they will drink the cup as he did, love the way he did, accept the cross as he did, live in humility as he did, and depend solely upon the Father as he did.

We adore the Lord when we deny ourselves, says Eudes, because "he himself first did what he asks of you, having given you the perfect example of self-abnegation. While he was on earth, he never acted according to his own desires, but rather he did the will of his Father. He never sought his own satisfaction nor his own interests, but those of his Father. 'For Christ did not please himself' (Rom 15:3)."[19] The disciple should imitate the master, the icon should copy the prototype, the member should image the head, and the Christian should live the life of liturgical abnegation that Jesus lived, which Frederick Faber says was one of oblation, victim, incense, priest, imprisonment, silence, weakness, and poverty.[20] Put succinctly, Bourdaloue can say, "what does he ask of me that he has not already practiced?"[21] To participate in Jesus's liturgy, we must also participate in Jesus's self-abnegation.

At this point I have struggled with whether I have made a distinction without a difference. I refer to Jesus living the first Christian life instead of simply saying we are to "imitate Christ," as the tradition has put it so brilliantly. Is anything to be gained by doing so— approaching the topic from above rather than from below, so to speak? Why concentrate upon Jesus's own liturgical life of abnegation? My answer is that both Christology and anthropology become more profound when Jesus descends nearer to us than we thought he would, and we are called to ascend higher than we thought we

---

18. Bourdaloue, *Sermons and Moral Discourses*, vol. 1, 178.

19. John Eudes, *The Priest: His Dignity and Obligations* (New York: P. J. Kenedy & Sons, 1947), 191.

20. Frederick Faber, *Bethlehem* (London: Thomas Richardson and Son, 1860), 79–83.

21. Louis Bourdaloue, *Spiritual Exercises: Readings for a Retreat of Seven Days. Translated and Abridged from the French of Bourdaloue* (London: Joseph Masters, 1868), 95.

could. Christology is taken more seriously because Jesus does not simply walk ahead of his people in his divinity, leaving us to make inferior copies in our humanity under our own power of imitation. And anthropology is taken more seriously when we learn that deification is our end, but only arrived at through the same abnegation Jesus practiced for the glorification of his Father in heaven.

Henri Brémond offers me some help when he observes a contrast that is not an opposition, but which still makes a difference. He juxtaposes the genius of Ignatius of Loyola with the brilliance of Bérulle, and insists that between the two points of view "there is no opposition, but they are distinct."[22] The first speaks more often of an imitation of Christ, the second far more often about a union with the Incarnate Word. "It may be no more than a question of *nuances* of thought; imitation engenders union and vice versa; yet the two conceptions are and remain different, each ... implying its own particular philosophy."[23]

I will categorize the two schools, or conceptions, as *moral imitation* versus *liturgical abnegation*. They are related, yet, to borrow Brémond's language, one inculcates energy, the other submission and annihilation. Union with the Mystery of the Incarnation is a divine act that we must *bear* and *receive*, and this, concludes Brémond, "is far beyond what the most energetic *askesis* could arrive at. But the Incarnate Word is ready to accomplish it all in us."[24] So this invites us to be alert to our language. "The one school *imitates* Christ, the other *lays bare* the soul, *leaves it* to him, working and moving in him. In the latter case the *askesis* is half-passive, and human activity has no other role than to join itself in absolute self-effacement to the Divine Activity; the term *askesis* is indeed here improperly used; apprenticeship or mystic initiation would be more exact."[25] The reason for adding abnegation to imitation is to move

---

22. Henri Brémond, *A Literary History of Religious Thought in France*, vol. 3: *The Triumph of Mysticism* (London: Society for Promoting Christian Knowledge, 1936), 228.
23. Ibid., 232.
24. Ibid., 111.
25. Ibid., 128.

from transitory ascetical acts to mystical liturgical apprenticeship. This is summed up neatly by François Guilloré:

> But here it is needful to observe that to imitate Christ and to "put on" Christ [are] not one and the same thing. We imitate our Blessed Lord when we try to do the like actions with him, and when, by our own operation, we produce a resemblance or expression of his actions in ourselves, either inwardly or outwardly. But to "put on the Lord Jesus," is to appropriate and apply his actions, so that, as St Paul says, it is no longer you that act, but Christ dwelling in you.[26]

Saying that Jesus is the first to lead the Christian life is intended to affirm that *imitatio Christi* is possible. He lets himself be found in the conditions of his mortal life, says Fénelon, and his mortal life was lived "in solitude, in silence, in poverty and suffering, in persecutions and contumelies, in the cross and in annihilations. . . . To be Christians is to be imitators of Jesus Christ. In what can we imitate him except in his humiliations?"[27] Riddle: How can a human being imitate God? Solution: God becomes a human being. We are not asked to imitate his miracles, says Gaetano de Bergamo, "nor to astonish the world by marvelous enterprises, but to be humble of heart. . . . Innumerable things are worthy of imitation in the Incarnate Son of God, but he only asks us to imitate his humility."[28] We can imitate Christ because his abnegation has made him imitable. He who professes to be a disciple of Jesus should live as he lived, and this we can do because he first lived as he intends us to live. Bona says he can become our lesson because "we learn to be meek and humble after his example. So great, so difficult a thing was lowliness, that we could not learn it, but from the humiliation of the highest."[29]

26. François Guilloré, *Spiritual Guidance* (London: Rivingtons, 1873), 192.
27. François Fénelon, *Christian Perfection* (New York: Harper & Brothers, 1947), 44.
28. Gaetano Maria de Bergamo, *Humility of Heart* (Mandeville, LA: Founding Father Films Publishing, 2015), 2–3.
29. Giovanni Bona, *Precepts and Practical Rules for a Truly Christian Life* (London: Printed by M. Clark, 1678) 66–67.

Jesus is guide of his flock, head of his members, and archetype of his disciples, which is why Bossuet can call Jesus our Model.

> It was the will of our Heavenly Father that the laws imposed upon Christians should in the first place be written in Jesus Christ. We must indeed be formed according to the model set forth in the Gospel, but then that Gospel itself was formed upon Jesus Christ. . . . Though his teaching is indeed our law, yet the primal law is his most holy life. He is truly our Master and our Teacher, but before all things he is our Model.[30]

Didactic Christianity is different from Liturgical Christianity, as moral imitation is different from liturgical abnegation, because the primal law is Jesus's holy life mystically shared with us. This prototype animates his image. Saint-Jure says Jesus sent his disciples into the world (John 7:13) in order "to work and suffer there as I did, that they may be vivified by My Spirit and resemble Me as an image resembles its prototype; for their perfection consists in the resemblance they shall have to Me."[31] He goes on to say we should live (interiorly and exteriorly) according to the pattern which Jesus has given us.

> Our Savior made himself our Model because he loved us. Let us therefore, for love of him, become copies of that Model; let us work continually for this end, so that Jesus may be represented in us, imprinting upon our hearts the features and lineaments of his humility, of his patience, of his obedience.[32]

That's what models are for, Saint-Jure concludes.

> A model always serves a twofold purpose: first, that a copy may be taken from it; and, secondly, that it may condemn that copy if badly made. . . . The reprobation of the wicked will be founded on

30. Bossuet, *Great French Sermons from Bossuet, Bourdaloue, and Massillon*, ed. Denis O'Mahony (London: Sands and Co., 1917), 50.
31. Jean Baptiste Saint-Jure, *Christ Our Teacher* (Baltimore: McCauley & Kilner, 1891), 96.
32. Saint-Jure, *Christ Our Teacher*, 192–93.

their want of resemblance to this Divine Model. And it is for this reason that St John calls them anti-christs.[33]

Jesus is the model for his Church. A model is a preliminary work to serve as a plan from which a final product is to be made: deified persons should be modeled upon this God-Man. Jesus's humanity yielded to the promptings of his divinity in the Hypostatic Union, and we are to become mystic apprentices of his submission to the Father. Charles Gay describes it as Jesus living his divine life under borrowed forms, and in this hypostatic union he is "the finished model of the supernatural state, of the state of grace, of the Christian state, in its substance and in its source."[34]

In what follows I would like to identify three themes proposed by the theologians of liturgical abnegation about Jesus's life of abnegation, as they appear in his kenosis, the cross, and the paschal mystery. Liturgical abnegation will run throughout.

The Incarnation: the Word's kenosis

François Nepveu is speaking for all when he says Christ's very incarnation was an act of annihilation. "He humiliated himself in the Incarnation, even to annihilation, in uniting himself to human nature, in despoiling himself of all his greatness and glory to clothe himself with our weaknesses. He desired to be born of a poor mother, in an abandoned stable, and to be cradled in a manger. He received in his circumcision the work of sin, and the character of the sinner, thus subjecting himself to the greatest of humiliations."[35] Our liturgical abnegation honors his incarnational abnegation. His kenosis was a stripping of glory and submission to a lower state, something Bossuet says we are amazed enough to see in a human being, much less a God.

If it is a spectacle that always strikes us afresh to see *men* remaining content with a naturally low station, it is a far more wonderfully

33. Saint-Jure, *Christ Our Teacher*, 193–94.
34. Gay, *The Christian Life and Virtues*, vol. 1, 21.
35. François Nepveu, *The Spirit of Christianity, or the Conformity of the Christian with Christ* (New York: Edward Dunigan & Brother, 1859), 133.

new thing to see *a God*, stripping Himself of His supreme greatness, come down from the height of His throne and voluntarily
annihilate Himself.... That Son, equal in eternity to the Father,
undertakes to become his Father's servant: that Son, raised infinitely above man, puts himself on an equality with all men. Well,
indeed, may the prophet declare that the Creator has done *a new
thing*: for never before has God had such a subject, or man such a
companion.[36]

Our own entry into Christianity should imitate Christ's entrance
into the world; or, to say it in reverse with Louis de Ponte, "his first
entrance into the world was, as St Cyprian saith, a pattern of our
first entrance into Christian religion, that his disciples might enter
by the way he entered, exercising those virtues which he exercised.
And to this end he left all that the world most loves, and seeks: and
sought after all that which the world abhors and flies."[37] And the
condition of his birth set the pattern of his life: his incarnation set-
tled "the foundation of that evangelical perfection, which he was to
preach."[38]

This theme fascinated Pierre de Bérulle. If *we* were planning salvation history, he thinks we would do it all differently. He imagines
a dialogue wherein we give God advice about how to go about saving the world. First, we would advise, if you are going to become
man, don't use Adam's flesh. "If, by an adorable secret of your love,
you prefer the lowest nature to the highest; do not choose this flesh
drawn from the body of sin.... Create a man apart, not derived
from men, and create a new world and paradise for this new
Adam."[39] Second, if you still insist on going through with this, make
the flesh you take impassible and exempt from the effects of sin.

36. Jacques-Bénigne Bossuet, *Devotion to the Blessed Virgin: Being the Substance
of all the Sermons for Mary's Feasts throughout the Year* (London: Longmans, Green,
and Co., 1899), 70–71.

37. Louis de Ponte, *Meditations on the Mysteries of Our Holy Faith*, vol. 2 (London: Richardson and Son, 1852), 159.

38. Ibid.

39. Pierre de Bérulle, *Discourses on the State and Grandeurs of Jesus: The Ineffable Union of the Deity with Humanity* (Washington, DC: The Catholic University of
America Press, 2023), 254.

"But at least—O great God!—since you will and you deign to take on human flesh, flesh derived from Adam, honor this flesh, raise this humanity up in its state, condition, and qualities, in this life already! Let it not be passible! Let it not suffer!"[40] And third, think of creation, and what it desires. "If it could speak, its voice and clamor would reach the heavens, petitioning the eternal Father for its Liberator, for deliverance and release from this abject condition."[41]

But the Creator has very different thoughts, concludes de Bérulle. "He wills that his Son be abased to our wretchedness. He wills that he bear our cross and sins. And he wills that we see the one who is life, our life, dead on a cross and in a grave, and that in his death we may regain life."[42] Therefore, the way the Incarnation actually happens is that "God, all-powerful and eternal God, wills to join himself to nothingness and unite himself to man and become flesh as man is. . . . In addition he wills to take on the flesh descended from sinners and covered with the darkness of sin, and to bear it heavy-laden with grief, suffering, and the marks of sin; for the flesh of Jesus is truly flesh descended from sinners."[43] Jesus is the first New Man—the first man of a new race—and the head communicates his life to his members.

De Ponte says the Incarnation honors precisely those virtues that accompany abnegation. In a word, the Son of God becomes man so he can practice human abnegation. Since the Son, as God, could not suffer "poverty, tears, and persecutions, he would descend from heaven, and make himself man, to practise the acts of these excellent virtues, and to discover to us the divine treasures enclosed within them."[44] Happiness depends upon knowing how to live, and Frederick Faber says it was so important for man to know "how to behave himself as a creature, that it was necessary the Creator should take a created nature, and come Himself to show him how to

---

40. Ibid., 256.
41. Ibid., 257.
42. Ibid., 258–59.
43. Ibid., 254.
44. Louis de Ponte, *Meditations on the Mysteries of Our Holy Faith*, vol. 3 (London: Richardson and Son, 1852), 124.

wear it. . . . Thus one of the many known reasons of the sublime mystery of the Incarnation was that the Creator Himself might show the creature how he should behave as a creature."[45]

God shows us how to wear our human nature. He models our humanity for us, even if it is an impudent thought, as Ullathorne notes: "It is an audacious thought, but who knows the power, or the goodness, or the condescension of God? . . . [W]hat if God were actually to come, as He has so often been imagined, in a mortal form, and to live with us, and to teach us what we are, and what we ought to be?"[46] An audacious thought that God would actually come to be first what we ought to be, to live first how we ought to live. Grace perfects nature; God perfects man; God becomes man to do first what man must do. "The life of humility, poverty, and self-abnegation is the most perfect of human lives," concludes Ullathorne, because it is lived "as depending on God alone, and as setting the things of this mortal life at their true value compared with the things of eternity."[47] Jesus is the first to live the perfect human life.

We copy Jesus's kenosis as if in a mirror when we adapt his abnegation to ourselves. He abnegated a glory that was truly his, and we must abnegate a glory we have falsely claimed. He has a true glory, we have a false pride. He denies himself the glory rightfully his, we must deny the boasting we wrongfully publish. We have not a glory like his to deny, but do we have a self-will that needs annihilation, which we must accomplish if we want to follow his example of having no desire except for the Father. To subdue our pride we imitate the one who had no pride to subdue, but who embraced humiliation and suffering nonetheless.

The Cross and Penitence

De Estella calls humility the "sweet spouse" of Jesus. "He came into the world with it, he lived in the world with it, he carried it with

45. Frederick Faber, *The Creator and the Creature, or, The Wonders of Divine Love* (London: Thomas Richardson and Son, 1858), 63.

46. William Ullathorne, *The Groundwork of the Christian Virtues* (London: Burns & Oates, 1890), 252–53.

47. Ibid., 196.

him up to the cross, and he died with it, never suffering it to depart from him."[48] Since this humility was practiced throughout Jesus's whole life, Nepveu challenges those who claim to be Christian to measure their abnegation against his:

> Christ was humble, thou art vain and proud; he shrank from honours, thou seekest them eagerly; he was gentle and meek, thou canst bear nothing; he forgave the heaviest wrongs, thou not the lightest; he loved his very murderers, thou not even thy brethren; he embraced a life of poverty, thou covetest the world's goods; his was a painful, self-denying life, thine is easy and self-indulgent; he denied himself the most innocent pleasures, thou allowest thyself the most dangerous and perchance, licentious; he was *obedient unto death, even the death of the cross,* thou wilt not obey in the easiest matters; he sought his own pleasure in nothing, thou in everything. Alas! the death of Christ will avail thee nothing if his life hath not been thy rule. His merits will not profit if thou hast not profited by his example. He cannot be thy Saviour if he has not been thy Pattern.[49]

Why were such humiliations accepted by Jesus? Grou says they "were decreed for him in the eternal counsels" and "he joyfully accepted and endured them." Why? "To glorify his Father and to expiate our pride." (There are those twin purposes of liturgy again.) To be his disciple "we should aspire to love the contempt and humiliation he so dearly cherished, and endeavor to view it as the livery, the ornament, and the distinguishing characteristic of a servant of Christ."[50]

The humiliation Jesus accepted is so deep that these theologians can even say Jesus practiced penitence—not for his sins, of course, but for ours. His consciousness of sin was very different from ours, notes Bourdaloue. "We bear our sins with haughtiness, and, far from feeling any confusion because of them, we glory in them, we

---

48. Diego de Estella, *The Contempt of the World and the Vanities Thereof* (1622), 329.

49. François Nepveu, *The Hidden Life* (London: J. Masters, 1871), 93–94.

50. Jean Grou, *The Interior of Jesus and Mary*, vol. 2 (Dublin: James Duffy, 1847), 64.

praise ourselves, and are puffed up because of them, we triumph in them. Yet this is what obliged the Divine Word to empty himself of his glory. The shameful insolence of some sinners could be repaired by nothing less than the humiliation of Jesus Christ."[51] God hates sin. Man should hate sin, but he doesn't. None but the God-Man could "feel a grief [over sin] corresponding to its malignity," none but the Incarnate One could measure the proportion between man's sin and God's holiness, "and consequently there was none but he who could make us learn to hate sin. It is for that very purpose that he came into the world . . . thus giving us the most excellent example of Christian penitence."[52] Incredibly, faith presents us not only with the spectacle of a suffering God, but also a penitent God. "When I say a penitent God," Bourdaloue concludes, "I mean a God touched with the most fervent contrition for the sin of man and satisfying for man's sin at His own expense and with all the rigor of justice—two obligations which the God-Man took upon himself from the first moment of his birth and which, as we shall see, he fulfilled perfectly at the time of his Passion."[53] Pope Leo the Great called the Passion of the Son of God the universal penance, the perfect penance, consummated for all the sins of men.

The penitence Jesus did not need to do, he felt; for sins he had not committed, he wept; for an alienation he did not know, he sorrowed. This was part of assuming our human nature and suffering for our sins. In Nepveu's words,

> Although he knew not sickness or infirmity, he condescended to take the remedies we so much need, that he might take from them all their bitterness, or at least abate our unwillingness to take them. . . . Although he was innocent—although he was holiness itself—he submitted to the severest punishment that was ever inflicted on the greatest criminals, in order that he might teach us to receive in a proper spirit the light punishment, which God's

51. Louis Bourdaloue, *Eight Sermons for Holy Week and Easter* (London: Wells Gardner, Darton & Co., 1884), 83–84.

52. Ibid., 84.

53. Bourdaloue, in *Great French Sermons from Bossuet, Bourdaloue, and Massillon*, 30.

mercy rather than his justice imposes upon us in place of the eternal pains which we have justly merited.[54]

It was such a horror for sin that moved love to come down. Eudes says that "Jesus Christ entertained in himself two widely opposed sentiments: one of infinite love for his Father and for you, the other of extreme hatred for everything opposed to his Father's glory and our salvation, namely, for sin."[55] We must continue those same sentiments in ourselves: loving God with all our might and hating sin with all our strength.

Grou protests that what disturbed Jesus in the Garden of Gethsemane was not the prospect of shame and torture on the cross; it was the experience of the sorrow mankind should have before God Almighty. As perfect man, Jesus had this sorrow perfectly. In Gethsemane, "his heart must needs experience a sorrow which should equal the enormity of so many iniquities, and correspond to the sovereign Majesty of God which was insulted by them; it must be that the innocent soul of Jesus should feel, by the sharpness of his grief, the hatred which God bears to sin, in order that from his heart to ours a piercing repentance might pass, a bitter sorrow, a detestation of sin, which should be the essential characteristic of Christian penance."[56] A sorrow passes from his heart to ours. Bourdaloue agrees. "[At Gethsemane] you shall see a God contrite, sore distressed, feeling all the bitterness of sin; [and at Calvary] you shall see the picture of a God offering himself a sacrifice for the reparation of sin, a dying God."[57]

As God-Man, Jesus experienced the broken heart man should feel, and the hatred of sin his Father in heaven does feel, and in this state he is the first to experience true Christian penitence. Unification in

---

54. Nepveu, *The Spirit of Christianity*, 41–42.

55. John Eudes, *The Life and the Kingdom of Jesus in Christian Souls: A Treatise on Christian Perfection for Use by Clergy or Laity* (New York: P.J. Kenedy & Sons, 1946), 12.

56. Jean Grou, *The Practical Science of the Cross in the Use of the Sacraments of Penance and the Eucharist* (London: Joseph Masters, 1871), 29–30.

57. Bourdaloue, in *Great French Sermons from Bossuet, Bourdaloue, and Massillon*, 30–31.

Christ's sacrifice is the only way to understand Christian abnegation. Therefore, the abnegation done by a Christian is a sort of abnegation different from all others, because it is not a moral or psychological self-disgust, it is a liturgical union with the hypostatic union. The door to the kingdom of God is the cross, as much for Jesus as for us; as much for us as for him. Thus Grou hears him saying to his apostles: "I prepare my kingdom for you . . . on the same conditions that my Father has prepared it for me. He willed that it should be at the cost of my Sacrifice; it must also be at the cost of yours."[58]

Paschal Unity

All this was part of the eternal plan, explains Charles Gay. God intended from the beginning to deify man; he acts upon his intention by making a God-man named Jesus; his life overflows him, and thus the Christian life enters his followers. "What is it, then, that God has ordained? That holy and beatified life of God, which is at once poured out entirely into this Man, as into an ocean that it fills, and in which, all-infinite as it is, it finds itself at ease; will it run over, will it rise above its limits and overflow them?"[59] Definitely. For the Word made Man will not be a solitary, a son keeping all the inheritance for himself, a temple closed, a treasure put aside and sealed. God commands the Word to travel through the world's history as "the commencement of an alphabet . . . as the head of an immense body (Col 1:18), as the eldest of a family whose members cannot be counted."[60] The alphabet of the Logos spells out the terms of eternal life, and abnegation is part of the progress of God in the creature, and part of the progress of the creature in God. The incarnate Eternal Word imprints his liturgical abnegation upon souls in various and innumerable ways. Our current life is the schoolroom, his cross is the textbook, and the final exam for graduation is mortification.

We are led to the conjugal union within a mystical ecclesiology: Jesus becomes Bridegroom to his Bride. And "do you know the

---

58. Grou, *The Practical Science of the Cross*, 184–85.
59. Gay, *The Christian Life and Virtues*, vol. 1, 23–24.
60. Ibid., 24.

nuptial hall in which Jesus unites himself with the Church?" asks Liebermann. "It is Calvary. It was there that he sacrificed himself for the Church to make her worthy of being his spouse. Since then, every soul that desires to be perfectly united with Jesus must expect that union to be accomplished in immolation."[61] Your union with Jesus will be accomplished in your immolation. The Spouse goes where the Bridegroom goes: this is the paschal mystery. The whole Christian life is a *Pasch*, a passage, whereby we accompany Jesus's return to his original home. This becomes our adopted homeland, for adopted sons and daughters. The Word came from the Father, alone, but he does not return home alone. As I risked expressing it once, "Normally a son receives more brothers when his father makes more sons; in this case, the Father receives more sons when his Son makes more brothers. Christ came down alone and returns as a crowd (*totus Christus*); he came as the Only Begotten Son and returns with a Mystical Body of siblings."[62]

Bossuet notes that Jesus does not run ahead of us, rather we travel together, side by side.

We know that the word *Pasch* means *passage*, or *passover*. . . . The first thing that we must notice is that we must make this Pasch, or this transition, with Jesus Christ. . . . Ah Jesus! I present myself to You to make my Pasch in Your company. . . . *The world passeth,* said Your apostle (I John 2:17). The figure of this world *passeth* (I Cor 7:31), but I do not wish to pass with the world; I wish to pass to Your Father.[63]

We do not undertake the Pasch under our own power. As the principle Christian, Jesus is the source and cause, the first form and quintessence, the archetypical and prototypical Christian. Jesus is the masterpiece, fixing and establishing his members in his rule of

61. Francis Libermann, *The Spiritual Letters of Venerable Francis Libermann to People in the World*, Spiritan Series 6, vol. 2 (Pittsburgh: Duquesne University Press, 1963), 305.

62. David W. Fagerberg, *Liturgical Dogmatics: How Catholic Beliefs Flow from Liturgical Prayer* (San Francisco: Ignatius Press, 2021), 36.

63. Jacques Bossuet, *Selections From Meditations on the Gospels,* vol. 2 (Chicago: Henry Regnery Company, 1962), 7–8.

life—a rule which consists of humility, modesty, meekness, loving enemies, and self-denial. Christ is unique, but he is not alone (one of the most profound theological antinomies). His Resurrection made him the first risen man, but not the last, reminds Bourdaloue: "Jesus Christ, after coming forth from the tomb, hath no longer lived as a mortal man, but as an heavenly, a risen man, and ... it is a law for us, that after our conversion we should no longer live like carnal and worldly men, but live a life quite spiritual, and agreeable to the blessed state into which men sincerely and thoroughly converted find themselves raised by grace."[64]

The wisdom of God stands in stark contrast to the wisdom of the world. Worldliness counsels the accumulation of honors, esteem, dignity, riches, and sensual pleasure, which is why St Paul says that if anyone have true wisdom, he will be thought a fool by the world, as de Estella explains: "The wisdom of God, which consists in true mortification and denying of ourselves, the world takes for foolishness.... The wisdom of Christ exceeds all our understanding, and therefore the world calls it folly, as we commonly call that folly which exceeds our capacity."[65] Deification certainly exceeds our capacity—until, that is, the Son breathes the Holy Spirit into his disciples. But that spirit is one of submission to God, lived in self-denial, so the world still feels liturgical abnegation as a stumbling block and foolishness.

Jesus's secondary occupation was carpentry, but "his chief and sovereign occupation was in adoring God," says Faber. "This was his incessant occupation."[66] Worship-by-abnegation was his whole life, it was his supreme work, it was his dominant state. I call it "liturgy on the cross," because it is done upon the cross, from the cross, by means of the cross, within the cross, and comes from embracing the cross. Liturgical abnegation is not motivated by practical stoicism, or self-improvement, or autonomous morality, or any kind of self-love. It is done in order to be a burnt offering to God, to please God, to adore God, to glorify God—I shall say to liturgize God. To

64. Bourdaloue, *Eight Sermons for Holy Week and Easter*, 208–9.
65. De Estella, *The Contempt of the World*, 158–59.
66. Faber, *Bethlehem*, 83–84.

liturgize is to commit liturgy in harmony with Christ, under the power of the Holy Spirit. Our liturgy is the activity of the mystical body of Christ, done with this prayer on our lips (from Charles Lebrun): "O Holy Father, O Divine Spirit, I offer you all the love and honor that my Jesus gave You throughout his life by all his divine thoughts, words and deeds, by the divine use he made of all the parts of his body and soul."[67] By union with Christ, I offer You what Jesus gave You first. His abnegation was part of his liturgy, our abnegation is part of ours.

Conclusion

I should end with a word to my audience. And although I hesitate as a layman to give any advice to you seedlings of the hierarchy, I will make two observations.

First, your entire formation should be a training in abnegation. Margaret of the Blessed Sacrament surveys the whole project from the heights she reached: "We must forget ourselves for the love of God, so that He can raise our soul out of ourselves, to be wholly His, for it is easy to see that there is not much room for Him in us, if we are continually taken up with ourselves."[68] Make room for Him whose instrument you are becoming. Take up His cause by ceasing to be taken up with yourself. You are becoming servants of a master whom Eudes says "only reigns in those in which sin, the world, and vanity are dead and in which pride, self, and the will are thoroughly subjugated, or at least so enfeebled that they do not prevent Him from being master."[69] Love is the basis for abnegation; love is the heartbeat of liturgy; love should be the operative motivation for your vocation. The self-denial and self-emptying that my authors have spoken about will have to find expression during countless exercises of patience during your ministry. I will make an educated guess that the priests you admire most—the ones who inspired you

---

67. Charles Lebrun, *The Spiritual Teaching of St John Eudes*, 128.

68. Margaret of the Blessed Sacrament, quoted in Henri Bremond's *A Literary History of Religious Thought in France*, vol. 2: *The Coming of Mysticism* (New York: The Macmillan Company, 1930), 256. She is Marguerite Acarie, second daughter of Madame Acarie, now known as Blessed Mary of the Incarnation.

69. Lebrun, *The Spiritual Teaching of St John Eudes*, 89.

on the path to ordination—are ones who practiced the most brilliant displays of self-abnegation. Libermann wrote volumes of letters to seminarians, and in one he warns a young man that his view of perfection was more imaginary than real because it rested on an interior sense of exaltation and enthusiasm. Libermann says all this remains imperfect "until the soul enjoys true peace.... To obtain this, much time is required, and the soul will need constancy and perfect perseverance in self-denial—especially denial of its self-love and pride, which is the greatest and last obstacle to be overcome."[70] I think he has described the purpose of your formation.

Second, when your people wonder how they will ever copycat a Son of God, give them the words Segneri overhears Jesus saying: "I am not a proud but a humble Master, so that unlike the world, I do not disdain to submit myself to the law which I enjoin on others."[71] Give them Jesus as a brother, an elder brother, the first Christian. Riddle: how can a human being follow a God? Solution: Jesus is not taking *his* path, he is taking *our* path, first. You pastor a flock along a pathway to heaven—and what does it consist of, asks de Sales, but "to attach ourselves to our Savior's cross, meditate on it, and bear in ourselves His mortification. There is no other road to Heaven. Our Lord travelled it first."[72] St Paul likens our Christian life to a race that requires self-control (abnegation), and Segneri says we can win the imperishable prize because a Giant has run it first. "Thou must run in the right manner, and not act according to thy humour, but follow in the sure footsteps of those who have happily preceded thee, of the patriarchs, the prophets, the martyrs, and above all, of Christ, who was the Giant of the course."[73]

---

70. Libermann, *The Spiritual Letters of Venerable Francis Libermann*, Spiritan Series 7, vol. 3, Letters to Clergy and Religious (Pittsburgh: Duquesne University Press, 1963), 93–94.

71. Paul Segneri, *The Manna of the Soul: Meditations for Every Day of the Year*, vol. 2 (New York: Benziger Brothers, 1892), 193–94.

72. Francis de Sales, *The Sermons of St. Francis de Sales for Advent and Christmas* (Rockfort, IL: TAN Books and Publishers, Inc., 1987), 15.

73. Segneri, *The Manna of the Soul*, vol. 1 (New York: Benziger Brothers, 1892), 160. Connecting Paul's admonishment to run the race in order to receive the prize (1 Cor 9:24) with Psalm 19:5 "like the strong man runs its course with joy."

The Giant does not run a different course than us; neither does he run so far ahead of us that we cannot keep up with him. He stays close to us. The mortification we practice is performed in concert with Jesus. He did not say, "here is your yoke; I have my own." A yoke is made for two, Francisco de Osuna reminds us, and "the one with the highest collar does most work and draws the heavier weight. Christ first undertook his part and is figured by Saul who had higher shoulders than the rest of the people and consequently, in his extreme humility and meekness, did more work."[74] The yoke is sweet because the Lord carries the chief part. He says, "take *my* yoke—the one I bore first, the one I am still bearing, and we will share it together."

Christ bore the yoke with invincible constancy for thirty-three years, without accepting or even desiring the least exemption from it. Now he yokes himself to you. Here is that distinction without a difference, except for the nuance that opens up new horizons. Moral imitation yokes you to Jesus; in liturgical abnegation, Jesus yokes himself to you. "The yoke of Christ," says Ullathorne, "is the discipline of humility in self-abnegation.... We are no longer under the yoke of Satan, no longer under the yoke of the world, no longer under the yoke of pride; we bear the yoke of Christ, whose yoke is sweet and his burden light."[75] Abnegation is the renunciation of our first father, Adam, who gave us death, so we can be children of the New Adam, who gives us life. This abnegation arises from liturgical joy, not legal rigor. We do not imitate Jesus under our own power, we enter a mystical participation in Christ, and that is why you are ordained to a sacramental ministry, not given a counselor's certificate or a morality manual. You are ordained to celebrate the Eucharist, where de Sales especially sees this liturgical abnegation at work.

Oh! my daughter, those who communicate according to the spirit of the Heavenly Bridegroom annihilate themselves and say to our

---

74. De Osuna, *The Third Spiritual Alphabet* (New York: Benziger Brothers, 1931), 360.
75. Ullathorne, *Groundwork of the Christian Virtues*, 201.

Lord: feed on me, change me, annihilate me, convert me into thyself. . . .

Well, our Lord has condescended to this excess of love, namely, to give himself to us for our food; and as for us, what ought not we to do in order that he may possess us, that he may feed on us, that he may make us what he pleases?[76]

What liturgical abnegation ought we not embrace that he may possess us?

---

76. John Camus, *The Spirit of St Francis de Sales* (London: Burns, Oates & Washbourne, Ltd., 1925), 396.

Since many of these authors are unfamiliar, here is a brief identification.

Alacoque, Margaret Mary. 1647–1690. French Visitation nun.
Bona, Giovanni. 1609–1674. Italian Cistercian, cardinal.
Bossuet, Jacques-Bénigne. 1627–1704. French bishop.
Bourdaloue, Louis. 1632–1704. French Jesuit preacher.
Bruyère, Cécile. 1845–1909. French Benedictine.
Camus, John. 1584–1652. French bishop.
Croiset, John. 1656–1738. French Jesuit.
De Bergamo, Gaetano Maria. 1672–1753. Italian Capuchin.
De Bérulle, Pierre. 1575–1629. French Cardinal, founder of the French Oratory.
De Estella, Diego. 1524–1578. Spanish Franciscan.
De Granada, Luis. 1504–1588. Spanish Dominican.
De Ponte, Louis (Luis de la Puente). 1554–1624. Spanish Jesuit.
De Sales, Francis. 1567–1622. French Bishop of Geneva.
Eudes, John. 1601–1680. French founder of the Eudists.
Faber, Frederick. 1814–1863. English Oratorian.
Fénelon, François. 1651–1715. French Archbishop of Cambrai.
Gay, Charles-Louis. 1815–1892. Auxiliary Bishop of Poitiers, preacher.
Grou, Jean. 1731–1803. French Jesuit.
Guilloré, François. 1615–1684. French Jesuit.
Libermann, Francis. 1802–1852. French Spiritan.
Nepveu, François. 1639–1708. French Jesuit.
Olier, Jean-Jacques. 1608–1657. French founder of the Sulpicians.
Pollien, François. 1853–1936. French Carthusian.
Saint-Jure, Jean Baptiste. 1588–1657. French Jesuit.
Ullathorne, William Bernard. 1806–1889. Bishop of Birmingham.

Bibliography

Alacoque, Margaret Mary. *The Autobiography of Saint Margaret Mary.* Charlotte, NC: TAN Books, 2012.

_____. *The Letters of St. Margaret Mary Alacoque*, Kindle edition. Charlotte, NC: TAN Books, 2012.

Baker, Augustine. *Holy Wisdom, Or Directions for the Prayer of Contemplation Extracted out of more than Forty Treatises*, edited by R. F. Serenus Cressy. New York: Burns & Oates, 1911.

_____. *The Inner Life of Dame Gertrude More*, volume 1. London: R. & T. Washbourne, Ltd., 1911.

Barbanson, Constantine. *The Secret Paths of Divine Love.* London: Burns Oates & Washbourne, Ltd., 1928.

Benedict of Canfield (William Benedict Fitch). *The Holy Will of God: A Short Rule of Perfection.* London: Thomas Richardson and Sons, 1878.

Blosius (Louis of Blois). *A Book of Spiritual Instruction: Institutio Spiritualis.* St Louis: B. Herder, 1900.

_____. *Comfort for the Fainthearted.* Westminster: Art and Book Company, 1908.

_____. *A Mirror for Monks.* London. C. J. Stewart, 1872.

_____. *Spiritual Works of Louis of Blois*, edited by John Edward Bowden. New York: Benziger Bros., 1903.

Bona, Giovanni. *The Easy Way to God: A Manual of Ejaculatory Prayer*, translated by Henry Collins. London: Burns Oates & Washbourne, Ltd., 1876.

_____. *Manductio ad Coelum: or, a Guide to Eternity.* London: printed for Henry Brome, 1672.

_____. *The Principles of Christianity.* London: printed for C. Dilly, 1783.

_____. *A Treatise of Spiritual Life.* Poplar Bluff, MO: the author, 1893.

Boudon, Henri-Marie. *The Book of Perpetual Adoration; or The Love of Jesus in the Most Holy Sacrament.* London: R. Washbourne, 1873.

_____. *The Hidden Life of Jesus: A Lesson and Model to Christians,* translated by Edward Healy Thompson. London: Burns, Oates, & Co., 1869.

Bruyère, Abbess Cécile J. *Spiritual Life and Prayer According to Holy Scripture and Monastic Tradition.* New York: Benziger Brothers, 1905.

Camus, Jean-Pierre. *The Spirit of St. Francis de Sales.* London: Burns, Oates & Washbourne, Ltd., 1925.

Challoner, Richard. *Considerations Upon Christian Truths and Christian Duties.* Philadelphia: Eugene Cummisky, 1874.

Crasset, Jean, and De Sales, Francis. *The Secret of Sanctity According to St. Francis De Sales and Father Crasset.* New York: Benziger Brothers, 1892.

Crasset, John. *Christian Considerations; or, Devout Meditations for Every Day in the Year.* New York: P. O'Shea, 1864.

_____. *The Devotion of Calvary; or Meditations on the Passion of Our Lord and Saviour Jesus Christ.* Liverpool: Booker & Co., 1844.

_____. *Meditations for Every Day in the Year from the Christian Considerations of Father John Crasset, S.J.: Pentecost to Advent.* London: R. Washbourne, 1888.

Croiset, Jean. *Devotion to the Sacred Heart of Jesus.* London: Burns & Lambert, 1863.

De Bergamo, Gaetano Maria. *Humility of Heart.* Mandeville, LA: Founding Father Films Publishing, 2015.

de Bernières-Louvigny, Jean. *The Interior Christian in Eight Books.* New York: The Catholic Publication Society, 1843.

De Castañiza, Juan. *The Spiritual Conflict and Conquest.* London: Burns & Oates, 1874.

De Caussade, Jean-Pierre. *Abandonment to Divine Providence.* St. Louis: B. Herder Book Company, 1921.

De Chantal, Jane. *Meditations for Retreats Taken from the Writings of St. Francis de Sales.* New York: Benziger Brothers, 1900.

De Granada, Lewis [Luis]. *A Memorial of a Christian Life.* New York: The Catholic Publication Society, 1870.

_____. *Considerations on the Mysteries of the Faith.* London: Joseph Masters, 1862.

_____. *Counsels on Holiness of Life: Being the First Part of The Sinner's Guide.* London: Rivingtons, 1869.

_____. *The Sinner's Guide*. Philadelphia: Henry McGrath, 1845.

De la Colombière, Claude. *Sermons*, volume 1, *Christian Conduct*. DeKalb, IL: NIU Press, 2014.

De Liguori, Alphonsus. *Alphonsus de Liguori: Selected Writings*. New York: Paulist Press, 1999.

_____. *The Great Means of Salvation and of Perfection*. New York: Benziger Brothers, 1886.

_____. *The Holy Eucharist*, volume 6 of *The Complete Works of Saint Alphonsus de Liguori, The Ascetical Works*. New York: Benziger Brothers, 1887.

_____. "Meditations for a Private Retreat of Eight Days," in *Saint Alphonsus de Liguori: Selection*, Kindle edition. No location: Aeterna Press, 2016.

_____. *Preparation for Death*. Philadelphia: J. B. Lippincott & Co., 1869.

_____. *Uniformity with God's Will*. Rockford, IL: TAN Books and Publishers, Inc., 1977.

De Lombez, Ambroise. *Lettres Spirituelles sur La Paix Interieure*. Paris: Chez Herissant, 1774.

_____. *A Treatise on the Joy of the Christian Soul*. London: S. Anselm's Society, 1894.

De Montfort, Louis. *True Devotion to Mary*. Bay Shore, NY: Montfort Publications, 1954.

De Osuna, Francisco. *The Third Spiritual Alphabet*. New York: Benziger Brothers, 1931.

De Ponte Louis. *Meditations on the Mysteries of Our Holy Faith*, volume 1. London: Richardson and Son, 1852.

_____. *Meditations on the Mysteries of Our Holy Faith*, volume 2. London: Richardson and Son, 1852.

_____. *Meditations on the Mysteries of Our Holy Faith*, volume 3. London: Richardson and Son, 1853.

_____. *Meditations on the Mysteries of Our Holy Faith*, volume 5. London: Richardson and Son, 1854.

_____. *Meditations on the Mysteries of Our Holy Faith*, volume 6. London: Richardson and Son, 1854.

De Ravignan, Gustave. *Conferences on the Spiritual Life*. London: R. Washbourne, 1873.

_____. *Ravignan's Last Retreat*. London: Burns & Oates, 1859.

De Sales, Francis. *Introduction to the Devout Life*. New York: Vintage Spiritual Classics, 2002.

————. *Letters to Persons in the World*. London: Burns & Oates, Ltd., 1894.

————. *Letters to Persons in Religion*. New York: Benziger Brothers, 1909.

————. *Maxims and Counsels of St. Francis de Sales for Every Day of the Year*. Dublin: M. H. Gill & Son, 1884.

————. *The Sermons of St. Francis de Sales for Advent and Christmas*. Rockfort, IL: TAN Books and Publishers, Inc., 1987.

————. *The Sermons of St. Francis de Sales on Our Lady*, Kindle edition.

————. *A Selection from the Spiritual Letters of S. Francis De Sales*, translated by H.L. Lear. New York: E.P. Dutton and Company, 1876.

————. *The Spiritual Conferences*. New York: Benziger Brothers, 1909.

————. *Treatise on the Love of God*. Blacksburg, VA: Wilder Publications, 2011.

De Sales, Francis and de Chantal, Jane. *The Mystical Explanation of the Canticle of Canticles by St. Francis de Sales*, and *The Depositions of St. Jane Frances de Chantal in the Cause of the Canonisation of St. Francis de Sales* (in one volume) in *Library of St. Francis de Sales*. London: Burns & Oates, 1908.

Elizabeth of the Trinity. *Complete Works*, volume 2, *Letters from Carmel*. Washington, DC: ICS Publications, 2014.

————. *Reminiscences*. New York: Benziger Brothers, 1914.

Eudes, John. *Man's Contract with God in Baptism*. Philadelphia: Peter F. Cunningham, 1859.

————. *Meditations on Various Subjects*. New York: P.J. Kenedy & Sons, 1947.

————. *The Priest: His Dignity and Obligations*. New York: P.J. Kenedy & Sons, 1947.

————. *St. John Eudes: Selections from His Writings*. London: Burns Oates & Washbourne, Ltd., 1925.

————. *The Sacred Heart of Jesus*. New York: P.J. Kenedy & Sons, 1946.

Faber, Frederick. *All for Jesus: or, The Easy Ways of Divine Love*. London: Richardson and Son, 1854.

_____. *Bethlehem*. London: Thomas Richardson and Son, 1860.

_____. *The Blessed Sacrament*. London: Burns Oates & Washbourne Ltd., 1861.

_____. *The Creator and the Creature, or, The Wonders of Divine Love*. London: Thomas Richardson and Son, 1858.

_____. *Growth in Holiness; or, The Progress of the Spiritual Life*. Baltimore: John Murphy & Co., 1855.

_____. *The Precious Blood; or, The Price of Our Salvation*. London: Burns & Oates, Ltd., 1860.

Fagerberg, David W. *On Liturgical Asceticism*. Washington, DC: Catholic University of America Press, 2013.

Fénelon, François. *Christian Perfection*. New York: Harper & Brothers, 1947.

_____. *The Complete Fénelon*. Brewster, MA: Paraclete Press, 2008.

_____. *Letters to Men*. London: Rivingtons, 1877.

_____. *Pious Thoughts Concerning the Knowledge and Love of God*. London: W. and J. Innys, 1720.

_____. *Spiritual Letters of François De Salignac De La Mothe-Fénelon [to Countess Gramont]*. Cornwall-on-Hudson, NY: Idlewild Press, 1945.

Gay, Charles. *The Christian Life and Virtues Considered in the Religious State*, volume 1. London: Burns & Oates, 1876.

_____. *The Christian Life and Virtues Considered in the Religious State*, volume 2. London: Burns & Oates, 1878.

_____. *The Christian Life and Virtues Considered in the Religious State*, volume 3. London: Burns & Oates, 1879.

Grou, Jean. *The Christian Sanctified by the Lord's Prayer*. New York: Thomas Whitaker, 1885.

_____. *The Interior of Jesus and Mary*, volume 1. New York: Benziger Brothers, 1893.

_____. *Manual for Interior Souls*. London: S. Anselm's Society, 1890.

_____. *Meditations upon the Love of God*. London: T. Baker, 1905.

_____. *Morality, Extracted from the Confessions of Saint Austin*, volume 1. London: J. P. Coghlan, 1791.

_____. *The Practical Science of the Cross*. London: Joseph Masters,

1871.

_____. *The School of Jesus Christ.* London: Burns Oates & Washbourne, Ltd., 1932.

_____. *Self-Consecration or the Gift of One's Self to God.* New York: E. & J. B. Young & Co., 1887.

_____. *The Spiritual Maxims of Pere Grou.* London: J.T. Hayes, 1874.

Huguet, Jean-Joseph. *The Consoling Thoughts of St. Francis de Sales.* Dublin: M.H. Gill & Son, 1877.

John of Ávila. *The Holy Ghost.* London: Scepter Limited, 1959.

John of St. Samson. *Prayer, Aspiration and Contemplation.* New York: Alba House, 1975.

John of the Cross. *The Ascent of Mount Carmel,* in *The Complete Works of Saint John of the Cross,* volume 1. London: Longman, Green, Longman, Roberts & Green, 1864.

_____. *The Obscure Night of the Soul,* in *The Complete Works of Saint John of the Cross,* volume 1. London: Longman, Green, Longman, Roberts & Green, 1864.

_____. *A Spiritual Canticle* in *The Complete Works of Saint John of the Cross,* volume 2. London: Longman, Green, Longman, Roberts & Green, 1864.

_____. *Spiritual Maxims,* in *The Complete Works of Saint John of the Cross,* volume 2. London: Longman, Green, Longman, Roberts & Green, 1864.

Lacordaire, Jean-Baptiste Henri. *Conferences of the Rev. Pere Lacordaire, Delivered in the Cathedral of Notre Dame, in Paris.* New York: P. O'Shea, Publisher, 1853.

_____. *God and Man. Conferences Delivered at Notre Dame in Paris.* London: Chapman and Hall, 1872.

_____. *Life: Conferences Delivered at Toulouse.* New York: P. O'Shea, 1875.

Leen, Edward. *Progress Through Mental Prayer.* New York: Sheed and Ward, 1935.

_____. *What is Education?* New York: Sheed and Ward, 1944.

Libermann, Francis. *Living with God.* New York: Catholic Book Publishing, 1949. Publication of *Instructions for Missionaries,* https://dsc.duq.edu/spiritan-rc/1/.

_____. *Letters to Religious Sisters and Aspirants,* Spiritan Series 5, volume 1. Pittsburgh: Duquesne University Press, 1962.

_____. *Letters to People in the World*, Spiritan Series 6, volume 2. Pittsburgh: Duquesne University Press, 1963.

_____. *Letters to Clergy and Religious*, Spiritan Series 7, volume 3. Pittsburgh: Duquesne University Press, 1963.

_____. *Letters to Clergy and Religious*, Spiritan Series 8, volume 4. Pittsburgh: Duquesne University Press, 1964.

_____. *Letters to Clergy and Religious*, Spiritan Series 9, volume 5. Pittsburgh: Duquesne University Press, 1966.

Massillon, John-Baptist. *Sermons by John-Baptist Massillon, Complete in One Volume.* London: Printed for Thomas Tegg, 1839.

Olier, Jean-Jacques. *Catechism of an Interior Life.* Baltimore: Murphy & Co., 1852.

_____. "Introduction to the Christian Life and Virtues." In *Bérulle and the French School*, edited by William M. Thompson, 262–63. New York: Paulist Press, 1989.

Pollien, François. *The Interior Life Simplified and Reduced to its Fundamental Principle*, edited by Joseph Tissot. London: Burns Oates & Washbourne, Ltd., 1927.

Rodríguez, Alphonsus (Alonso). *St Alphonsus Rodríguez: Autobiography.* London: Geoffrey Chapman: London, 1964.

Rodríguez, Alphonsus (Alfonso). *The Practice of Christian and Religious Perfection*, volume 1. London: James Duffy, 1861.

_____. *The Practice of Christian and Religious Perfection*, volume 2. London: James Duffy, 1861.

Saint-Jure, Jean-Baptiste and de la Colombière, Claude. *Trustful Surrender to Divine Providence: The Secret of Peace and Happiness.* Rockford, IL: TAN Books and Publishers, Inc., 1983.

Saint-Jure, Jean-Baptiste. *The Spiritual Man; or, The Spiritual Life Reduced to its First Principles.* London: Burns & Oates, 1878.

_____. *A Treatise on the Knowledge and Love of Our Lord Jesus Christ*, volume 1. New York: P. O'Shea, 1870.

_____. *Union with Our Lord Jesus Christ in His Principal Mysteries for All Seasons of the Year.* New York: D. & J. Sadlier & Co., 1876.

Scaramelli, John Baptist. *The Directorium Asceticum; or, Guide to the Spiritual Life*, volume 1. New York: Benziger Bros., 1902.

_____. *The Directorium Asceticum; or, Guide to the Spiritual Life,* volume 2. New York: Benziger Bros., 1902.

_____. *The Directorium Asceticum; or, Guide to the Spiritual Life*, volume 3. New York: Benziger Bros., 1902.

_____. *The Directorium Asceticum; or, Guide to the Spiritual Life*, volume 4. New York: Benziger Bros., 1902.

Segneri, Paul. *The Manna of the Soul: Meditations for Every Day of the Year*, volume 1. New York: Benziger Brothers, 1892.

_____. *The Manna of the Soul: Meditations for Every Day of the Year*, volume 2. New York: Benziger Brothers, 1892.

_____. *The Devout Client of Mary*. London: Burns & Lambert, 1857.

Surin, Jean-Joseph. *Foundations of Spiritual Life*. London: James Burns, 1844.

Thérèse of Lisieux. *Thoughts of the Servant of God Thérèse of the Child Jesus*. New York: P. J. Kenedy & Sons, 1915.

Tronson, Louis. *Examination of Conscience upon Special Subjects*. London: Rivingtons, 1870.

Ullathorne, William. *Christian Patience: The Strength and Discipline of the Soul*. New York: Catholic Publication Society, 1886.

Vianney, John. *The Little Catechism of the Curé of Ars*. Rockford, IL: TAN Books, 1951.

_____. *Thoughts of the Curé of Ars*, Kindle edition. Charlotte, NC: TAN Books, 1984.

_____. *The Sermons of the Curé of Ars*. Chicago: H. Regnery, 1960.

Vianney, Joseph. *The Blessed John Vianney, Cure D'Ars, Patron of Parish Priests*. New York: Benziger Brothers, 1906.

Von Cochem, Martin. *The Four Last Things: Death, Judgment, Hell, Heaven*. New York: Benziger Brothers, 1899.

www.ingramcontent.com/pod-product-compliance
Lightning Source LLC
Chambersburg PA
CBHW022007080426
42733CB00007B/503